Centre for Educational Research an

EDUCATIONAL FINANCING AND POLICY GOALS FOR PRIMARY SCHOOLS

COUNTRY REPORTS

Volume I

AUSTRALIA CANADA GERMANY

ORGANISATION FOR ECONOMIC CO-OPERATION AND DEVELOPMENT
1979

The Organisation for Economic Co-operation and Development (OECD) was set up under a Convention signed in Paris on 14th December 1960, which provides that the OECD shall promote policies designed:
- to achieve the highest sustainable economic growth and employment and a rising standard of living in Member countries, while maintaining financial stability, and thus to contribute to the development of the world economy;
- to contribute to sound economic expansion in Member as well as non-member countries in the process of economic development;
- to contribute to the expansion of world trade on a multilateral, non-discriminatory basis in accordance with international obligations.

The Members of OECD are Australia, Austria, Belgium, Canada, Denmark, Finland, France, the Federal Republic of Germany, Greece, Iceland, Ireland, Italy, Japan, Luxembourg, the Netherlands, New Zealand, Norway, Portugal, Spain, Sweden, Switzerland, Turkey, the United Kingdom and the United States.

The Centre for Educational Research and Innovation was created in June 1968 by the Council of the Organisation for Economic Co-operation and Development for an initial period of three years, with the help of grants from the Ford Foundation and the Royal Dutch Shell Group of Companies. In May 1971, the Council decided that the Centre should continue its work for a period of five years as from 1st January 1972. In July 1976 it extended this mandate for the following five years, 1977-82.

The main objectives of the Centre are as follows:
- *to promote and support the development of research activities in education and undertake such research activities where appropriate;*
- *to promote and support pilot experiments with a view to introducing and testing innovations in the educational system;*
- *to promote the development of co-operation between Member countries in the field of educational research and innovation.*

The Centre functions within the Organisation for Economic Co-operation and Development in accordance with the decisions of the Council of the Organisation, under the authority of the Secretary-General. It is supervised by a Governing Board composed of one national expert in its field of competence from each of the countries participating in its programme of work.

THE OPINION EXPRESSED AND ARGUMENTS EMPLOYED IN THIS PUBLICATION ARE THE RESPONSIBILITY OF THE AUTHORS AND DO NOT NECESSARILY REPRESENT THOSE OF THE OECD

© OECD, 1979
Queries concerning permissions or translation rights should be addressed to:
Director of Information, OECD
2, rue André-Pascal, 75775 PARIS CEDEX 16, France.

TABLE OF CONTENTS

PREFACE 5

AUSTRALIA
    by K.R. McKinnon and G.A. Hancock 7

CANADA (Province of Ontario)
    by E. Brock Rideout, Lawrence M. Bezeau and David Wright 57

FEDERAL REPUBLIC OF GERMANY
    by Peter Siewert and Helmut Köhler 109

PREFACE

This volume is one of a series of three reporting ten country studies: Australia, Canada (the province of Ontario), the Federal Republic of Germany, Italy, the Netherlands, Norway, Sweden, the United Kingdom (England and Wales), the United States (Florida and California), and Yugoslavia, prepared during 1976 to investigate the relationship between modes of finance for primary schools and educational policy objectives. They are the outcome of the first phase of activity in the CERI project on educational financing and educational policy and as such they have attempted to fulfil a number of purposes. The first was to provide a description of the history of primary educational finance arrangements in order to frame the context within which present educational finance arrangements operate. A second was to present current policy objectives and to describe the linkage between these objectives and the financial instruments which are used to achieve them. Finally, the country studies were intended to provide some insight into the effectiveness of these instruments—or lack of it—in achieving their intended purposes. Each of these studies is meant to stand independently, useful in itself as a country description and analysis of the choice, use and effectiveness of current financing arrangements in achieving policy goals for primary schools.

The presentation of these ten country studies in three volumes is as follows:

Volume I:	*Volume II:*	*Volume III:*
Australia	United Kingdom	Netherlands
Canada	United States	Norway
Germany	Yugoslavia	Sweden
		Italy

A general comparative report, based on the data and judgements provided by the authors of the country studies, is also being published. This report summarises the variety of approaches that individual countries use to finance their primary schools and describes major trends in school finance policy in each country. It then compares and contrasts the diverse arrangements which countries have developed to accomplish a number of educational policy objectives. These include equality in educational resources and/or equity in access to resources, provision for special educational needs, decentralisation of control in educational decision-making and enhancement of parental (or student) choice among educational alternatives. Findings from this report will form a basis for further work to be undertaken in the area of educational finance and organisation.

AUSTRALIA

by

K.R. McKINNON
and
G.A. HANCOCK
*Schools Commission
Canberra*

CONTENTS

Chapter I
THE AUSTRALIAN CONTEXT OF SCHOOL FINANCING

BACKGROUND	11
THE STATES	12
Government school systems	12
Non-government schools	12
THE COMMONWEALTH	14
DISPARITIES AND TENSIONS	15

Chapter II
SOURCES OF SCHOOL FINANCE

COMMONWEALTH SOURCES	19
STATE SOURCES	21
PRIVATE SOURCES	22

Chapter III
FINANCIAL INSTRUMENTS FOR SCHOOL-LEVEL EDUCATION

COMMONWEALTH	23
Specific purpose ("section 96") grants to government school systems	24
Specific purpose ("section 96") grants to non-government schools and systems	25
Specific purpose ("section 96") grants for joint programs	26
Student assistance ("section 51 xxiiiA") grants	26
STATE GOVERNMENTS	26
General budgetary allocations	26
Student assistance	27
Capital expenditure	28
PRIVATE SOURCES	28
Government schools	28
Non-government schools	28

Chapter IV
SELECTED POLICY ISSUES: AUSTRALIAN PERSPECTIVES

EQUALITY	30
SPECIAL GROUPS	32
Rural dwellers	32

Aborigines	32
Migrants	33
LOCUS OF CONTROL	33
DIVERSITY AND CHOICE	35

Chapter V
SELECTED COMMONWEALTH GOVERNMENT FINANCIAL INSTRUMENTS AND THEIR IMPACT ON ASPECTS OF EDUCATIONAL POLICY

PROGRAMS FUNDED UNDER SECTION 96 OF THE CONSTITUTION	36
General Recurrent Grants for government and non-government schools	36
Disadvantaged Schools Grants	38
TAXATION CONCESSIONS FOR EDUCATION EXPENSES	39

Chapter VI
SELECTED STATE GOVERNMENT FINANCIAL INSTRUMENTS AND THEIR IMPACT ON ASPECTS OF EDUCATIONAL POLICY

THE STATE BUDGET	41
CASH ALLOCATIONS TO INDIVIDUAL GOVERNMENT SCHOOLS	43
PER CAPITA RECURRENT GRANTS TO NON-GOVERNMENT SCHOOLS	44

Chapter VII
SELECTED PRIVATE FINANCIAL INSTRUMENTS AND THEIR IMPACT ON ASPECTS OF EDUCATIONAL POLICY

PRIVATE OUTLAYS ON GOVERNMENT SCHOOLS	46
PRIVATE OUTLAYS ON NON-GOVERNMENT SCHOOLS	47

Chapter VIII
LIKELY DIRECTIONS OF SCHOOL FINANCE

THE ROLE OF THE FEDERAL GOVERNMENT IN FUNDING SCHOOL-LEVEL EDUCATION	49
Centralising tendencies	49
Fiscal federalism	50
Statutory commissions	51
DEVOLUTION FROM THE STATE TO REGIONAL AND LOCAL LEVELS	52
PRIVATE INITIATIVES AND CHOICE	52
SHAPING FUTURE POLICY	53
BIBLIOGRAPHY	55

TABLES

Chapter I

1. Distribution of Australian population: 30 June 1975 ... 13
2. Australian urban and rural population: 30 June 1971 ... 13
3. Approximate annual recurrent expenditure from State sources per primary and secondary student in government schools, by State, 1974/75 ... 13
4. Proportion of total capital outlays by State governments spent on government schools and annual expenditure per head of population, 1973/74 - 1975/76 ... 14
5. Population not born in Australia at 30 June 1971 ... 15
6. Annual rate of growth of Australian population 1961-1975 ... 15

Chapter II

7. Commonwealth payments to the States, 1975/76 19
8. Commonwealth government outlays on education 1972/73 to 1975/76 (actual) and 1976/77 (estimate) 21

Chapter III

9. Summary of Commonwealth specific purpose grants for schools in the States by program and sector 1976 24
10. Typical benefits provided by State governments to school students 27

FIGURES

Chapter II

1. Sources and magnitude of recurrent funds for typical Australian primary schools   17
2. Sources of school finance in Australia 18

Chapter I

THE AUSTRALIAN CONTEXT OF SCHOOL FINANCING

BACKGROUND

The Commonwealth of Australia, a federation of six States, was formed in 1901 from British colonies which were established between 1788 and 1859. The written Constitution on which the federation is based defines the role of the national (Commonwealth) Government and, by implication, those of the States, a factor which has been very important in shaping the financial instruments applied to education.

"Free, compulsory and secular" education Acts had been passed in each of the colonies between 1872 and 1893, reflecting the nineteenth century liberal desire to provide universal access to elementary education. The private organisations and religious denominations which ran the existing schools were not coping with the provision of services throughout the areas of scattered settlement and in any case the "free and secular" philosophy meant that it was unacceptable to rely on religious denominations to provide these services universally. Consequently, systems of public (government) schools were established and public financial assistance to private and denominational schools was abolished.

In general, the Protestant denominations accepted the principle of secular schools provided by the State, though some Protestant and non-denominational private schools continued operations and a few new ones were established. However, the Catholic schools network was maintained and expanded: the Catholic church was firmly resolved to continue its educational role despite the lack of State aid, a feasible objective at the time because of the services contributed by its many religious staff.

The basic pattern of centralised State responsibility for primary and secondary schools through the direct administration of government (public) systems and general overview of non-government schools which existed at the time of federation has been maintained to the present. In addition the Commonwealth Government has in recent years assumed responsibility for the school systems in the two mainland Federal Territories (the Australian Capital Territory and Northern Territory) which had until then been conducted by neighbouring States on behalf of the Commonwealth. Public provision is common to many services in Australia, including roads and transport, telegraph and postal facilities, and hospitals: it has been dictated by geographic conditions and circumstances of early settlements, together with a concern for the egalitarian provision of essentials.

Of the 9 400 schools in Australia, 2 100 are non-government. Eighty-five per cent of these are Catholic, operating either as part of diocesan "systems" or as separate schools run under the aegis of a religious order. Most of the other non-government schools are also operated by religious groups. There are approximately 5 750 government primary schools and 1 400 non-government primary schools: in addition, 450 government and 400 non-government schools enrol both primary and secondary students (this study is concerned with the primary level of education).

In 1975 there were 2.9 million primary and secondary students, of whom 1.8 million were at the primary level. The proportions of primary school students enrolled in government, Catholic and other non-government schools were 80.3, 17.5 and 2.2 per cent respectively. The primary stage consists of seven years.

The minimum school leaving age is fifteen years in all States except one (where it is sixteen), although more than 50 per cent of students remain at school beyond sixteen years.

In 1975/76 the estimated total outlay on schools by all State and Commonwealth governments was $2 840 million (10.5 per cent of all public outlays) of which $475 million were Commonwealth special purpose grants for schools in the States. The total outlay as a proportion of Gross Domestic Product was estimated to be 6.5 per cent, having risen from 4.3 per cent in 1970/71. The average cost per student in government primary schools in 1975 was about $600, an increase of more than 20 per cent in real terms over the previous three years.

THE STATES

Government school systems

The State systems of public education are administered centrally by the chief executive officer of each Department of Education, known as the Director-General. He is responsible to a Minister who in turn is answerable to State Parliament. The responsibilities of the Departments, until relatively recently, have been very wide: they have covered the training and allocation of staff, prescription of texts, distribution of materials, provision of building facilities and supervision (inspection). Changes in the traditional pattern are now occurring.

Some administrative decentralisation has been initiated, especially over the last decade, ranging from the delegation of some head office functions to regional levels, to the devolution of some organisational and financial authority to individual schools. Similarly, responsibility for the training of teachers has been transferred to autonomous tertiary education institutions.

Despite the general similarity in the pattern of educational provision throughout the nation, there are variations among the States in their educational services. This is reflected in organisational and curriculum patterns and in student retention. The differences in size, geography, demography (see Tables 1 and 2), degree of development and economic capacity have created different priorities and pressures which have led to unequal expenditure on education at the primary and secondary levels (see Tables 3 and 4).

Non-government schools

Any group of citizens has the right to start a non-government school but most State governments monitor and approve standards of curricula and physical facilities. Eligibility for public financial assistance and the official recognition of courses is generally dependent on such approval. In recent years the organisation of Catholic schools, which was based on parish self-sufficiency, has

Table 1. **Distribution of Australian population: 30 June 1975**

State	Persons ('000)	Per cent
New South Wales	4 793.2	35.5
Victoria	3 667.7	27.2
Queensland	1 998.5	14.8
South Australia	1 235.0	9.1
Western Australia	1 125.8	8.3
Tasmania	406.1	3.0
Northern Territory	88.7	0.7
Australian Capital Territory	191.9	1.4
Australia	13 506.9	100.0

Source: Australian Bureau of Statistics, Ref. No. 4.16.

Table 2. **Australian urban and rural population: 30 June 1971**

(Per cent)

State	Urban Greater than 100 000	Urban Less than 100 000	Total urban	Rural	Migratory	Total
New South Wales	69.05	19.51	88.56	11.32	0.13	100.00
Victoria	71.65	16.07	87.72	12.22	0.07	100.00
Queensland	44.79	34.46	79.25	20.55	0.20	100.00
South Australia	68.97	15.61	84.58	15.26	0.16	100.00
Western Australia	62.28	19.25	81.53	18.21	0.25	100.00
Tasmania	33.28	40.89	74.17	25.72	0.11	100.00
Northern Territory	..	64.14	64.14	35.43	0.43	100.00
Australian Capital Territory	97.78	..	97.78	2.22	..	100.00
Australia	64.50	21.06	85.56	14.31	0.14	100.00

Source: Australian Bureau of Statistics Yearbook for 1973, p. 135.

Table 3. **Approximate annual recurrent expenditure from State sources[a] per primary and secondary student in government schools, by State, 1974/75**

$ (Dec. 1974)

State	Primary	Secondary
New South Wales	510	850
Victoria	520	935
Queensland	520	815
South Australia	520	965
Western Australia	505	965
Tasmania	540	1 015
All States Average	515	895

a) Includes administrative, superannuation and student transport costs but excludes specific purpose grants for primary and secondary education from Commonwealth sources.

Source: State statistical returns to Schools Commission.

Table 4. **Proportion of total capital outlays by State governments spent on government schools and annual expenditure per head of population, 1973/74 - 1975/76**

State	Proportion of total capital outlay %	Per capita expenditure $ (Dec. 1975)
New South Wales	23.6	20
Victoria	26.1	23
Queensland	19.2	16
South Australia	17.2	24
Western Australia	15.9	18
Tasmania	16.2	37
All States Average	21.5	21

Source: Schools Commission.

become more co-ordinated and for the last three years Commonwealth Government funds to the diocesan systems have been disbursed through Catholic education commissions within each State. Other non-government schools are by and large the responsibility of individual school councils.

THE COMMONWEALTH

Despite the fact that a specific "education" power was not vested in the Commonwealth at the time of federation the Commonwealth participated increasingly in education since World War II, initially in the tertiary field, but gradually extending to the school level both through grants to the States and through its responsibility for schools in the Territories. This involvement was facilitated by the Commonwealth progressively acquiring control of the major sources of public revenue, in particular income tax. This major taxing power (transferred by the States in war-time conditions by the Uniform Taxation Agreement of 1942) gave the Commonwealth the responsibility of collecting and allocating uniformly levied income taxes and has had a profound effect on federal financial and political relationships.

The main authority for the Commonwealth becoming involved in educational activity in the States has been section 96 of the Constitution (the grants to the States provision), which permits the Commonwealth to offer grants to the States under terms and conditions determined by the Commonwealth Parliament, and section 51 of the Constitution (the social services provision), which under subsection *xxiii*A permits the Commonwealth to provide cash or services to students and thus affords considerable scope for direct federal government participation in education. Constitutional responsibility for such matters as Defence, Immigration and Aboriginal welfare has provided other authorisation and reasons for Commonwealth involvement in schooling, through provisions for the education of soldiers and their children, migrants, and aborigines. Similarly, concessional deductions for educational expenditure can be authorised only by the Commonwealth because it alone has the taxation power. Less directly, the Commonwealth has for many years also given assistance to education through means such as the educational radio and television services provided by the Australian Broadcasting Commission. Section 116 of the Constitution, which prevents the establishment of religion, has a significant bearing on the focus of Commonwealth assistance to church-sponsored non-government schools.

DISPARITIES AND TENSIONS

As a result of a variety of factors common to most countries but including post World War II population growth, expanded immigration (see Tables 5 and 6 for details) and economic prosperity, Australian expenditure on education has accelerated dramatically over the past twenty-five years. Although increasing proportions of States' budgets have been devoted to education it has not proved possible to avoid deficiencies in provision within, and inequalities among, States. What the public has seen as insufficient total resources has led to continuous agitation for increased outlays for schools, particularly to overcome the substandard educational provision in such places as inner-urban areas and the remote inland. Many non-government schools have also been functioning under similarly inadequate conditions and with similar financial stress.

Political pressure has mounted on successive Commonwealth governments to have them accept that there have been national needs which should be met from the Commonwealth's superior financial resources. The Commonwealth has responded with financial programs which, because the more substantial of them depend upon section 96 of the Constitution, have had to be channelled through the States. This approach would be necessary in any case as overall controls and priorities in expenditure are determined by the States. So in spite of the Federal Government's financial supremacy its involvement has not been unfettered. In addition the States have not always welcomed national initiatives, arguing that their own priorities and plans tend to be distorted by the conditions imposed by Commonwealth programs and that the special purpose grants, even when made to individuals or non-government schools, may reflect unacceptable educational or social policies.

Table 5. **Population not born in Australia (at 30 June 1971)**

State	Total 000's	Proportion of total State or Territory population %
New South Wales	893.0	19.4
Victoria	797.7	22.8
Queensland	231.5	12.7
South Australia	280.1	23.9
Western Australia	283.3	27.5
Tasmania	40.3	10.3
Australian Capital Territory	36.6	25.4
Northern Territory	16.8	19.5
All States	2 579.3	20.2

Source: Australian Bureau of Statistics Census Bulletin No. 4.

Table 6. **Annual rate of growth of Australian population 1961-1975**
(Per cent)

Year	Natural Increase	Migration	Total
1961-70 (av.)	1.19	0.83	2.02
1970-71	1.26	0.81	2.07
1971-72	1.27	0.33	1.60
1972-73	1.12	0.22	1.34
1973-74	1.02	0.56	1.58
1974-75	0.94	0.29	1.23

Source: Australian Bureau of Statistics, Ref. No. 4.11 and 1973 Yearbook, p. 132.

Chapter II

SOURCES OF SCHOOL FINANCE

To gain a clear picture of the sources of educational finance in Australia it is necessary to consider the ways in which funds are raised by governments, the factors influencing allocations to education and the ways in which funds flow among levels of government. Apart from the small proportion of contributions from individuals the resources available to government schools derive from governments and even in the non-government sector, where private contributions are higher, government sources of funding are very important.

There are no specific education taxes nor are particular sources of government revenue earmarked for educational purposes. Both Commonwealth and State governments consolidate the revenue available to them and then allocate a portion of the consolidated revenue to each government function.

The Commonwealth obtains its funds from a wide range of sources, the most significant of which are taxes on personal income (paid on a graduated scale according to level of earnings) and on company profits (a fixed percentage); excise and customs duties, sales taxes and surpluses on public business undertakings are other major revenue sources.

State governments derive their revenue from Commonwealth government financial assistance and from State taxes, most of which, since the transfer of income taxing responsibility to the Commonwealth in 1942, have been non-growth in nature (for example, motor taxes, probate and stamp duties), payroll tax being the significant exception. State taxes currently constitute about 40 per cent of all State revenue. Loans are raised on both the Australian and international markets for capital works.

Although the major sources of general revenue are in the hands of the Commonwealth it must reallocate some of the revenue to the States. Similarly the States must depend in part on the Commonwealth for funds despite the fact that they are responsible for the services. Both levels of government are remote from individual tax payers and local schools. In these circumstances it is not surprising that decisions about the magnitude of educational finance and the uses to which it will be put are determined in Australia by a complex interaction in which interest groups, the media, government agencies, academics and political parties are all involved. Proposals for new policies emanate from various quarters but they need general support before they are seriously considered or adopted. Teacher associations, parent organisations and church affiliated bodies are increasingly successful at mobilising opinion within their own organisations and even linking with one another to build an influential political base.

While Parliament is ultimately decisive in making allocations of funds (at both State and Commonwealth levels) most budgetary decisions are taken by the

Cabinet of the ruling political party. Although these decisions are taken in the light of specific policies which led to the Government's election and in the light of the balance of public pressures, in Australia as in other countries the permanent public service exerts a strong influence. In the schools field, public officials are most often professional educationists who have strong policy viewpoints which they put to their political masters.

The dependence of schools (whether government or non-government) upon centrally raised and allocated funds means that financing patterns are largely influenced by the constraints of the general administrative and financial framework of government. For example, finance for schools must be arranged in ways which meet the requirements of Treasury and Audit Acts; and government employing authorities such as Public Service Boards and Teachers' Tribunals control the salaries and working conditions of people engaged in education and hence have considerable independent financial influence. Consideration of alternative sources and methods of educational funding is thus influenced by administrative and fiscal mechanisms as much as by assessments of educational effectiveness.

The sources and magnitude of funds flowing to typical primary schools in 1976 are shown in Figure 1. For government schools it can be seen that most of the funds come from State sources with Commonwealth support being significant though relatively small, and private contributions being negligible. Private sources of finance (including contributed effort) constitute somewhat less than half of the total budget of most non-government primary schools, the remainder being made up through government subsidies. While there are common sources of funds for all non-government schools, the relative volumes of funds flowing from these sources vary markedly according to the traditional levels of service, the fee structures and the institutional backing of the schools. (It is emphasised that the overall magnitude of funds flowing to any particular school can vary markedly from these norms—particularly in the non-government sector.)

Figure 2 sets out the major interrelationships among sources of educational finance.

Figure 1. **Sources and magnitude of recurrent funds for typical Australian primary schools**

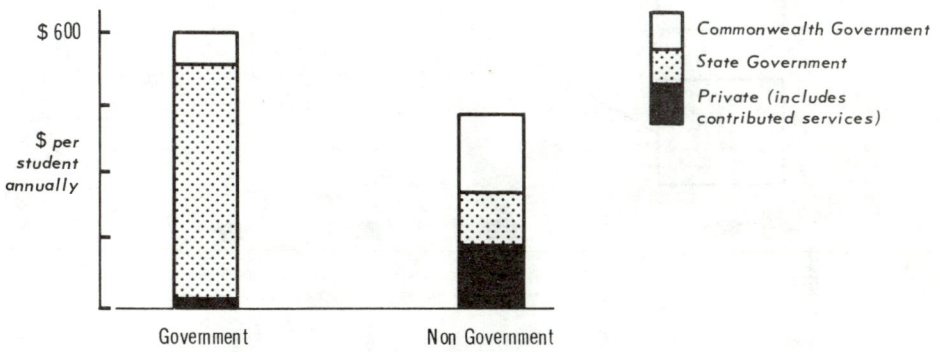

Figure 2. Sources of school finance in Australia

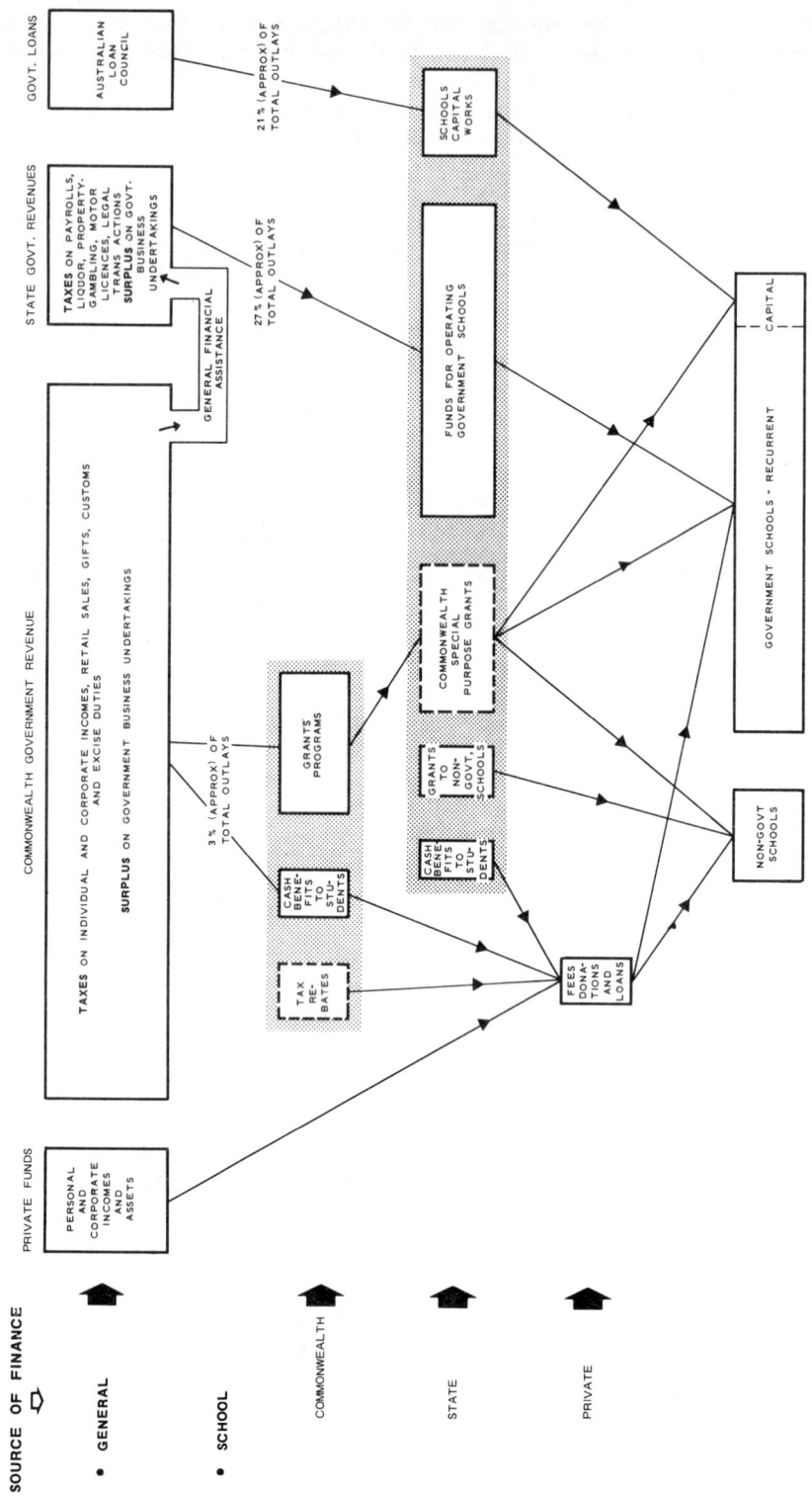

COMMONWEALTH SOURCES

From the revenue available to it the Commonwealth Government meets the costs of the public services it provides and the cash benefits it gives to individuals and organisations, as well as the grants it makes to other levels of government. It is through the device of transfer payments to the States that the Commonwealth is a major source of funds for schools.

There are three types of general grants provided to the States as "untied" subventions to their budgets: in addition there are grants for capital works. The largest of these general grants are the *financial assistance grants* which are paid to all States and were until fifteen years ago termed "tax reimbursement grants" because they were conceived in the late 1940s as a tax reimbursement to the States for their having agreed to cease collecting income tax. These grants are now based upon a formula which is usually reviewed every five years. It takes into account population increases, wage increases and betterment factors and other adjustments such as offsetting the financial effects of shifts in responsibilities between Commonwealth and State governments. As the level of funds derived from State government taxes is relatively fixed Commonwealth financial assistance grants (see Table 7) which currently comprise about 35 per cent of all State revenue are a significant determinant of State government resources. These grants, which assist States to meet their general commitments (one of the most demanding being education), are not restricted by conditions and thus do not predetermine priorities in States' spending activities. However, they are in practice used for recurrent rather than for capital purposes.

Table 7. **Commonwealth payments to the States, 1975/76**

$m

Nature and Type	Amount
GENERAL PURPOSE:	
Financial assistance	3 073
Special	39
Capital works (including Loans)	1 139
Total	4 251
SPECIFIC PURPOSE:	
Education	1 461
Health	1 083
Transport	495
Housing	363
Urban and Regional Development	263
Social Security and Welfare	182
Total	3 847
OTHER:	
Assistance related to State debts, Local Government and Special Revenues (e.g. natural disaster relief)	152
TOTAL GRANTS (net of repayments)	8 250

Source: Payments to or for the States... 1966/77, AGPS 1976 (1976/77 Budget Paper, No. 7).

Some States in a weak financial position can seek *special grants*, the amount depending upon the extent to which a "claimant" State is assessed to be lagging behind "standard" States with respect to its capacity to provide equivalent services.

A Commonwealth Grants Commission has, since 1934/35, undertaken the recommendation of this assistance. Since the grants themselves are untied despite the detailed consideration given to special factors there is no obligation upon a State to allocate such additional funds to schools. Nevertheless there is an acknowledged, if indirect, relationship to school financing inherent in this funding mechanism. Only one State presently benefits from special grants and then only by a relatively small amount.

Occasionally the Commonwealth makes *special revenue assistance grants* to compensate particular States for unexpected events, usually related to natural disasters, such as floods or drought. These grants are unimportant as far as the overall flow of funds is concerned and have no particular bearing on finance for education.

With respect to finance for capital works, the Australian Loan Council, representative of the Commonwealth and State Governments, approves the annual borrowing programs of all levels of government. Until 1970/71 funds for State capital works and housing programs were met entirely from the loans program, but since then a proportion (currently one-third) of the total loans program for State governments is provided as an interest-free *capital grant* by the Commonwealth Government. This modification was made to assist the States in expenditure on capital works from which debt charges are not recovered, that is, on non-revenue-producing assets such as schools. Because there is no specification of the capital purposes for which the grants are to be used, the capital grants are regarded as general rather than specific purpose grants.

Over recent years Commonwealth grants to the States have been channelled increasingly through instruments specific (or "tied") to a particular activity: this approach is characteristic of funds applied to education. One reason for this trend in the schools area is that a number of *specific purpose grants* were established because the Commonwealth accepted a particular national responsibility (for example, the welfare of Aborigines) which had educational implications. Second, some financial responsibility for schools in the States has been acknowledged by the Commonwealth Government since 1964/65 when specific grants were offered for the improvement of science teaching facilities for both government and non-government secondary schools. A third reason is that there has been growing community and political pressure on the Commonwealth to increase its responsibility for school financing as in other non-traditional areas such as transportation. As the Commonwealth wishes to be seen as having a direct influence on improvements to schools in the States and, presumably, to retain some control over expenditure, specific purpose grants provided the means. Although specific purpose grants for education are tied, in that they must be spent on education, most of the funds are distributed to suit the preferences of the recipient, according to broad guidelines.

Whereas in 1970/71 specific purpose grants formed approximately 25 per cent of total grants to the States, by 1975/76 they constituted 48 per cent. Education payments grew from making up 27 per cent to 36 per cent of all specific purpose grants over this period. Some of this growth can be attributed to the Commonwealth's assumption of full responsibility for financing tertiary education in place of a previous system whereby State governments were obliged to provide matching funds from their own sources in order to receive grants. In addition, and as indicated in Table 8, there has been a marked increase in commitment of Commonwealth funds to school-level education, especially from the 1974 calendar year when funds recommended by the Schools Commission began to be applied to schools.

In all, the Commonwealth specifically contributes, on average, approximately 14 per cent of the total funding of government schools and some 35 per cent

Table 8. **Commonwealth government outlays on education 1972/73 to 1975/76 (actual) and 1976/77 (estimate)**

$m

Level	1972-73 Actual	1973-74 Actual	1974-75 Actual	1975-76 Actual	1976-77 Estimate
Universities	190	331	552	604	673
Colleges of Advanced Education	72	193	393	435	507
Technical and Further Education	19	41	71	102	122
Schools	124	227	528	610	690
Pre-schools	1	7	46	65	74
Special groups	29	47	66	77	59
General administration	10	12	17	21	22
Cost supplementation	—	—	—	—	60
Total (less recoveries)	443	857	1 672	1 912	2 204

Source: Budget Paper No. 8 of 1975/76 and No. 1 1976/77.

of non-government schools in the States through State Grants legislation by authority of Section 96 of the Constitution.

Besides specific purpose grants there are some *indirect* sources of Commonwealth government finance for school-level education. Income tax concessions available to persons spending upon certain items of education are a case in point. Whilst there is no outlay of funds the cost in terms of forgone taxation has been considerable, for example, approximately $120 million for concessional deductions in 1973/74 (the latest data available: this cost would currently be much larger). Also, funds for programs operated through portfolios other than education for the benefit of particular groups such as handicapped persons or for particular purposes such as health education have an impact on schools, although not one of great significance.

STATE SOURCES

State governments in 1975/76 are estimated to be on average the source of about 84 per cent and 15 per cent of the expenditure on government and non-government schools respectively. Educational funding by the States occurs through the overall budget rather than by means of discrete financial instruments because the financing of schools is an integral and major aspect of State government activities. Funds are authorised through general appropriations for teacher salaries, materials, scholarships and so on, instead of by special purpose legislation and with the previously discussed Commonwealth grants. Nevertheless the structure of the State budget makes this important source of funds a powerful financial instrument. As there is no specifically designated "schools" tax the financial resources directed to education depend upon the relative priority accorded to schooling when State budgets are formulated. The national average proportion of total State revenue devoted to school-level education in the last decade has moved from 21 per cent in 1966/67 to 27 per cent in 1975/76.

Each State government has its annual borrowing program approved by the Australian Loan Council (see page 20) and is free to allocate these funds for whatever capital purposes it chooses. Over the past three years some 21 per cent of total capital outlays by the States have been devoted to schools. States tend not to augment the capital program funds raised from loans with consolidated revenue funds.

Specific purpose recurrent grants received from the Commonwealth for schools flow mainly through five programs of the federal Schools Commission (General Recurrent Grants, Disadvantaged Schools Special Education, Services and Development and Special Projects). A Capital Grants Program is based on the States' particular building needs with respect to general facilities, disadvantaged schools, special education and libraries but may in fact be spent by the States as they determine. Some 80 per cent of the Commonwealth funds are contained in general resources programs which do not restrict the application of funds to particular educational purposes.

PRIVATE SOURCES

A small proportion of the costs of operating government schools (generally some 2 to 3 per cent) is raised from private sources to meet their locally identified needs. As government schools do not have the legal right to demand fees (although in some States small levies are made), the extent of the contributions made by parents are broadly related to socio-economic (neighbourhood) factors. Non-government schools rely upon fees from parents and upon financial support and frequently contributed services from community (especially religious) organisations to operate and to build schools.

To supplement private effort non-government schools which fulfil minimum legal and/or educational requirements receive public financial assistance from both State and Commonwealth sources. State governments provide recurrent per capita payments to parents or schools, bursaries and, with one exception, interest subsidies on building loans. The Commonwealth Government makes recurrent and capital grants to schools via State governments for both general underpinning and specific program purposes.

Chapter III

FINANCIAL INSTRUMENTS FOR SCHOOL-LEVEL EDUCATION

Having described the major sources of funds for school-level education in Australia particular financial instruments used to apply funds can now be discussed in more detail. Any specific structure or flow of funds for education is regarded for this purpose as a financial instrument. Thus the term instrument is applied to a financing arrangement whether or not it has been devised with deliberate policy intent. It is not always easy to discern whether a particular financial action is integral or peripheral to the accompanying legal, administrative and informational moves which together make a policy thrust. In the discussion, however, the potential and limitations of the financial aspects will be distinguished as far as possible.

For instance, government school-teachers' salaries are listed as a line item in State budgets and this is a convenient way of making clear the purposes for which funds are to be used. This centralised salary provision allows not only the payment of teachers but also staff appointments and promotions to be organised on a State-wide basis. While facilitating equality of educational services for all students in the State, such a provision inevitably inhibits diversity.

It is characteristic of Australia that the State financial instruments have remained essentially unchanged for many years so that their connection with specific policy issues has not always been seen to be close. But as recent Commonwealth action has shown, nothing prevents the development of new financial instruments if the political will exists, and if it is desired to approach particular policy objectives more directly and explicity. In the discussion of Commonwealth, State and private instruments which follows, the importance of existing instruments, the influence of the newer Commonwealth initiatives and the impact on policy which emerges from the overall complex of funding instruments, are of considerable interest.

COMMONWEALTH

Commonwealth programs are obviously financial instruments because they tend to operate in a defined and identifiable way within specific enabling legislation and often arise from public investigations (for example, by the Schools Commission) which define the rationale and purposes of the grants. To the extent that they are effective, this effectiveness stems in part from their relative newness and openness to change and in part from the fact that most of them are intended to operate in a co-ordinated way so that increased general resources are accompanied by staff development, support for innovation, encouragement of new structures and continuous appraisal. Their importance is also partly due to the fact that they work at the margin where their influence is disproportionate to their size. Given that most educational finance is tied up in annually recurring commitments, any increase in the relatively small amount of funds available for new projects or purposes has a highly visible effect. The programs are discussed in sequence according to their degree of effect upon educational expenditure. Only those having a significant bearing on primary education are taken up.

Specific purpose funds for government primary schools did not become available until 1972. Table 9 sets out the distribution of funds allocated for 1976 by program, State and sector. Although allocations for primary and secondary levels are determined separately, the amounts flow to States as a single grant to be used at their discretion. Over the last three years there has been periodic supplementation of grants to offset the effects of inflation.

Table 9. **Summary of Commonwealth specific purpose grants for schools in the States by program and sector 1976**

$m (June 1975 prices)

Program	Amount	Program	Amount
GOVERNMENT SCHOOL PROGRAMS		PROGRAMS AVAILABLE FOR ALL SCHOOLS	
General Recurrent Grants	163.9	Special Education:	
Disadvantaged Schools	13.5	Training	0.8
Special Education	8.2	Replacement	5.8
Capital Grants	100.0	Development Activities:	
Total	286.4	Training	6.1
		Replacement	1.9
NON-GOVERNMENT SCHOOLS PROGRAMS		Education Centres:	
General Recurrent Grants	131.7	General Support	0.9
Disadvantaged Schools	2.1	Facilities	0.4
Special Education	3.0	Special Projects	3.6
Capital Grants	21.0	Total	19.5
Total	157.8	ALL PROGRAMS	463.7

Source: States Grants (Schools) Act 1976.

Specific purpose ("section 96") grants to government school systems

The *General Recurrent Grants Program* provides funds to each government school system to augment expenditure on staff and other operating items provided by the State's own sources. It is essentially a resources supplementation and equalisation program. The level of resource availability for schools in each State is compared and grants are provided to increase those resources, more being allocated where services to students are poorer. The tied nature of the grants ensures that they go towards raising the overall level of services to students even in States which assign a low priority to schools in their spending. The only portion of the $164 million Program earmarked in any way is an amount of $15 million designated for the special educational needs of non-English speaking migrant children and those arising from other aspects of the multi-cultural Australian environment.

A substantial allocation is made as a *Disadvantaged Schools Program* to cater for the special needs of government schools in poorer areas whether these are in the country, the inner city, or outer suburbs. State allocations are decided on socio-economic criteria. A major strategy of this Program—which recognises the educational implications of socio-economic disadvantage and seeks to address them—is to encourage the school and its community to participate in the development of approaches catering for the particular learning needs of its children. The lump sum grants are administered by task forces which distribute funds to eligible schools on the basis of projects put forward by the school community.

Special Education Program funds are available for additional educational assistance to handicapped children for whom special schools tend to be the most frequent provision. The Program is also intended to encourage arrangements which will lead to an increasing number of these children being integrated into ordinary schools.

Grants to government school systems through the *Capital Grants Program* meet a wide range of purposes including the provision of new places and a greater variety of facilities and the restoration and improvement of existing buildings. Funds are used at the discretion of the State, which is asked to observe notional allocations for particular needs (for example, disadvantaged and special schools).

Specific purpose ("section 96") grants to non-government schools and systems

The major Program for non-government schools is for *General Recurrent Grants,* which currently provides non-government schools and systems with extensive subsidies. To determine grants the cost of conducting non-government schools is considered in relation to their size and type of enrolment (primary, junior and senior secondary students) and the school or school system is assigned one of six levels of subsidy per pupil depending on the amount of private resources available (that is, the "need" of the school). Commonwealth subsidies are decided independently of State payments but the combination of the two sets of grants at present ranges between 30 per cent and 50 per cent of the operating costs for similar government schools.

Non-government *disadvantaged schools* are funded through a Program which applies similar criteria to those applied to government schools. *Special education* funds for the non-government sector have a double purpose: grants are made to the States to allow them to give additional assistance to meet the needs of handicapped children enrolled in non-government special schools, or to allow them to accept into the public system those non-government schools wishing to be taken over. The policy thrust is that governments should assume responsibility for the schooling of all children whose parents wish it, even for those handicapped children for whom government school provision was not previously available.

Commonwealth *capital grants* account for about one-half of all expenditure on non-government school buildings in Australia. In each State and Territory a committee of the Schools Commission makes recommendations to the Commission on the allocation of funds. Recommendations are based on two factors, the relative educational need of the school for a particular facility and the amount of government subvention necessary to mount the project. A specific amount is then allocated to a school, usually indicated as a proportion of the estimated final cost of a building project. The educational need for the facility governs its provision, not the capacity of the school to contribute funds.

In summary, grants to non-government schools are characterised by their significance in terms of their proportionate contribution to the overall operating costs of the non-government sector and the freedom of individual schools or systems to deploy funds in any manner consistent with the particular purpose for which they have been allocated.

Specific purpose ("section 96") grants for joint programs

Table 9 also shows that there are a number of inter-sector (government and non-government) programs funded by the Commonwealth. The *Services and Development Program* caters for the in-service training of teachers for special education and for teacher-librarians. It also caters for the planning of support services to schools on an intersystemic basis, for development activities for teachers, other school staff and parents and for the support of autonomous Education Centres.

The *Special Projects Program* (often referred to as "Innovations") is intended to foster change by encouraging fresh approaches and local participation—whether on an individual or group basis. This is the only example of the Commonwealth making grants direct to schools in the States. Projects are chosen according to the merits of proposals put forward by schools in their own context. Grants are usually small (on average $5 000) but as they are approved after local consultation and via a "second channel" outside the normal authority hierarchy they are very popular. The Program uses less than one per cent of Commonwealth specific purpose funds for schools but is currently sponsoring projets in more than 1 000 schools. Funds are also provided within this Program for nation-wide projects and evaluation studies. Action research projects in key areas of special need have been initiated, including the education of Aboriginal and country children and of girls.

Student assistance ("section 51 xxiiiA") grants

The Commonwealth Department of Education administers a scheme of Assistance for Isolated Children which provides boarding and correspondence education allowances and assists in other cases of special hardship as, for example, where handicapped children are forced to live away from home. That Department also administers the Aboriginal Study Grants and Secondary Grants Schemes which, because they are age-related, are sometimes received by older students attending primary classes. The Department of Repatriation administers a Soldiers' Children Education Scheme and the Department of Social Security administers a Handicapped Child's Allowance, both of which apply in part to the primary school. These direct benefits provided to parents of selected primary school students are, in terms of both scope and money, relatively minor financial instruments in comparison with other grants, though not of course as far as individual recipients are concerned.

STATE GOVERNMENTS

General budgetary allocations

The annual budget of each State Government is made up after consideration, on the one side, of the resources available to it, including funds from the Commonwealth Government both untied and tied, and on the other side, of its existing commitments and promises in all areas including education. Within the total allocation for schools, funds are allocated to functional areas such as salaries, transport, equipment or student assistance. The allocations are intended to sustain existing policies or give effect to policy promises. A common practice in each State education department is to pay all staff on a central payroll and to deploy staff throughout the State according to school entitlements based on enrolments. Similarly equipment is often allocated to schools on a formula basis (dependent on the size of the school). It is not customary for States to use legislation, other than the annual legislation, to appropriate the budgets for government departments, as a means of relating finance to educational policies.

It has been customary for the annual financial allocations to be divided within education departments according to the head office divisions (primary, secondary or special education) rather than integrated regional allocations. There are regional directors of education within every State but recurrent resources come to them in forms other than cash, such as staff quotas or authority to let transport tenders within policies determined at headquarters. They have little power and schools have even less to re-arrange the priorities across spending categories, or even, in some cases, to authorise and pay for goods and services from local suppliers. Financial transactions are subject to State treasury regulations and audit requirements. These invariably put a high premium on precisely and minutely stated (in government gazettes) headquarters directives, on substantial documentation and on supervision of transactions by Treasury. Permanent heads of education departments cannot initiate new financial channels without long and tortuous negotiations and in the ultimate the sanction of treasuries.

The power that centralised budgetary processes gives to government school system authorities to post their teachers to any locations means that no gross inequalities need occur as a result of the State funding mechanism. To date the mechanism has not however been administered in ways which make it seem strong enough to overcome the natural tendency for experienced and more senior teachers to seek positions in schools in favoured regions; they tend to work in more attractive areas, while less popular (lower socio-economic and distant rural) areas generally find it somewhat more difficult to obtain equivalent staff. Nor until recently did authorities seek to discriminate positively in favour of schools which experienced the greatest difficulty in raising supplementary resources by their own efforts, those schools almost invariably being schools with the greatest need. The possibilities and limitations of this instrument will be further analysed in *Chapter VI*.

Student Assistance

Schemes for direct assistance to students are not of great significance at the State government level, with the exception of per capita payments for students attending non-government schools. Different types of assistance currently available are set out in Table 10. The fact that they can be paid in the form of cash, in direct support of a particular policy, and directly to the intended beneficiary does illustrate that State budgets can in fact be flexible financial instruments.

Table 10. **Typical benefits provided by State governments to school students**

Type of assistance	Description
Conveyance allowances	Free transport, rebates or subsidies
Textbook allowances	Sometimes means tested, often paid directly to schools
Special bursaries	Varying levels of assistance, variously awarded
Remote area allowances	Varying criteria (such as distance from nearest school) sometimes supplementary to Commonwealth allowances
Special education allowances	Awarded to handicapped children sometimes supplementary Commonwealth allowances
Per capita grants	To non-government schools, or to parents sending their children to such schools

Capital expenditure

Each State government has traditionally been responsible for building government schools and providing other capital resources where and when required. States have interpreted this obligation as necessitating central decision-making about major capital allocations. The need for this approach was probably reinforced by rapid expansion in school enrolments after 1950, leaving little discretion to States other than to try to assess where the most pressing needs for new, additional or upgraded improvements lay. The Department of Education in most States is a client of the Department of Public Works, which is the construction authority. While the use of private architects is not common the use of private sector builders, through the tender system, is widespread. The only significant variation from this broad pattern has been a recent development in Victoria where the structure of decision-making with respect to priorities among building works has been altered to incorporate various local, regional and State levels of responsibility for allocation of resources. Local communities are rarely consulted on the detailed planning of new school facilities.

State governments do not provide initial financial assistance to non-government schools when they embark on building programs but operate schemes which provide various levels of interest subsidy (usually around 7 per cent) on loans raised for approved projects.

PRIVATE SOURCES

Government schools

There are few distinctive "official" financial instruments operative at government primary schools with respect to private sources of finance, though Parents and Citizens' Associations operate extensively as fund raising bodies. A common means for raising revenue is through voluntarily contributed general fees and this is usually supplemented by levies imposed for the hire or purchase of books, sporting equipment, excursions and so forth. In addition a wide range of other revenue generating activities are engaged in, such as school fetes. It is the responsibility of parents to provide sets of uniforms for children: these are not compulsory, but accepted in many schools. Funds raised by Parents and Citizens' Associations may be spent either on priorities determined by the Association or (more often) on projects proposed by the school principal.

Non-government schools

In addition to Commonwealth and State grants to non-government schools (and other sources of income if the school is linked with a church community) these schools must raise income through school fees. The fee structure at the primary school level is fairly uniform within individual schools across the range of grades as there is not usually a major differences between the type of educational provision made for classes at the primary level. There are, however, considerable differences among primary schools in the levels of fees charged, the current charges ranging between $50 and $1 000 per annum.

It is not unusual, especially in some religious affiliated schools, to operate family concessional rates if more than one child from the same family attends the school or if the family is deemed to require special consideration on the grounds of economic hardship. Some schools provide scholarships for open competition, or bursaries for needy students. Overall, the distribution of schools according to amounts of fees collected is biased heavily towards the low-fee end of the scale. In 1974 more than 50 per cent of primary schools collected $50 or less per student in fees, which was about 10 per cent of equivalent government primary school running costs for that year.

Non-government schools also need to raise funds for capital purposes, their sources varying according to their clientele. The organisation of some schools into co-ordinated systems has enabled the formation of central building funds which have helped harness the resources of supporters and facilitate access to private sector finance. In more recent years a far greater proportion of capital funds has been provided from the Commonwealth Government for these purposes, and interest subsidies by State governments on loans have reduced the financial impost on the schools themselves.

Chapter IV

SELECTED POLICY ISSUES: AUSTRALIAN PERSPECTIVES

EQUALITY

Educational discussion in Australia has reflected the international preoccupation with "equality". Does equality relate to opportunity offered, resources disbursed, or benefits received? The Australian interest also reflects its traditional egalitarian concerns. There is nation-wide awareness that problems relating to the education of Aborigines, migrants, the poor, country dwellers, girls and the handicapped are issues of equality.

In earlier discussion reference was made to the way in which the States have traditionally striven to provide equality of opportunity through equalisation of resource provision and access through State-wide systems of government schools. That approach has been complemented by Commonwealth fiscal arrangements which have sought to equalise capacity between the wealthy and less wealthy States. Most Australians have held as a strong belief that equality rests on equal access to equal resources and that achievement and social mobility depend largely on the exploitation of such access and on the development of individual potential. Such beliefs were certainly important in fostering the extension of opportunities for secondary schooling which occurred in the 1950s and 1960s.

The type of schooling provided—that is, universally comprehensive at the primary school level and generally comprehensive at the secondary level—reflects the general view of equality. Nevertheless, in some States a few academically selective secondary schools have been retained; and in most States, within the "secondary comprehensive" framework streaming and tracking have been common after the initial year or two.

Despite general community support for egalitarian principles, evidence has emerged which suggests that in Australia, as elsewhere, higher socio-economic groups remain relatively favoured in proportion to the general population on general indices of school success.

The Commonwealth's involvement in education at the school level following the creation of a federal Schools Commission in late 1973 has also rested in part on an equality of opportunity perspective. This perspective accepts that schools have limited impact on social mobility but nevertheless supports the view that current evidence about the effectiveness of schools only deals with what has been, not with what might be; accordingly there is a need for schools to continue to be concerned with both individual and group success. It is a special responsibility of schools to help students develop the competencies which give them power over their circumstances. The nation cannot be satisfied for some to succeed while many are pushed aside through repeated failure while in school. The view is that all young people should leave school confident that they can not only cope with the workings of the adult world but also participate in shaping it. This aspect of the general perspective has provided the rationale for the increases in the levels of resources of the past three years, in the hope that better resources would enable schools to provide more adequately for the needs of every student.

In relation to equality among groups, the view is that schools should make a more significant contribution to equalising the life-chances of children from differing social backgrounds by responding to the circumstances of students, giving special assistance where out-of-school conditions are least supportive of formal learning. Similarly, school experience should not contribute to a lowering of the aspiration and attainment of groups of children whose upbringing and family situations are unlike those of the usually most successful. Groupings of children whose backgrounds are normally associated with lower than average school success is in itself an added disadvantage. Such schools need special attention and superior resources.

Accordingly, stress is being placed on the need for positive discrimination towards the less favoured groups. An "activist" public policy of assisting all individuals to acquire basic competencies is being applied to primary education in particular and especially to demonstrably disadvantaged groups such as the handicapped, country students, girls, migrants and Aborigines.

Although these perspectives on equality are not shared by everyone the thrust of the special purpose grants provided by the Commonwealth and the ideas advanced in Schools Commission reports have been generally well received. Yet there is continuing imbalance in spending at different educational levels, which ensures that the traditionally favoured social groups, who stay on at school longest and achieve entry to tertiary institutions, have several times as much public money spent on their education as those who leave early. Some adjustment to the balance of government spending on primary, secondary and tertiary education has begun to redress this inequity, but the movement is as yet slight.

There is also considerable agreement that although additional resources are necessary they are not sufficient in themselves to ensure equality of opportunity. Promoting the quality of education is, thus, of major concern at present, particularly as there is a small but vocal group within the community arguing that current concepts of equality of opportunity inevitably lead to a general decline in excellence and intellectual aspiration. The practical problem is to ensure that concern for equality of opportunity is also concern for individual and group excellence, that a discussion about means is not interpreted as a disagreement about ends.

Ironically, the denial of public financial aid for many years to the more than 20 per cent of children in private schools has provided the political anvil for hammering out a national view of equality of opportunity. Beginning in the 1950s and accelerating in the 1970s, aid has been extended to prevent the collapse of the part of the non-government sector which had been affected by the reduction in contributed service of religious staff and by inflation. Despite massive increases in support the gap between the resources of those schools and those of government schools has not been closed and the controversy continues about the degree of responsibility which should be accepted by governments, whether State or Commonwealth, for ensuring equal opportunities for all within a framework of choice between government and non-government schooling.

SPECIAL GROUPS

Several minority groups in Australia have suffered particular educational disadvantage. The groups which will be discussed briefly here are rural dwellers, Aborigines and migrants. The list is by no means exhaustive (for example, the particular educational needs of girls and of handicapped children are not dealt with), but an effort has been made to focus on issues which are particular, if not unique, to Australia.

Rural dwellers

Australia is a vast land and despite the major concentration of population in the State capital cities many children are remote from settlement or totally isolated. All States have developed "correspondence" schooling (in 1974 over 15 000 students were receiving their education by correspondence) which in some cases is supplemented by "schools of the air"—direct radio contact between teacher and pupil. The estimated number of school children living in rural areas or in towns of 5 000 or less is approximately 60 000 or some 3 per cent of all school students. Some of these children attend private boarding schools or State hostels. The provision by States of boarding allowances for isolated students has been common though Commonwealth allowances have created a nation-wide provision (more than 20 000 students currently benefit from this allowance). Consolidation of small rural schools, allied with subsidies for travel and provision of school transport have been widespread practices in most States, aimed at improving the quality of the educational experience as well as containing expenditure.

By maintaining control over teacher posting State education authorities have been able to ensure that teachers are available for rural areas. However, teacher turnover in these areas is high and many experienced teachers have been reluctant to face what they have regarded as prolonged "exile" from large centres. Cultural facilities are few and expectations of country children are circumscribed by their environments. While Australia has undertaken many and varied initiatives to alleviate the educational disadvantages of rural dwellers few feel that the problems have as yet been overcome.

Aborigines

Aborigines (and Torres Strait Islanders) represent the one per cent of Australia's population about whose educational needs, until the last ten years, there has been grossly insufficient concern. They live in a variety of circumstances ranging from nomadic tribal groups to fully integrated city dwellers. Many of their educational problems have arisen from poverty, inadequate health care, geographic and social isolation and a distinctive cultural ethos. Though access by Aborigines to ordinary schools is not debarred in any way, or subject to legal discrimination, difficulties have arisen because the social and economic handicaps experienced by many of them have rendered this access ineffectual, especially as many groups are either isolated or itinerant.

Governments have, particularly over the last ten years, expressed increasing practical concern for particular requirements of Aboriginal education. The States are attempting to develop appropriate curricula and to provide suitable staff and physical support. Expenditure on Aboriginal education at the Commonwealth level has, following a referendum in 1967 which gave the Federal Government particular responsibility for Aborigines, increased considerably: between 1971/72 and 1974/75 there was a fourfold increase in Commonwealth expenditure to approximately $33 million.

The problems surrounding Aboriginal education overlap in many ways with issues related to education of small minority groups in special need. There has in the past been a general lack of appreciation for Aboriginal culture and a non-acceptance of cultural diversity. Aboriginal languages and social and cultural traditions were not generally woven into schooling for Aborigines. In addition, there has been a lack of cultural reciprocity or even sensitivity about Aboriginal culture among white Australians.

Migrants

Since World War II there has been a large intake of migrants to Australia. In 1971 there were more than two and a half million foreign-born residents, over 20 per cent Australia's present population, which is now approaching fourteen million.

Provision for education of migrants developed uncertainly. In the past governments have espoused pluralism and tolerance, but little understanding of the social and cultural problems or the educational difficulties faced by a large number of migrant children (as well as Australian-born children of migrant parents) was evident during the early years of accelerated intake—the 1950s. Migrants have tended to be concentrated in inner-urban areas with many schools having large proportions of children without any facility in English. A 1974 Victorian Education Department study, for example, estimated that only 30 per cent of students in need were receiving tuition in specially formed classes. In some schools up to three quarters of the total enrolment included such children.

The general approach to assisting migrant children has been to organise "withdrawal" classes, offering periods of language assistance apart from normal classroom activities. This approach was supported by the Commonwealth Government in a 1971 policy initiative—the Child Migrant Education Program—sponsored under the Immigration (Education) Act. Recently, however, criticism has been levelled—by educational authorities, groups and individuals concerned with migrant education—at the policy of withdrawal, on the grounds of instructional ineffectiveness as well as of the implicit neglect of cultural identity and the stress placed on cultural assimilation. There is a growing realisation that further work is necessary to devise adequate learning methods, and above all, that Australia should view itself as a multi-cultural society, accepting the cultural consequences and benefits of its diverse population.

LOCUS OF CONTROL

In Australia the question of locus of control is focused in two ways, in relation to Commonwealth-State relationships, and in relation to the possibilities for devolution of authority within centralised school systems to lower levels. The question arises out of concern for educational effectiveness and financial accountability but is also related to power. The States and non-government school authorities sometimes claim that the financial resources of the Commonwealth allow it to arrogate power over education denied to it under the Constitution, yet equally within State systems parents and teachers claim that the central office bureaucracy retains a tight grip on power which should be devolved to lower levels.

Devolution is a popular concept. Its advocates claim that local involvement will help reduce social alienation, promote identification with the school and allow participation in the formulation of objectives. They say decentralisation of authority will increase administrative efficiency and responsiveness to local needs and place responsibility for expenditure on those best able to judge local requirements. There has, however, been little systematic examination of the relationship between the source of funds and legal responsibility for educational policy. As it is unlikely that there will be either new sources of funds below that of the State level or the devolution of State political power, movements in the locus of control to the local level are likely to occur only through delegations of retrievable financial and administrative authority. Not only are the possibilities limited, but it is also questionable what real power there is in a situation where decisions can be over-ruled further up in a hierarchy.

Administrative decentralisation on a regional pattern is practised by almost all States but this rarely extends to devolution of authority to initiate policy. However, limited steps are being taken in some States to devolve some policy matters in respect of staffing and facilities to the regional and even school level. Also, since there are no external examinations at the primary level some devolution of curriculum responsibility to the local level has been possible.

Tensions have arisen in some teachers' unions between a desire to maintain centralised administrative machinery for ease of industrial negotiations and a wish to establish local professional autonomy in curricular activities. The desire for professional autonomy has in turn conflicted with the interest of some assertive parent and community groups—raising the issue of where the barriers between professional and community control, co-operation and autonomy lie.

In considering the extent and form of public financial assistance to schools—whether they be government or non-government schools—the impact of associated controls is important. Some people fear that increased assistance (say, federal aid to State government schools, or State aid to non-government schools) will lead to increased control over the sort of educational services provided: teaching methods, curriculum patterns and so on. But the general power structure of Departments of Education, public examination boards, teacher training institutions, teachers' unions and parent organisations often have the effect of pushing more vigorously than financial instruments towards common practices.

In Australia government finance is not a prerequisite for government control of non-government schools. As the States already have regulatory powers by statute the offer by them of public financial assistance does not automatically involve additional regulations or controls. On the other hand, State regulatory powers have been used sparingly, enabling schools to see themselves as independent in all practical respects. Financial assistance has more threatening potential in relation to control. Schools want to keep maximum autonomy but recognise that increasing financial dependence in practice weakens their autonomy. The possibility, rather than any direct threat, of diminishing assistance is an important factor encouraging compliance with the wishes of the financing authority. The potency of financial instruments in determining the point of control becomes equally obvious when the programs of the more radical alternative schools being financed within government systems become a matter of public debate.

At both Commonwealth and State levels there have been set up advisory bodies to assist in the definition and fulfilment of needs and priorities in education. It is generally accepted that some sort of educational planning is desirable because the characteristics of Australia's economic and political system prevent educational services from reaching maximum efficiency without some external interference. Government involvement is justified on the grounds that its intervention improves the allocation of resources so that society's preferences will be met, that economic stability is promoted and that something highly valued by society—schooling—is given public support.

Some would argue that the very existence of planning bodies with briefs to define national or regional priorities further inhibits devolution of authority whether to State, regional or school levels; for the consequences of autonomy are variety and non-conformity, without any guarantee that established objectives will be satisfied. It is also argued that the establishment of national or State bodies which allocate funds to system authorities which in turn disburse them in fact strengthens already over-centralised educational bureaucracies at the expense of devolution. Moreover, it is already evident that administrative mechanisms necessary to distribute block grants within hitherto loosely organised systems (for example, Catholic schools) has resulted in the strengthening of central authority at the expense of previously existing school autonomy. In short, the financial mechanism is effecting a transfer of power to the centre despite the traditions of local responsibility: the costs and benefits of this transfer have yet to be assessed.

Those who advocate planning agencies point to the difference between planning and bulk resource distribution responsibilities and the operational powers of school system authorities. They cite overseas experience which suggests that an outside stimulus is necessary if centralised systems are to be persuaded to improve. They claim on social and economic grounds that central planning of certain functions allied to local determination and implementation of priorities is eminently desirable and practicable.

DIVERSITY AND CHOICE

The issues of diversity and choice as they relate to schools in Australia include definition of the range of choice there can be within government systems as well as between the government and non-government sectors.

Australian arguments in favour of diversity and choice are based on the desirability of variety, the possibility of generalisable benefits from experimentation and the meeting of desires of parents who for religious, social or educational reasons prefer an alternative to the government school system. The dangers of a monopoly of education have also been advanced as reasons for encouraging a variety of schools. Some also believe that choice within and between sectors of schooling will cause "poor" schools to be exposed and "good" schools to flourish.

The practical possibilities and problems of increasing the range of choice of schooling both on the administrative level and in terms of consequences for society are now being seriously discussed in Australia for the first time. Financial instruments to promote choice would be novel in the Australian context: in assessing alternative strategies for such a purpose most analysts would want to take into account experience with recent Commonwealth specific purpose financial instruments.

While it is recognised that vouchers, modified in particular ways to ensure social equity and paid to all parents, may open up the widest choice there is considerable caution in Australia about the free market approach. There is a widespread belief that any method of assistance to promote diversity and choice through public financial aid must take into account the level and type of service offered and the openness and access to that service in order to guard against unjust discrimination among children according to parental income and preference. Any policy which makes non-government schools less expensive for their users facilitates the choice to move out of public school systems but does nothing about choice within them. Choice within public school systems is not extensive at present for they have not yet been able to abandon geographically zoned entry criteria; but abandonment would amount to little unless there were genuine alternative programs from school to school. Given the State-wide appointment and promotion procedures for teachers which prevent selective appointment of staff with particular views, distinctive school philosophies within State systems do not seem very likely. Indeed it may be more feasible to have a variety of possibilities within an individual school than to promote choice between them.

Chapter V

SELECTED COMMONWEALTH GOVERNMENT FINANCIAL INSTRUMENTS AND THEIR IMPACT ON ASPECTS OF EDUCATIONAL POLICY

PROGRAMS FUNDED UNDER SECTION 96 OF THE CONSTITUTION

General Recurrent Grants for government and non-government schools

The Commonwealth Government introduced general recurrent grants as a major means of supplementing funds provided by State Governments and private sources for the operation of schools. By progressively increasing the resources available to schools (primary schools having the proportionately greater increase) it was planned that all government and non-government schools in Australia would reach specified target standards of resource usage within six years. The Commonwealth judged that the States and non-government schools lacked the capacity to provide sufficient additional resources to remedy the deficiencies in schooling and that it had a responsibility to become involved.

A survey of schools undertaken by the Interim Committee for the Australian Schools Commission provided the necessary confirmation of the existence of deficiencies in school services and the imbalance in the provision of resources not only across States but also between the government and non-government sectors.

The effectiveness of the general recurrent grants instrument depends upon the parties involved continuing to accept it as an appropriate financial mechanism, not an easy requirement given the multiple and competing interests at stake. As funds are provided to the States to be used at their discretion within government school systems they facilitate achievement of the goals of both the Commonwealth and the States. In that they are used for schools, they fulfil Commonwealth purposes; in that the States determine the priorities for their use, they achieve States' goals. From a federal perspective there needs to be a conviction that the schools do require the additional resources when balanced against the capacity and willingness of the nation to support schools in the light of competing demands on the public purse. From the State Government point of view usefulness of the grants depends on the degree to which they are really accepted as being responsive to State priorities. As far as parents and teachers are concerned the effectiveness of the instrument is determined by the extent to which it helps to fulfil their goals.

Some States query the desirability of specific purpose grants for general recurrent expenditure on schools. It is accepted that the needs of schools justify additional Commonwealth grants for educational purposes in the broadest sense.

Their doubt relates to the justification for a continuing specific purpose schools grant in contrast to a more general education grant or, alternatively an increase in the level of Commonwealth assistance to State finances as a whole thus allowing the States themselves to determine whether the funds should be applied to schools. The instrument appears to them as a limitation on their autonomy.

When the grants were introduced it was assumed that States were reaching the upper limit of their capacity to increase resource levels from their own sources. It was considered reasonable to expect States to maintain their own effort while the Commonwealth would provide differential grants allowing all States to improve the standards of their schools, with the lagging States being assisted to catch up. A difficulty with such an approach is that it has benefited most those States which have had least concern for education. Moreover, subsequent assessments based on the level of services offered would result in relatively smaller grants for States which have done more than simply maintain effort compared with grants to those who have allocated no more than the minimum to fulfil the maintenance of effort requirement. In short, the approach penalises State self-help.

One alternative would be some form of matching grant by agreement between Commonwealth and State. The general effect would be a compounding of the increases in school resources in those States with a high preference for education. The States with most need would continue to provide less service and the primary objective for Commonwealth assistance, a national concern to ensure an acceptable level of educational service for every school student in Australia, would be undermined. Thus both approaches have short-comings. The Commonwealth Government has accepted a recommendation by the Schools Commission that from 1977 it operate on the dual principles of ensuring a minimum level of services in schools nationwide by supplementing grants to the below-average States, while at the same time maintaining a basic level of support for all States.

One other point in support of the use of this instrument in preference to, say, channelling the same volume of funds through general financial assistance grants is that the public reports embodying the grants recommendations link discussion of the educational policy rationale for the grants with the method of assessment. This is of major significance because the public record of the principles and data upon which the grants are based allow interested parties access to ideas and otherwise inaccessible information which can be used to promote debate about the effectiveness of specific instruments for particular purposes.

Non-government schools have, in general, welcomed the additional benefits they have obtained as a result of Commonwealth general recurrent grants. Most schools have been enabled to maintain a level of operation otherwise unattainable, especially at a time of declining numbers of religious staff and rapid salary increases of lay staff. Many see the Commonwealth as being more responsive than the States to representations of needs, although the explicit linking of grants to specific policy issues such as equality of opportunity is to some schools a threatening omen. Separate grants by the Commonwealth and the States also permit public comparisons of the generosity of particular governments and consequently an increase of pressure on the less generous ones. In general, however, the grants have been restricted in their effectiveness only by the limits on the total volume of funds available.

Criticism of the instrument as it presently applies to non-government schools has been mounted on two fronts. The first relates to the criteria by which schools are assessed for measuring need. Their financial needs are assessed in terms of the resources available in average government schools, with an allowance for size of school and for the composition (that is, primary, secondary, senior secondary) of students enrolled. The validity of this approach depends on acceptance of the comparability of the cost structures of government and non-government schools and on the validity of measuring the services available to students rather than the capacity of parents to pay. There is a clear difference of stance between those who believe that the educational services available to students should depend on the level of resources their parents can pay for and those who believe that resource levels should relate basically to student needs irrespective of parental capacity or willingness to pay.

The second criticism relates to whether the Commonwealth should continue with a system of differential grants to non-government schools. Alternatives posed are either a system of uniform per capita payments to non-government schools or vouchers to ensure a specified minimum level of public assistance to all school pupils whether they are enrolled in government or non-government schools. The arguments for these views are usually based on the grounds that all parents make taxation payments which enter a common public revenue pool and all are entitled to benefit from the normal range of services funded from that pool.

This instrument has a bearing on the four policy issues discussed in Chapter IV. It is concerned with *equality,* through the provision of an acceptable level of resources for all schools and systems; it focuses on *school-level control* of resources; it draws attention to the needs of *special groups,* by encouraging the selective and differential application of additional resources; and it fosters *diversity and choice* through the "un-earmarked" nature of the grants. Internal tensions arise among these four objectives: allocation decisions which attempt to achieve equality of basic resource provision across schools and to cater for the needs of special groups often conflict with financial incentives to locate control at the local school level and to encourage choice and diversity in schooling.

Disadvantaged Schools Grants

This specific purpose Program is seen by the Commonwealth as an instrument to provide supplementary inputs of resources to schools catering for low socio-economic groups, primarily in the hope of improving educational outcomes through the development of relevant and enjoyable school activities. The Program epitomises moves from a major concern with inputs to consideration of the way resources are related to the processes of and outcomes from schooling. A link between certain socio-economic factors and the range of educational experiences of students was accepted, and it was an integral aspect of the political and social philosophy of the then Federal Government to strive for greater equality of outcomes across groups. There was considerable evidence of the existence of concentrated educational disadvantage in inner-city and some rural areas. Data were gathered from the 1971 national census and school authorities about which schools might be identified as drawing pupils from homes of socio-economic disadvantage.

Some State governments are wary of the methods of operation of the Disadvantaged Schools Program seeing it as possibly threatening traditional patterns of power and influence, in spite of the fact that the funds are paid through State treasuries and the decentralised administration of the Program minimises the direct involvement of the Commonwealth. The threat appears at two points. First, the juxtaposition of publicly stated policy initiatives with the provision of funds encourages public surveillance, even when funds are not legally tied; and second, funds are provided with the intention that States will employ participatory decision-making procedures. Teachers, parents and, where appropriate, students are expected to discuss needs, consider strategies and then develop or area-based committees set up by the State, the school community itself will implement. Since the pattern of devolved decision-making was insised on by the Commonwealth when the grants were first made the States were put under pressure to operate in ways they might not have adopted if there had been no program.

In the short run effectiveness depends upon continued Commonwealth and State commitment to these values—that is, the search for the appropriate learning through the involvement of individual schools and a responsiveness to what is seen as a way to solve local problems. In the longer run the test will be whether those ways of allocating resources and making decisions are seen to be ways of increasing the effectiveness of schools. The acid test will be the degree to which experience gained through the Program affects traditional patterns of administration: that is, the degree to which schools and school systems extend the principles of the Program to the allocation of the majority of their resources. If so, the need for this distinctive financial instrument, which is in any case limited in application to about 12 per cent of schools, will diminish over time.

Whilst evaluation of the Program to date is still in progress there is evidence to suggest that it is achieving its intended effects in relation to means as well as ends. Greater resources are being allocated to schools with the greatest need. There is more participative decision-making and more responsiveness by all those involved.

The extent to which Federal Government objectives are achieved by operating through school systems over which they have no managerial control will always depend upon the attitudes of those systems and the effectiveness of the actions taken by monitoring committees and individuals who are implementing particular projects. Federal level objectives will certainly be modified because the instrument is one by which resources are applied to schools after passing through several intermediate layers of administration. On the other hand Commonwealth commitment to the importance of co-operation and devolution as means to more effective schooling in Australia implies that its own instruments should exemplify the approaches it hopes will be adopted generally, even if there will inevitably be some loss of efficiency in its own instruments.

Thus this financial instrument relates to the four policy issues upon which attention is being focused: aspiration towards more *equal outcomes* from those schools enrolling students from lower socio-economic levels compared with other schools; emphasis on *school-level control* of the Program; treatment of a *particular socio-economic group* which is deserving of special attention; and stimulation of *diverse approaches* instead of continuing established procedures in an uncritical way.

TAXATION CONCESSIONS FOR EDUCATION EXPENSES

Taxation concessions are used to compensate taxpayers for education expenses incurred from private sources. The structure, purpose and effects of this instrument have varied in its almost twenty-five years of operation. Over most of that period, however, it has taken the form of a reduction in taxable income, the benefit being related to the amount spent on education (up to a specified limit) and the level of taxable income of the taxpayer: the higher the rate of income tax payable, the greater the benefits received in response to expenditure on education. This instrument was therefore of selective benefit, being of greater value to the more prosperous, especially those parents who sent their children to high-fee private schools.

The original purpose of the taxation concession was to assist private schools and other educational institutions because it first related only to actual payments to institutions rather than to educational outlays in general terms. At its inception there were very few forms of government assistance to non-government schools and it was considered desirable at that time to develop a financial means of encouraging private sector educational expenditure. Perhaps, too, it was regarded as an efficient means of increasing educational expenditure other than by governments having to bear all the additional financial burdens directly.

Since the operation of the concession benefited mostly those with the greatest capacity to allocate private resources to education, the highest income earners, the instrument served a fiscal purpose of increasing expenditure on education from private rather than government sources as distinct from an educational policy objective (such as equity). Others believe it was introduced simply as a result of political pressure from those groups being denied assistance from the Government for expenditure on private schools. In this view, any educational effects are largely a by-product of, or perhaps even the rationale for, actions having wider political ramifications.

In the period 1952 to 1974 the maximum concessional deduction was increased periodically and the scope of items permitted to be included as concessions was widened to encompass expenditure other than that directed to institutions. Thus parents with students enrolled in government schools gained some benefits from its operation, although generally not to the same extent as those parents with students enrolled in more expensive non-government schools.

In a time of rapid inflation the maximum permissible concession was not increased in proportion to increases in non-government school fees, thus diminishing the instrument's effectiveness. On the other hand, personal income inflation means that all taxpayers moved to a higher point on the progressive taxation scale and therefore gained relatively larger concessions for each dollar spent on education.

In 1974/75 the Federal Government reduced the maximum concessional deduction from $400 to $150 per annum. This move made it virtually a basic concession for all taxpayers undertaking educational expenditure on behalf of their children, although higher income earners still gained most benefit from the way that the concession operated. In 1975/76 the instrument was replaced by a rebate scheme whereby a taxpayer could deduct a flat 40 cents in the dollar from his taxation liability to a maximum educational expenditure of $250, thus removing the anomaly whereby higher income earners gained greater advantage from a given level of expenditure than a lower income earner. Through these changes the instrument has now become equitable between income earners at different points of the income taxation scale.

Direct payments to schools have replaced this instrument as the major thrust of the Commonwealth Government's financial assistance of schooling. In addition, State governments have generally increased their per capita payments to non-government schools, and this too has changed the context within which this instrument operates. Thus for many taxpayers the relative importance of the instrument has declined: it no longer has the influence that it once had as an incentive for parents to enrol their children in non-government schools. Also, to the extent that the rebate, in contrast to the concessional deduction, treats all taxpayers the same, regardless of income, the instrument no longer has the effect of exacerbating disparities.

Chapter VI

SELECTED STATE GOVERNMENT FINANCIAL INSTRUMENTS AND THEIR IMPACT ON ASPECTS OF EDUCATIONAL POLICY

Although State government financial instruments are not separately defined in the same ways as the Commonwealth section 96 specific purpose grants, their importance derives from the fact that they are the means by which the majority of funds are made available for schools. South Australia is discussed as an example of approaches common to most States.

THE STATE BUDGET

As mentioned in Chapter II, the schools' share of the public purse, including Commonwealth general and specific purpose grants, flows through the State budget which an Act of Parliament authorises as the principal State financial instrument. As States are sovereign, the degree of flexibility in the use of funds depends on their traditions and desire for change.

While State parliaments formally appropriate funds for education in each State, State treasuries exercise considerable influence in the allocation and control of financial resources. The financial year in Australia operates from 1 July to 30 June. The State budget is debated and enabling legislation passed by the Parliament in August/September of the financial year. The funds for all educational services for schools are included in the budget and each item of expenditure is approved by the Parliament.

In South Australia, the State Treasury receives in the first part of each calendar year budget expenditure estimates from each government department. The Department of Education prepares details of its needs, which are mainly focused on personnel, because 89 per cent of recurrent expenditure on its own schools represents outlay on salaries. Following discussions between Treasury and the Department, agreement is reached about the amount of revenue which will have to be allocated to maintain current services in the next year, to cater for any expansion which may arise as a result of increased student enrolments, and to support other desired improvements. Then the Director-General, on the advice of his senior officers, decides upon the precise allocation of teachers and other staff among the various divisional demands which will have been specified at the pre-budget stage of the departmental submissions to Treasury. Details appear in the published budget papers of primary, secondary, and special schools' financial allocations for various types of personnel.

Once the allocation of funds and of a total number of teachers is completed, appointment of individual teachers for the new school year takes place. State-wide criteria for the selection and appointment of teaching staff are centrally determined and staff are appointed to particular schools. It is the responsibility of the head office to fill all promotions positions and to replace teachers resigning, proceeding on leave, or retiring, although the co-operation of five regional offices is sought in completing this task. A representative of each region will discuss with head office staffing personnel the determination of the total number of teachers required for allocation to the region. The regional office is able to locate and to recommend to head office the appointment of replacement staff from local sources.

The authority of the head office to appoint all teachers has been reinforced traditionally by the fact that permanent appointment to the State teaching service has entailed a commitment to teach anywhere in the State. All trainee teachers in receipt of financial assistance have been required to enter into a bond to serve wherever they are appointed. Now very few teachers in South Australia enter the service under bond, but as there will soon be a surplus of teachers in Australia and as the economic recession has resulted in fewer alternative job opportunities for teachers little difficulty is expected in obtaining sufficient staff for schools.

The interaction between equality of resource provision and school-based decision-making may be illustrated with respect to the South Australian staffing formula which is devised and made known to school principals as early in the financial year (October) as is practicable. There are three basic categories of staff: "general" teachers (that is, those whose major activities are centred on classroom teaching); teachers of small groups (for example, art, music); and teachers whose presence in the school does not appreciably influence class sizes (for example, principals, librarians). The first two categories comprise the basic staffing allocations, which favours schools which need proportionally more small groups. In addition to a relatively small favourable adjustment for senior staff (who it is intended should devote more time to non-classroom teaching activities), schools are invited to negotiate for an additional number of teachers to meet special needs: for example the school might have a difficult physical layout; be still developing; be "disadvantaged"; or have an "experimental" curriculum.

Thus the allocation of teachers is aimed at achieving equality and consistency of staffing and yet is capable of adjustment to meet the specific proposals of individual schools. There is no deliberate staffing policy for class sizes as exists in some other State systems. School principals in South Australia are consulted where possible by regional and central office authorities about staffing decisions affecting their schools, but consultation falls far short of the control over staff selection given to school principals in some other countries.

The major financial load for the treatment of special groups rests with the State education departments and depends upon the priority given to these areas in relation to other schooling and the total level of funds available for schooling in general.

In South Australia, 2.4 per cent of all primary school children are receiving specific supplementary support due to a physical or intellectual handicap. In addition some 3.4 per cent are benefiting from the Child Migrant English Program. Teachers involved with migrant children are funded by the Commonwealth Government, as are the salaries of some of the teachers involved with handicapped children. The overall level of provision in South Australia, and the degree of integration of handicapped with normal children compares favourably with the other States. Nevertheless, there has not yet been a thorough assessment of the incidence of students requiring particular types of support, or the capacity to provide teachers sufficient to meet all identifiable needs.

The South Australian Department of Education recently commissioned a study of the feasibility of extending school-based management responsibility to match the increasing professional autonomy of schools, but significantly the report was not in support of financial allocations being made to schools to enable permanent staff to become a resource controlled at the school level. The stated reasons related more to presumed administrative and financial efficiency than to educational policy costs and benefits.

A transfer from central to school level of the power to choose resources, and hence the devolution of real management authority, need not necessarily conflict with the ultimate responsibility of the State for the maintenance of standards and the operation of appropriate public accountability procedures. There is little evidence to support the view that school-based decision-making leads to less efficiency or accountability in the handling of resources than head office decisions made on behalf of all schools. Nor is devolution necessarily difficult to reconcile with industrial matters such as guaranteed employment of staff.

Some claim that the traditional Australian approach is a viable means of achieving equality of educational services in public school systems where there is a wide geographic spread and even more widely varying regional financial capacity. But a comment often made about the centralised State budget is that it has negative consequences: for example, that its hallmark is inflexibility, that it ensures conformity in resource provision and that it prevents local control and diversity in educational offering. Whilst such outcomes do occur, they are not always the consequences of the financial instrument itself but rather of the way it is used. It can be employed flexibly and with local variation. In some aspects, however, it is difficult to overcome inherent rigidities; overall categorisation of expenditure by function such as salaries, equipment, transport, which facilitate accounting procedures, is universal. Allocations to programs or regions or individual schools to be spent according to the priorities determined by specified objectives and perceived needs are unknown.

CASH ALLOCATIONS TO INDIVIDUAL GOVERNMENT SCHOOLS

Despite the absence of staffing autonomy for schools, there is a trend for individual government schools to be given some direct financial responsibility. For example, primary schools in South Australia receive cash allocations: each school has a Council, an incorporated body, which receives grants for grounds maintenance and equipment amounting to some $5 per student. If a school is new it receives a foundation grant to enable the development of a basic book stock. An average primary school benefits from an annual text book allocation valued at about $10 per student. An average secondary school (of 1 000 students) receives $35 per student to operate a book loan scheme and to provide materials. The school has the discretion of choosing whether or not to purchase through the State supply scheme, so it is able to select the type and range of books which best suit its individual needs. In addition a school of this size and type will usually obtain up to $10 per student as a compulsory parental input to the school. Another $8 000 is made over in cash and $4 000 in requisitionable items by the State Education Department to cover other costs such as maintenance of grounds and equipment, cleaning and stationery materials: the school must make a declaration that money has been spent for the purposes named, and accounts are subject to audit. While there is Ministerial approval for primary schools in South Australia to have a "points" allocation for various types of ancillary staff, and consequently some discretion over the particular mix of these resources utilised, the scheme has not been fully implemented (as it has for secondary schools). Besides, there is no ability to exchange these resources for other kinds. Schools retain a major proportion of fees obtained from the hire of their facilities.

Similar initiatives are being taken elsewhere. Moves have been made to decentralise the administration of schools: the division of States into regions; provision for school councils which will have limited powers of decision in relation to school programs and resources; and allowances for students paid directly to schools for the purchase of learning materials.

While the level and extent of payments described above have only just begun, some school administrators are expressing doubts about the capability of individual schools to use discretionary power even in the narrow confines of non-teacher resources within a school. However, this does not reflect on the general support that exists for such moves: the unpreparedness of those who make decisions at the school level can be overcome through appropriate development activities.

PER CAPITA RECURRENT GRANTS TO NON-GOVERNMENT SCHOOLS

State governments, motivated by a complex of political, social and philosophical factors, have conceived of per capita recurrent grants as being essential for the continuation of the non-government sector of schooling. The declared reasons for the construction and implementation of the instrument centred around the financial difficulties of many non-government schools and their declining enrolments. Political factors including the activity of pressure groups and the need for parties aspiring to government to attract and retain votes were no doubt influential. The classic economic argument of reducing the schooling financial burden on the State by providing incentives for private investment, has not loomed large.

Cost factors such as the rising costs of schooling (especially the teacher salary component) had their effect, particularly in relation to the Catholic schools which were being forced to employ proportionately more (and relatively more expensive) lay staff. The inflow of migrants from countries where enrolment in church affiliated schools was common and where extensive State aid had been provided, were causing financial tensions as migrant parents wanted to enrol their children but not pay high fees. Finally, the spread of settlement to areas having no non-government schools, and hence the prospect of large capital costs to initiate them, together with the fact that they would have had to have high fees since few contributed (voluntary) services would be available, increased the leverage for an extension of State aid.

The instrument has enabled non-government schools to continue functioning, both by partially relieving the financial burden on parents and by assisting to raise unacceptably low standards.

State per capita grants are an interesting example of the State budget as a financial instrument and of the way it relates to the issue of locus of control. Although grants are paid from a line in the State budget, without specific legislation, they are paid direct to schools in cash and are used to meet all kinds of operating expenses, a discretion not granted to public schools. Governments do not try to influence the operation of non-government schools through these grants. A set of minimal criteria only must be met by a school before funds are granted to it, the school usually needing to be certified as providing an adequate educational service. The grants are also a means of facilitating choice between government and non-government schooling, and thereby encouraging diversity:

but the choice can be exercised only by those who can afford or who are willing to pay school fees and who can obtain entry to the non-government school of their choice.

It is difficult to assess this financial instrument in terms of the extent of the choice it facilitates for parents, or the amount of diversity of schooling actually it promotes, because the distinctive effects of State per capita grants are confounded with those of Commonwealth aid. For example, in South Australia the nature of the Commonwealth Government's scheme led to an adjustment by the State Government of its scheme. If it had continued to distribute funds to schools on an assessed basis of need without regard to changes that had been taking place in the form of Commonwealth payments, the two schemes, running in parallel, would have promoted inequities. Nevertheless, the scope of the instrument ensures its importance; from being means-tested and limited in most States, it has grown in size and importance to the extent that it is now a vital general subsidy, being of the order of 20 per cent of the per pupil running cost of equivalent government schools.

Chapter VII

SELECTED PRIVATE FINANCIAL INSTRUMENTS AND THEIR IMPACT ON ASPECTS OF EDUCATIONAL POLICY

PRIVATE OUTLAYS ON GOVERNMENT SCHOOLS

A long-standing tradition in government school finance has been that a (virtually compulsory) private educational outlay can be relied upon from parents of children attending them. State governments appear to have regarded local levies on parents as a means whereby direct parental interest and involvement in local schools is sustained and particular needs are met. Expenditure by parents has been necessary in order to maintain their children at school, since expenditure on books, fees, school uniforms, and many other incidental expenditures does not come from public sources. This instrument, therefore, relates especially to the policy issues of equality and locus of control. The practice has been allowed to continue by governments of differing political persuasion, so it is not so much attributable to an ideological position over whether schooling is a private or public good, as to financial necessity and convention.

In South Australia, for example, only relatively few parents of students fail to make this input to schools. At the primary school level, textbooks are selected by government schools from a central pool and provided at no direct cost to parents, although the notional cost is currently some $10 per head. However, parents are obliged to pay for all their children's stationery and art and craft materials, and must meet library and sports fees. These expenses vary from school to school depending upon location and activities engaged in, but comprise a compulsory annual payment to the school of between $15 and $25. There is no restriction upon the voluntary contributions which schools and (more typically) their parent bodies can request, and the primary school is dependent upon parents and the school council for financial assistance for unavoidable minor expenses. At the secondary school level, government grants for discretionary purposes mean that rather less reliance need be placed upon private contributions than at the primary school level. Requests can be made of parents for voluntary contributions as well, and parents may undertake additional expenditure on books.

Some view compulsory payments as a means of achieving a minimum level of parental support higher than that which would obtain under a voluntary scheme. All schools including those drawing students from families with lower income capacities have some disposable income under their control and, it is argued, can thus provide a better service than would be the case without compulsory levies. On the other hand inequalities among schools in different areas are not overcome since voluntary additional contributions are more easily obtained in some areas than others. Moreover many believe that any retreat from the principle of all compulsory education being free must be harmful for those worst off in the community.

Considerable inequality of educational provision can result from widely varying levels of fees being paid in different schools. For those children attending government schools in inner-city and some rural areas, the level of resource use provided by parents and the local community is less than that of government schools in other areas. The necessity for private inputs may be a contributing factor in deterring poorer families from continuing their children's education for the same length of time as do wealthier families (especially when considerable family income is forgone once children are old enough to join the workforce).

The effectiveness of private levies in achieving the intended result of parental interest and commitment to the work of the school, as well as the generation of funds from private sources, depends upon a judgment as to whether parental involvement is best achieved by imposing financial obligations or by some other means. Prescription of a uniformly low and virtually compulsory fee has reduced one major source of inequality but reliance on this instrument does in general condone inequality. Fortunately there are additional instruments which counteract inequalities and which have reduced its importance, amongst which the following may be included: textbook grants to students; conveyance payments; isolated children's allowances for educational expenses; and increased direct grants to individual schools.

PRIVATE OUTLAYS ON NON-GOVERNMENT SCHOOLS

Private outlays are the means whereby parents can exercise their preference for educational services alternative to those provided by the government sector, and by implication, if not by design, are an effective way in which decision-making can be focused at a local level. This instrument therefore relates to the policy issues of diversity and choice and locus of control. In the (nineteenth-century) context of its origin, it was used simply because of the absence of educational provision by government authorities. Today it is the instrument employed by those parents whose educational preferences for their children are for other than government operated schools, and who are able and willing to exercise their choice of selecting and contributing towards an educational service to their own liking.

The instrument is effective in ensuring that decision-making occurs at the local level, by permitting the functioning of schools and systems which are relatively free from State and bureaucratic controls. As a result some schools do exhibit distinctive characteristics which suggest that local control is being used creatively, as measured for example by atypical curricula, teaching methods and organisation. However, most schools do not, as is evidenced by adherence to State-wide curricula and organisational patterns. Despite their apparent fiscal and organisational independence, the need to prepare students for public examinations and the general tendency for the community to "rate" schools on common criteria combine to induce in non-government schools a high degree of conformity and uniformity.

As the costs of education have increased substantially over recent years and as government school standards have improved, proportionately fewer parents have been able or willing to meet the costs of non-government education. Consequently, there is a tendency for high standard, high fee non-government schools to become increasingly the prerogative of children of wealthier parents, and low standard, low fee schools to be for the less affluent who have felt impelled to seek alternative schooling for their children on personal grounds. Thus, increasing inequalities of educational provision have emerged, both within the non-government sector and between it and the government sector.

Modifications to the instrument have occurred, especially in the last decade, insofar as private outlays on non-government education have increasingly been supplemented by a range of State and Commonwealth government instruments (for example, by matching grants and interest subsidies for buildings, per capita grants for general operating purposes), so that for most non-government schools in Australia contributions from private sources is no longer the prime source of revenue.

Chapter VIII

LIKELY DIRECTIONS OF SCHOOL FINANCE

The preceding discussion has explored the bearing particular financial instruments have had on the distribution of educational resources in Australian and, to some extent, the effectiveness of those instruments for achieving particular educational policies. In this section we further explore their effectiveness by relating them to broader trends within Australian society.

THE ROLE OF THE FEDERAL GOVERNMENT IN FUNDING SCHOOL-LEVEL EDUCATION

The expanding role of the Commonwealth in school financing should be viewed in the context of two divergent tendencies, one a general movement towards centralisation, the other a demand for increased local participation in decision-making. Centralising tendencies have been greatly strengthened by technological developments which make efficient central management much more feasible, but other advances, especially in the communications field, ensure wide and speedy dissemination of information about central decision-making processes and lead to demands for more local involvement in those processes. The tension between the two tendencies should be kept in mind in examining the changing Commonwealth role.

Centralising tendencies

The Commonwealth's growing influence vis-a-vis that of the States is one of the themes running through the history of the Australian federation. Several factors have fostered this: judicial decisions have tended to add power to the Commonwealth and to diminish that of the States; national referenda have also augmented Commonwealth influence; but the most forceful factor has been generated by the Commonwealth-State arrangements for the Commonwealth to collect income taxes on behalf of itself and the States. The Commonwealth has increasingly used fiscal leverage to mount programs and to induce States to undertake Commonwealth-inspired activities. When public concern about education became a major political factor in the 1960s, federal politicians became more and more education-oriented, resulting in specific purpose grants for schools in the States. In so doing the Commonwealth came to assume more of a nation-wide role in the formulation and *de facto* implementation of school policy.

Fiscal federalism

For Australia to be regarded as a truly federal system it would need to satisfy at least two important fiscal criteria. First, fiscal authority would be located with the level of government which is best able to appraise available options. Second, if specific purpose payments from the national to a State level of government are to be made, they should not unwittingly or mischievously distort State resource allocation decisions.

Because the Commonwealth has revenue raising devices which in the main take more from those most able to pay and are of a growth kind, as distinct from State taxes which tend to be of a regressive and non-growth nature, it seems necessary for the Commonwealth to be prepared to supply most of the finance for schools through the various financial instruments discussed earlier. However, on "federal" grounds the case for specific State or locally based revenue for schools is strong. A State or local education tax would, despite possible drawbacks of an equity and efficiency kind, have a direct impact on spending by the private sector and could therefore be expected to reflect more validly what the community is prepared to pay for the schooling of its children. Such a change is not likely in Australia where no level of government has ever had or seriously contemplated a school tax, although it is interesting to note that at the national level a health insurance tax on personal incomes has been imposed and there is a suggestion that a nation-wide superannuation scheme might be financed by means of a levy.

A popular objection to the present shared responsibility between the Commonwealth and the States for the financing of schooling is that it often leads to a pattern of services which neither level of government, if left to its own devices, would choose. Moreover because the interplay of politics and administration is so complex, implementation of tied grants programs in the precise manner intended is easier to envisage in theory than in practice. With shared responsibility, conflicts over status and power are inevitable and the possibility of reduced effectiveness of financial allocations must be accepted as a consequence of the arrangements.

Nevertheless given particular electoral promises and a commitment to provide resources for purposes such as to promote a national priority and to ensure minimum levels of performance, it is questionable whether the Commonwealth could in fact have adopted any method of assistance other than specific purpose grants when it became involved in financing school-level education. The Commonwealth is now so deeply involved that it will almost certainly remain so. The question that it now faces is not so much one of constitutional propriety as one of determining how it can efficiently and equitably channel funds without unduly distorting State preferences and without becoming directly involved in the management of schools.

The present Commonwealth Government has a policy of revitalising federalism by rearranging existing financial patterns. It is proposed that this include cost-sharing arrangements with the States and the absorption of some specific purpose grants into general financial assistance grants—to be renamed tax reimbursement grants—in selected areas of activity, perhaps those covering (parts of) education. The move is intended to increase State budget flexibility, reserving specific purpose grants for agreed areas of national need or to meet special situations.

It is not intended that States revert to raising the major portion of their own income taxes although they will have a restricted right to nominate limited surcharges or rebates as a component of the national tax collection. The financial adjustment to equalise revenue capacity among States is to be included in the formula for general financial assistance to the States. Commonwealth payments to the States will include their share of national tax revenue and any amounts they are entitled to receive as a result of the formula for equalising capacity. But even if no specific purpose grants were made, the Commonwealth would still be in a position to control the total amount of revenue to be made available to the States, so the question of how much more authority and responsibility will in fact go to the States will still be in the hands of the central government. Clearly, the conditions for continuing conflict will remain.

The original Australian concept of federalism as a sharp division of powers and functions between State and Commonwealth governments is no longer viable; new distributions of powers are progressively evolving. Yet depite its superior financial strength the Commonwealth does not always attain its goals. In politically sensitive areas—and this certainly includes education—a degree of tension between levels of government is to be expected and strategies to improve federal relations must take this conflict into account: for example, by institutionalising it through some form of truly inter-governmental machinery or by agency arrangements. This is especially so as a number of today's problems in education seem to be less attributable to inherent limitations of the federal system itself than to a reticence to exploit the full range of techniques (informational and financial, as well as legal, instruments) for priority determination and policy implementation.

Statutory commissions

One of the major Commonwealth devices for allocating funds for schools is the Schools Commission, which exemplifies the type of machinery which has over the years come to play a significant role in public administration in areas in which the Commonwealth has adopted full or part responsibility for what were previously regarded as State functions. Because a principal task of such agencies is to analyse needs in physical terms and then to translate these into dollar amounts, they can operate most effectively where the number of cases to be assessed and compared is sufficiently small for judgments about relative need to be seen as fair and reasonable. This may partly explain why Australia makes use of statutory agencies (commissions, bureaux) to make recommendations on a range of intergovernmental fiscal matters while larger federations (in terms of population and governmental units) tend to adopt a straight formula method of allocation.

There are other issues relating to the potential effectiveness of "independent" agencies. For example, a concern to ensure that assessments of need are made on an impartial basis raises the question of defining an appropriate set of relationships between a commission and the legislative (parliamentary), political executive (ministerial) and administrative (public service) arms of government—especially if some members of the Commission are interest group leaders. Also, a commission which is set up by and reports to one level of government on matters having jurisdictional spillovers does not operate readily as an inter-governmental agency: in the case of the Schools Commission this is so despite the fact that it is chiefly concerned with making recommendations on financial assistance to the States for school-level education which is conceded to be basically a State responsibility and which involves considerable State expenditure. Key issues for the future are whether a commission can have both an advisory and an executive/administrative role and how it might best make a contribution to the work of all governments concerned with its statutory responsibilities.

DEVOLUTION FROM THE STATE TO REGIONAL AND LOCAL LEVELS

State government policies increasingly favour devolution of authority to schools. Decentralisation of administration and moves towards the devolution of curriculum responsibility to schools and their communities have implications for patterns of school resource allocation. The policies will only become a reality when financial authority is devolved concurrently with administrative and curriculum authority, for real decision-making must involve the power of choice over the type and mix of resources, as well as the way they will be used.

The pivotal financial problem is not necessarily the creation of new sources of finance for schools (for example, a local education tax) but whether there can be genuinely devolved authority for planning the use of funds. With such devolution, resources could still come from central sources and be supplemented to a minor extent by local fund-raising activies. Responsibility for supplying basic finances efficiently and equitably would remain with the State Government while schools would have the resources and the freedom to shape their services to meet the needs of their students. But while a State Minister for Education must answer to the Parliament for every event in every public school in his State, it is difficult to visualise devolution of significant responsibility for policy matters. Although devolution opens up the possibility of schools developing divergent philosophies it also exposes the Minister and his Government to political pressure from those in the community who oppose what a particular school is doing, with consequent pressure to withhold funds. Centripetal forces can only be resisted if policy making powers and the concomitant financial resources are devolved in some non-retractable way, preferably by legal means, and in ways which transfer the need to be publicly responsive and accountable from State Ministers to some equivalent organ at the level to which power has been devolved.

It is difficult to predict exactly where the present evolution is leading. It is safe to say, however, that the pendulum which has for so long been swinging in the direction of uniform resources and services through central provision is now moving back toward more diverse patterns. Efforts are being made to devolve management and policy responsibility. In consequence the tensions and contradictions between ministerial responsibility and devolved power are being exposed. Redefinition of the limits of ministerial responsibility for ensuring equality of opportunity and for preventing intolerable diversity will be necessary before the limits of the movement can be established.

PRIVATE INITIATIVES AND CHOICE

The "free, compulsory and secular" principle which helped create the centralised State systems and the policy of withholding public aid to non-government schools have been progressively modified, particularly in recent years as political compromises have been reached as a consequence of interest group activity against a background of threatened collapse of the non-government sector and as tolerance has grown in the community for schools based on either religious or "alternative" philosophies. During the period when the financial assistance given was small, the importance of the policy issues involved in deciding the amount and pattern of assistance could be minimised. As dependence on government aid has grown it is becoming more obvious that the relationship between public responsibility for schools and private initiatives has to be progressively resolved. The possibility of basing policy on concern for containing public expenditure on schooling, or facilitation of choice, or tolerance for religious obligations, or reduction of parental burdens, will have to be weighed against the traditional rationales for public schooling, especially as acceptance of additional policy considerations (such as increased choice) may involve increased financial outlays.

The Australian electorate is clearly willing to continue subsidising non-government schools and so to underwrite their existence; but it is less clear whether future support will be based more or less on achieving equality of opportunity as distinct from facilitating choice. Financial instruments supporting the principle of choice could widen disparities in the resource levels among schools and thus negate equality of opportunity. The issue is a politically live one at present because of uncertainty as to whether the form of government grants to non-government schools should or will be essentially of a uniform per capita kind or differential amounts based on one or more of a variety of criteria: the discrepancy between the resources which a school has and a target standard which can be sustained for all schools; the assessed educational needs of individual children enrolled in a particular school; or the degree of accessibility of a school, as defined by fee levels, to the socio-economic spectrum of potential users.

An even more important consideration in the long run is the growing dependence on public support of non-government schools. Many of these schools raise a very small proportion of their costs through fees and as voluntary or contributed services become more scarce and it becomes less acceptable to have inadequate resources they must turn increasingly to governments for increased aid. The level of subvention might have to be raised to the point where it is feasible for groups hitherto prevented from starting their own schools because of economic factors, including the lack of an institutional base, to operate them. There will then be pressure both to allow government schools to become more like such heavily subsidised schools and to relate the rights and obligations of these schools to government ones.

A new financial instrument being proposed in Australia is a scheme of guaranteed assistance to a school to allow it to operate with an acceptable level of resources—the "Supported Schools" concept. While the scheme has been proposed by the Schools Commission to meet the problems of existing low-fee, low-resource non-government schools it could by inference be applicable to the financing of all schools providing there was an acceptable nation-wide policy on the tolerable limits of choice and diversity. Another proposal, with the critical distinction from the one above that government funds would go to individuals rather than schools, has been made for the introduction of a voucher system. Such a system would need to be introduced by, or at least be acceptable to, State governments. Given the traditional reluctance of States to introduce new financial instruments, widespread implementation of these proposals cannot be considered very likely in the immediate future.

SHAPING FUTURE POLICY

Inevitably these developments point up the issues of equality of opportunity, choice and locus of control. The sharp divisions between government and non-government schools, and between the responsibilities of State governments and the Commonwealth Government, have become increasingly blurred as aid from the Commonwealth has been extended to both government and non-government sectors and as total public support for non-government schools has increased.

At the State level policies have tended to be stated separately from considerations of cost and the financial instruments required to give effect to them:

the main financial instrument for the funding of both government and non-government schools has continued to be the general State budgetary mechanism. The advent of explicit Commonwealth financial instruments has initiated a process of examination of the relationship between the financial instruments and the outcomes intended, attracting attention not only to the practices of the Commonwealth Government but also to the policy implications of State procedures. In addition, the interplay of State and Commonwealth instruments has revealed how difficult it is to define a financial instrument in precise enough terms to ensure that its attention is not susceptible to subversion through administrative processes.

Thus recent school financing trends in Australia have arisen as a result of the introduction by the Commonwealth Government of financial instruments explicitly aimed at intended policy outcomes and subject to regular evaluation and public reporting. These initiatives have encouraged greater scrutiny of State instruments and policies. Moreover, the increased flow of information and the ongoing debate about desirable policies and ways and means of bringing them about have increased the public participation in shaping the educational priorities of the Commonwealth and State governments. Modifications to the processes of collecting and allocating financial resources which are remote from individual citizens may not occur in the next few years but as it is likely to be a period of economic stringency as well as debate about educational standards and outcomes concern for effectiveness will be high. The major trend will probably be a search for ways of accommodating this heightened public interest and involvement.

SELECT BIBLIOGRAPHY OF RELEVANT AUSTRALIAN MATERIALS

L.M. Alwood. *Australian Schools; The Impact of the Schools Commission.* Melbourne, Australia International Press and Publications, 1975.

Australia. Department of Education. *Inquiry into Schools of High Migrant Density; 1974 Study Based on Schools in New South Wales and Victoria.* Canberra, AGPS, 1975.

Australia. Department of Education. *Transition from School to Work or Further Study; a Background Paper for an OECD Review of Australian Educational Policy.* Canberra, 1976.

Australia. Senate. Standing Committee on Education and the Arts. *Report on Education of Isolated School Children.* July, 1976.

Australian National University. Centre for Research on Federal Financial Relations. *1975 Report, and Review of Fiscal Federalism in Australia.* 1976.

G.F. Berkeley. Financing Education in Queensland, the State-Commonwealth Mix. (Mimeographed paper, 43 p., prepared for a Seminar of the Brisbane Group of the Centre for Research on Federal Financial Relations on Friday, 12 December, 1975).

I.K.F. Birch. States' Rights in Education; Australia, the United States of America and West Germany. *Education Research and Perspectives.* Vol. 2, No. 1, June 1975, pp. 15-24.

R. Blandy and T. Goldsworthy. *Educational Opportunity in South Australia.* Flinders University of South Australia, 1975.

J.V. D'Cruz and P.J. Sheehan, eds. *The Renewal of Australian Schools.* Richmond, Vic., Primary Education, 1975.

P. Fensham, Ed. *Rights and Inequality in Australian Education.* Melbourne, Cheshire, 1970.

J. McLaren. *A Dictionary of Australian Education.* Ringwood, Vic., Penguin, 1974.

R.L. Matthews, ed. *Making Federalism Work; Towards a More Efficient, Equitable and Responsive Federal System.* Canberra, Centre for Research on Federal Financial Relations in association with the Centre for Continuing Education, ANU, 1976.

School-based Funding; a Report commissioned by the Education Department of South Australia and preparated by A.C. Burnell and B.F. McMillan of the School of Accountancy, South Australian Institution of Technology, April 1976.

Schools Commission: Reports and other publications.

Segall, Patsy and R.T. Fitzgerald. *Finance for Education in Australia; an Analysis.* Hawthorn, Vic., Australian Council for Educational Research, 1974. (Quarterly Review of Australian Education, Vol. 6, No. 4.)

D. Smart. The Commonwealth Government and Education 1945-76. (To be published in *Education News,* late 1976.)

P.D. Tannock, ed. *The Organization and Administration of Catholic Education in Australia.* St. Lucia, Qld., University of Qld. Press, 1975.

D. Tomlinson. *Finance for Education in Australia; Developments 1969-75.* Hawthorn, Vic., Australian Council for Educational Research, 1976. (*Australian Education Review,* No. 5.)

Patrick Weller. The Schools Commission, Political Resources and Federal-State Relations, in R.M. Burns and others. *Political and Administrative Federalism.* Canberra, Centre for Research on Federal Financial Relations, ANU, 1976, pp. 72-82. (Research Monograph No. 14.)

CANADA
(Province of Ontario)

by

E. Brock RIDEOUT
Lawrence M. BEZEAU
and
David WRIGHT

*Department of Educational Administration
The Ontario Institute for Studies in Education
Toronto*

CONTENTS

Chapter I
CONTEXT OF PRIMARY SCHOOL FINANCING IN ONTARIO	60
The historical context	60
The educational context	62

Chapter II
SOURCES OF FUNDS AND REVENUE PRODUCTION	64
Federal level revenue	64
Provincial level revenue	65
Local level revenue	67
Other sources of revenue	68

Chapter III
FEDERAL INVOLVEMENT IN ELEMENTARY AND SECONDARY EDUCATION IN CANADA	69
Direct involvement	69
Indirect involvement	70
Federal education policy	72

Chapter IV
FINANCIAL INSTRUMENTS USED TO CHANNEL FUNDS TO PRIMARY EDUCATION	73
Provincial grants	73
Grant on ordinary expenditure	73
Grant on extraordinary expenditure	76
Municipal tax levies	79
The valuation of property	79
Local taxation for public schools	79
Local taxation for separate schools	80
Limited power of boards to levy and collect taxes	80
Borrowing	80
Long-term borrowing	80
Short-term borrowing	80
Fees and other user charges	81
Limits placed on intergovernmental allocation of funds	81
Provincial	81
Municipal	82
MEETING RISING COSTS CAUSED BY INFLATION	83
COST CHANGES ARISING FROM YEAR-TO-YEAR FLUCTUATIONS IN ENROLMENTS	83

Chapter V
RATIONALE FOR PRESENT SYSTEM OF FINANCING AND THE DISPARITIES RELATED TO VARIOUS OBJECTIVES	85

Chapter VI

POLICY GOALS AND THEMES 89
1. Equality of educational opportunity 89
2. Decentralization of decision-making 89
3. Treatment of special populations 90
   a) Native population 90
   b) Special education 91
   c) Franco-Ontarians 91
   d) Early childhood education 91
   e) Compensatory education 92
   f) Geographically disadvantaged pupils 93
   g) Students from homes where neither English nor French is spoken . 93
4. Integration of public education with other public services 93
5. Access, selection and certification 94
6. Socialization 94
7. Innovation 95

Chapter VII

RELATIONSHIP BETWEEN POLICY GOALS AND FINANCIAL INSTRUMENTS 96
1. Equality of educational opportunity 96
2. Decentralization of decision-making 97
3. Treatment of special populations 98
   a) Native population 98
   b) Special education 98
   c) Franco-Ontarians 99
   d) Early childhood education 99
   e) Compensatory education 100
   f) Geographically disadvantaged pupils 100
   g) Students from homes where neither English nor French is spoken . 101
4. Integration of public education with other public services 101
5. Access, selection and certification 102
6. Socialization 102
7. Innovation 103
8. A general comment with respect to policy and forms of school finance . 103

Chapter VIII

PROPOSED CHANGES IN THE FINANCING SYSTEM 104
Handicapped children 104
Provincial funding of primary education 104
Combined public-separate school administration 105
Immigrant children 105
Weighting factors 105
Collective bargaining by teachers 105
Autonomy of individual schools 106
Federal equalization grants 106
BIBLIOGRAPHY 107

TABLES

2-1. Budgetary revenue of Ontario (interim 1975-76) 66
2-2. Percentage of provincial expenditures devoted to all levels of education 1961 and 1972 67
2-3. Percentage of provincial local expenditures on elementary and secondary education borne by the provinces 1954-1974 67
3-1. Federal direct and indirect assistance for elementary and secondary education as a percentage of total government expenditures on elementary and secondary education 1960, 1965, and 1970 71
3-2. Indexes of five provinces for personal income per weighted person aged 5-19 years in 1960, 1965, and 1970 71
3-3. Percent of federal revenues devoted to elementary and secondary education: 1960, 1965, and 1970 72
3-4. Percentage of total government expenditures on education coming from federal sources in 1960, 1965, and 1970 (Canada) 72

Chapter I

CONTEXT OF PRIMARY SCHOOL FINANCING IN ONTARIO

The British North America (BNA) Act of 1867 created the Dominion of Canada and with its various amendments, serves as the country's constitution. Section 93 of the Act placed upon the legislatures of the various provinces[1] exclusive power to pass laws respecting education. This power was granted subject to qualifications respecting the rights and privileges of denominational schools in each province. Education appears explicitly in the Canadian constitution because of the importance originally attached to it in preserving the religious and linguistic character of the separate provinces under the federal umbrella.

In Canada, the federal government provides educational services for native peoples, the population of the territories[2], and the children of members of the armed forces living on armed forces bases at home and abroad. All other educational services are provided by the provinces; there is no federal ministry of education.

THE HISTORICAL CONTEXT

The first schools in Ontario, built and run by the settlers through voluntary effort and subscriptions, were set up in the late 18th Century. The provincial government soon entered the field of education, and in 1807 passed the District Public School Act which provided grants for a school in each of the eight administrative districts of the province. These schools, however, were grammar schools operated for and by the economic elite in the larger towns. Rural settlers demanded that the provincial government accept its obligation to provide education for all the children of the province. This pressure resulted in the Common Schools Act of 1816 which provided legislative sanction to the informal schools established by groups of parents. The inhabitants of any town, township, village or place were given authority to unite and build a school, provided they could furnish a minimum of twenty pupils and would pay part of the teacher's salary. Apart from the government grant, all money required for the maintenance of a common (or elementary) school had to be raised by subscription. This Act also empowered the inhabitants to elect a board of three trustees who were given the authority

---

1. The original member provinces were Ontario, Quebec, New Brunswick, and Nova Scotia; to these have been added: Manitoba (1870), British Columbia (1871), Prince Edward Island (1873), Alberta and Saskatchewan (1905) and Newfoundland (1949).
2. Yukon and the Northwest Territories.

to appoint the teacher, and to make the rules and regulations for the government of the school. Local control of elementary education was therefore established from the outset. Not until the "Baldwin Act" of 1849 was a structure for municipal self-government set up in Ontario (then Upper Canada). With the passing of this Act, which made provision for the voluntary levying of property tax by local municipalities, tax-supported free public education became a real issue, although the primary schools did not become entirely tuition- free until 1871.

Ontario contains two publicly supported elementary school systems: the non-denominational public elementary schools, and the predominantly Roman Catholic separate school system. The BNA Act of 1867 guaranteed the right of any class of persons possessing denominational schools by law at the union to retain and extend such schools. The first legislative provision for separate schools had occurred in 1841 when the newly formed government of the United Province of Canada[3] provided for the establishment of schools by the religious minority (Protestant or Roman Catholic) which dissented from the authority of the local school trustees. This provision ensured the right of the large minority of Protestants in Quebec and of Roman Catholics in Ontario to conduct their own educational affairs. In practice, the first tax-supported school established in a school section was the public school and any subsequent school of the minority denomination was designated as a Roman Catholic or Protestant separate school.

The financial instruments utilized to fund elementary education in Ontario were developed as, and have remained, education specific. Two main reasons underlie this development. The first is the view, promoted since Ryerson became Assistant Superintendent of Education in 1844, that education is more of a provincial function than a municipal one. As the education system evolved, it was felt that for education to benefit the whole society and meet the aim of equality of educational opportunity for each individual, a greater measure of centralized control was necessary. In addition, administrative units for education had been initiated prior to those for other municipal functions and therefore the provincial government already had educational representatives at the local level. From the outset then, financing of education was seen as a specific and separate area by both the province and the local community. The necessity for this separation was accentuated by the existence of separate schools, which presents certain complications. In a municipal council, the majority of the members would likely be public school supporters. To give this majority control over the budget for both school systems could seriously affect the autonomy of the minority in that municipality. This is a further reason for the continued separation of educational and municipal finance.

The system of school finance in Ontario did not develop exclusively from reactions to internal pressures but was also influenced by external factors. Ryerson, who is credited as the architect of the present Ontario elementary school system, travelled extensively in Europe and personally investigated teacher training and the school systems of more than twenty countries, including Britain, Prussia, Sweden, Holland, and Switzerland. He was also intimately acquainted with educational practices in a number of American states. The Ontario system for many years bore the imprint of the ideas Ryerson picked up in his travels. The American state of New York, which borders Ontario, has had considerable and continuing influence on financing in Ontario. The province was originally settled by United Empire Loyalists from upstate New York, and later immigrants from New York and Pennsylvania brought with them a different perspective on education than did immigrants from Britain. One way in which school finance at the

---

3. A union of the provinces of Upper Canada (Ontario) and Lower Canada (Quebec).

local level differs from that in New York State and other parts of the United States is the lack of direct ratepayer involvement in the school budget. From the outset, Ryerson insisted that the school trustees have the final say over the budget of the local school. Only on questions involving money for school construction was there any Ontario tradition of voting by ratepayers, and even this privilege was revoked in 1969. The ratepayers select the trustees and the trustees run the schools.

In Ontario, the financing of private schools is non-govermental. Such schools are entirely responsible for their own financing and have no claim to direct aid from public funds. These schools are exempt from municipal property taxation except for rates imposed for local improvements. Many private schools were initially formed by denominational groups who desired a particular religious base in instruction. The inclusion of separate schools for Roman Catholics in the public school system has lessened the pressure for public finance of private schools which exists in some other jurisdictions. Private elementary enrolment is only 1.31 percent of all elementary enrolment in the province.

THE EDUCATIONAL CONTEXT

Education in Ontario is compulsory between the ages of six and sixteen, and is free in that it is entirely supported by public funds. Ontario, as of 1975 September, had 115 public elementary school boards, 60 Roman Catholic separate school boards, and two Protestant separate school boards in operation. These 177 elementary boards administered 4 017 schools with a total enrolment of 1 389 478. Elementary education is the term used in Ontario to describe the school system operating from junior kindergarten through grade 8. Although provincial curriculum guidelines consider junior kindergarten to grade 6 as "primary" education, it is administratively and financially inseparable from the elementary education described above. In addition, Roman Catholic separate schools are permitted to offer grades 9 and 10 as elementary education. Kindergarten was introduced in 1882 and was made an optional part of the elementary school system by the legislation of 1885. There was a rapid growth of such facilities in the cities and larger towns, but kindergartens were not practical in rural areas until the consolidation of school districts occurred in 1969. Kindergarten education for 5-year-olds is usually on a half-day attendance basis and is now almost universal in Ontario. A considerable growth in enrolment in junior-kindergarten classes for 4-year-olds has occurred since the 1969 reorganization. At that time, total enrolment in junior kindergarten was 7 666. This figure increased to 43 807 in 1975. At present, junior-kindergarten classes are concentrated in the urban areas.

Elementary and secondary education are financed separately in Ontario because of the existence of separate schools. At the time of Confederation, the common schools, of which the separate schools were a part, provided only elementary education and this system was frozen by the BNA Act. Thus, public- and separate-elementary school boards developed independently. The secondary education system, however, was created after Confederation as an entirely public school system. Public and separate school supporters are taxed separately for elementary school purposes. All ratepayers, however, are taxed at the same rate to support the secondary school system which is totally public. A Board of Education, therefore, has two different groups of ratepayers (for elementary and for secondary schools) which necessitates the keeping of two separate and distinct sets of accounts and budgets.

At present, a Board of Education is responsible for providing public elementary and secondary schooling within its area of jurisdiction. Within a board of education there are administrative units called "panels" which effectively function as distinct school boards. Each board has an elementary-school panel consisting of public school trustees assumed to represent the religious majority, and a secondary school panel consisting of the public school trustees plus one or more representatives of the separate school ratepayers. Separate school boards are responsible only for the governance of the separate (elementary) school system. The separate school representatives on boards of education are elected by separate school supporters.

The various school systems operate under the control of elected citizens who make up each system's board of trustees or school board. They have been assigned decision-making power to set the annual budget and establish the policies to be implemented by professional educators. While school boards have broad areas of legal discretion as to the type and level of services to be offered, they exist as a result of provincial legislation and operate within the limits set by the province's Education Act and Regulations. School boards provide educational programs, hire personnel for these programs, build suitable facilities, and manage the schools. Each school board negotiates a contract including a salary schedule with the locals of the teacher organizations represented on its staff. There is no provincial salary scale or contract, although negotiations and the right to strike are governed by provincial legislation. The province controls teacher training and approves textbooks, curriculum guidelines, and construction projects.

On 1st January 1969, the school districts of Ontario were reorganized and consolidated into much larger administrative units. The extent of this reorganization is witnessed by the fact that in 1960 there were 3 462 elementary school administrative units in Ontario. By 1966 this number had dropped to 1 408, and the 1969 reorganization reduced this figure to 190. There are at present 177 boards in Ontario operating elementary schools. In most cases, these educational jurisdictions are much larger than those of the municipalities. Five major cities — Hamilton, Ottawa, London, Windsor and Toronto — are administrative units in their own right. Metropolitan Toronto is a special case with a two-tier system. Since 1967, the Metropolitan Toronto School Board has consisted of members of the Toronto City Board of Education and of the boards of the five municipal boroughs. The Metropolitan Board studies each of the subsidiary boards' budgets and then allocates finances according to a set of allocation formulae. Apart from these five cities, the county is the basic administrative unit for public-elementary education in southern Ontario. In northern Ontario the province has created what are called "district boards of education" around centres of population. The remaining 34 cities are included within the appropriate county or district for educational purposes. Most of the units for Roman Catholic separate schools are coterminous with those of one or more public systems.

In general, the provincial education system has been in the process of change since 1968. There has been an increase in the size of the basic school administrative unit with a corresponding increase in the operating scope of the school authorities. This freedom, however, has been balanced between 1970 and 1975 by tighter provincial fiscal control. During this period, the province introduced expenditure ceilings which seriously curtailed the decision-making powers of the wealthier boards. These restrictions were removed in 1976.

Chapter II

SOURCES OF FUNDS AND REVENUE PRODUCTION

Education in Canada is financed by all three levels of government: federal, provincial, and municipal. The proportions contributed by each, however, vary depending on the province and the level of education. Historically, education is controlled by the provinces and administered locally.

A major factor in recent years in the finance of education, and more generally in provincial finance, has been federal revenue sharing. The sharing takes the form of federal-to-provincial transfers of taxation points of a tax utilized by both levels along with outright money grants to the provinces. For example, the fifty percent federal subsidy of university education operating costs is accomplished by a transfer to the provinces of points from the personal and corporation income taxes as well as cash grants [4]. The transfer of taxation points, whereby the federal government reduces its percentage of a certain tax and allows the provinces to increase their take by the same percentage, tends to become institutionalized over time so that the provinces regard the revenue as their own and not a federal transfer. Nevertheless, the amount of revenue each province obtains from the tax transfer is used for calculating the federal grant, which contains an equalization component based on university operating costs. There is precedent for provincial transfer of a federal tax transfer back to the original taxpayer, and also for provincial abandonment of a federal tax transfer. Neither of these examples involved revenue earmarked for education. In conclusion, it becomes rather difficult to designate transferred tax points as either federal transfers or revenue from provincial taxation. They have characteristics of both.

FEDERAL LEVEL REVENUE

Federal financial aid for education, in the form of transfer payments to the provinces, is a major source of funds at the post-secondary level. Federal aid to the secondary and elementary levels is less direct and considerably smaller. Nevertheless, in recent years the federal government has increased its participation in elementary education through contributions in two main areas: equalization payments and language programs. In 1972-1973 the ten provinces received 5.8 per cent of their gross revenue from equalization payments, although Ontario, along with Alberta and British Columbia, receives none. The language programs, which were started in 1970, are designed to provide an opportunity for members

---

4. This was changed late in 1976 to "Established Programs Financing" which is not tied to university education.

of an official language majority group to acquire a knowledge of their second official language, and for members of the official minority language group to be educated in their first language. In all provinces, with the exception of Quebec, the majority language is English and the minority language is French. Federal contributions are made in the form of partial reimbursement for language programs developed and administered by the provinces. Language programs constitute Ontario's only source of federal funds for elementary education. Ontario accounts for 60 per cent of the Francophone elementary school students in the nine English-speaking provinces, and in 1975-1976 will receive an estimated $28 million from the federal government to promote its French language programs at all levels. Of this, approximately $10 million is for elementary education. The total enrolment in French language schools in Ontario in 1975 September was 77 424, or 5.6 per cent of a total elementary enrolment of 1 389 478.

Seven of the ten provinces receive revenue from the federal revenue equalization system, which was developed to equalize the per capita revenue of each of the provinces. Under this system, the federal government makes unconditional grants to the provinces to bring the per capita yield for each of its revenue sources, including local school taxes, up to the national average in provinces where it falls below. If it is assumed that they contribute to elementary education in the same proportion as total provincial revenue then they make a substantial contribution. This is particularly so in the Atlantic Provinces where equalization payments constituted, on average, 21.2 per cent of the gross general revenue for each province in 1972-1973. The 1975 estimated payments to these provinces ranged from 21.5 per cent of New Brunswick's gross general revenue to 28.3 per cent for Newfoundland.

In addition to the above schemes, the federal government directly operates and supports a limited number of elementary education systems including those for Indians, Eskimos and Armed Forces' dependents. This, however, is negligible in relation to the amount spent on education in Canada.

PROVINCIAL LEVEL REVENUE

As described above, Ontario receives federal funding for elementary education only for its French language education programs. The Canadian constitution limits provincial and, by implication, municipal revenue production to direct taxation only. Tax sources are not earmarked for education in Ontario and hence all provincial revenue is assumed to contribute proportionately to the financing of education. Table 2-1 shows the provincial revenue from various sources for 1975-1976. Over half (57.9 per cent interim 1975-1976) of Ontario's budgetary revenue is generated through taxation. The Atlantic provinces, however, generate only one-third of their revenue in this manner and, as described above, receive large federal equalization payments to supplement their income. Alberta's main source of revenue is neither taxation nor federal support but royalties from natural resources which contribute almost half of its gross general revenue.

Taxation, then, is the most important method of revenue production in Ontario. In 1975-1976, over half of this revenue was produced by two taxes; 35.1 per cent was generated through personal income tax and 25.5 per cent was raised through retail sales tax. The income tax rate levied by Ontario is presently 30.5 per cent of federal basic tax. The present sales tax rate for Ontario is 7 per cent. This tax was first introduced in Ontario in 1961 at a rate of 3 per cent and was increased in 1966 to 5 per cent and in 1973 to 7 per cent. During 1975, the retail sales tax was temporarily cut to 5 per cent but returned to the 1973 level in 1976.

Table 2-1. **Budgetary revenue of Ontario (interim 1975-1976)**

Revenue item	Millions of dollars
TAXATION	
Personal income tax [a]	1 827
Corporation income tax	977
Retail sales tax	1 325
Gasoline and motor vehicle fuel taxes	585
Tobacco tax	102
Race tracks tax	38
Capital and premium taxes	160
Mining profits tax	62
Succession duty	64
Land transfer tax	52
Other taxes	13
	5 205
OTHER REVENUE	
Health insurance premiums	564
Liquor control board profits	337
Vehicle registration fees	214
Other fees and licences	95
Lottery profits	39
Fines and penalties	49
Royalties	44
Sales and rentals	38
Utility service charges (sales of electric power)	28
Miscellaneous	47
	1 455
Payments from the Federal Government	1 931
Interest on investments	391
TOTAL BUDGETARY REVENUE	8 982

a) Including $256 million federal revenue guarantee and netted by $387 million in tax credits.

The payments from the federal government to Ontario, 21.5 per cent of gross general revenue in interim 1975-1976, are all for shared-cost programs including medicare, hospital care, and social welfare. Only some $10 million were for elementary education in the form of French grants. Comparable data for determining the proportion of provincial expenditures that were devoted to education go back no further than 1961. No distinction is made in comparative reports between expenditure on elementary and secondary education and expenditure on post-secondary education. The figures in Table 2.2 should show accurate comparative figures, though in terms of total percentage they will not be directly comparable with other countries.

Estimated education expenditures as a percentage of gross general expenditure estimates of the provincial governments for 1974-1975 are also shown in Table 2.2.

The 1974-1975 estimates show that education accounts for the largest percentage of expenditure in the provinces of Newfoundland Prince Edward Island, Nova Scotia, New Brunswick and Quebec. Expenditures on health are in first place in the remaining five provinces, closely followed by education. Although health services (including socialized hospital care and physicians' services) are 50 per cent financed from federal funds, the money is all spent provincially; for this reason health has edged out education as the biggest expenditure

Table 2-2. **Percentage of provincial expenditures devoted to all levels of education, 1961 and 1972**

Year	Nfld.	P.E.I.	N.S.	N.B.	Que.	Ont.	Man.	Sask.	Alta.	B.C.	Canada
1961	24.8	20.6	23.0	14.3	24.5	24.8	22.5	25.6	30.1	22.4	24.5
1972	23.3	23.5	24.6	30.9	26.3	28.3	27.5	23.9	29.9	21.3	26.8
Est. 1974-75	26.2	27.6	24.8	27.0	25.6	25.5	20.8	21.6	23.6	19.2	24.5

Table 2-3. **Percentage of provincial/local expenditures on elementary and secondary education borne by provinces, 1954-1973**

Year	Nfld.	P.E.I.	N.S.	N.B.	Que.	Ont.	Man.	Sask.	Alta.	B.C.	Canada
1954	85	55	53	44	35	37	36	31	40	39	38
1964	89	67	52	34	58	49	43	48	50	47	52
1973	77	96	63	100	67	64	58	56	61	63	65.5

in the wealthier provinces. Table 2.3 shows the percentage of total educational expenditures borne by the provinces and their constituent school boards for elementary and secondary education 1954, 1964, and 1973.

LOCAL LEVEL REVENUE

Only the federal and provincial governments in Canada have constitutional powers to levy taxes for the support of public services. Local authorities are, however, assigned certain tax sources by the provincial government. In general, these are the sources which are most readily and efficiently administered at the local level. The most important of these is the real property tax which in 1974 accounted for 69.2 per cent of the revenue of municipalities from their own sources. The municipality's revenue is then supplemented by other revenue raised by the province through grants to both municipalities and school boards.

Revenue for elementary education derives from two main sources: local taxation on property and provincial government grants from general revenue. According to the various provincial acts governing the taxation of real property at the municipal level, only municipal councils and separate school boards have powers to levy taxes on ratepayers residing within the territory under their jurisdiction. In the last ten years the proportion of school revenue accounted for by local property tax has decreased considerably in all provinces to a present level of approximately 40 per cent of total operating costs. In Ontario, local municipalities were required to raise 37.4 per cent of their 1973 total expenditure for elementary education through this tax, compared with 48.0 per cent in 1970 and 69.6 per cent in 1966. The result of the decrease in revenue from local taxation has been a corresponding increase in the proportion of school revenues accounted for by provincial funds. In 1973, 58.5 per cent of Ontario school board revenues came from such provincial grants and subsidies.

A third local revenue source which is insignificant when compared with the property tax and provincial grants, but which is mentioned to complete the picture, includes miscellaneous items such as cafeteria profits (if any), laboratory breakage charges, and rental of school facilities to community groups. Revenue from these sources is extremely small and is often intented merely to defray extra costs associated with the respective activities.

Two other types of payments may appear in revenue statements of boards although neither is a true revenue source. Tuition payments from one board to another on behalf of students resident in one district but attending school in another, act as revenue for individual boards but are merely transfer payments in the aggregate sense. Because of the lumpy nature of school board cash flow, boards are permitted to enter into short-term borrowing to meet operating expenses. The amount borrowed must not exceed the board's currently uncollected revenue.

Almost all of Ontario school board revenue for investment in capital facilities, such as buildings, is obtained from the Ontario Education Capital Aid Corporation. This corporation was created by the provincial government in 1966 to overcome the problems of school boards and municipalities in financing large capital expenditure. These problems centred around a lack of sufficient resources to undertake capital expenditure except by recourse to borrowing. Under this program, the province uses funds generated by the Canada Pension Plan to purchase local school debentures. This program has resulted in a significant reduction in the rate of interest borne by such debentures.

There are four other, though lesser, sources of capital funds. School boards may secure capital funds from the current revenue fund. In this case, the expenditure is limited by the Education Act to an amount equivalent to one dollar per thousand of the equalized assessment. A second source is through provincial contributions from general revenue by which a school board may receive a provincial grant for part of the capital expenditure. This capital expenditure, however, must be capital expenditure approved by the Ontario Municipal Board, and in 1974 amounted to only 1.9 per cent of the total capital fund for all school boards in Ontario. Proceeds from the sale of land, buildings, and insurance is the third source of capital funding, and this accounted for 1.5 per cent of the total revenue for all Ontario school boards in 1973. Finally, a school board may borrow in the open bond market, but if it does so, it will receive grant assistance or repayment only with the approval of the Ministry of Education and the Ontario Municipal Board.

OTHER SOURCES OF REVENUE

Elementary schools which operate outside the public school systems exist throughout Canada. Alberta and Saskatchewan provide some form of financial assistance to private schools while Quebec has a system of public support for private education. In Ontario, they are operated and paid for by an individual, an association, or a corporation and receive only remission from property taxes usually remission from corporation taxes.

There is no legislation in Ontario to cover funds raised by individual schools for their own purposes. In general, however, publicly supported schools are not encouraged to raise money at this level. The result is that any funds raised depend on the needs and initiative of staff and students. In this area, funds are usually raised for special projects such as field trips or athletics. Home and School Associations and other similar groups also provide assistance. Donations are not now a significant source of funds in the public sector but continue to be used by many private schools.

Chapter III

FEDERAL INVOLVEMENT IN ELEMENTARY AND SECONDARY EDUCATION IN CANADA

The Canadian federal government has been involved in education in a small way ever since Confederation because of its constitutional responsibilities. Its involvement over the years has increased as federal power generally increased and as its superior taxing ability, both constitutional and political, became apparent. During this same period of time education became a more important and varied enterprise providing greater scope for federal largesse. Today the federal government is heavily involved in education, especially in its finance, in spite of limited constitutional authority.

DIRECT INVOLVEMENT

The federal government has been educating aboriginal persons and members of the armed forces for many years. It has been directly involved in the education of Indians and Eskimos ever since Confederation. Responsibility for their education was placed on the federal government by the BNA Act. The federal government has been directly involved in the education of the children of members of the armed services abroad since the end of World War II, and in the education of the children of members of the armed forces living on armed forces bases in Canada for at least that length of time. The latter involvement is by direct agreement with the provinces involved. In Ontario, the Department of National Defence provides the accommodation, and the Ontario Ministry of Education pays a grant of 50 per cent of operating costs.

The earliest federal involvement with the provinces was in the area of vocational and technical education. In 1919 "The Technical Education Act" was passed by the Parliament of Canada. This Act provided ten million dollars to the nine provinces (at that time) to be spent over a period of ten years on the construction and equipment of vocational secondary schools, with the provinces sharing the cost on a 50-50 basis. Ontario claimed 3 million dollars of this amount, its share based on population.

In 1960 the federal government passed "The Technical and Vocational Training Assistance Act" which funnelled some 382 million dollars of federal funds to Ontario school boards, alone, in the years 1962-1969 for the construction and equipping of vocational and technical schools. In both cases the federal government saw value in increasing the skill level of the labor force.

The first direct federal involvement in elementary education at the provincial level was through the Languages Programmes Branch of the Department of the Secretary of State, beginning in 1970. This was a consequence of the recommendations of the Royal Commission on Bilingualism and Biculturalism and was designed to make the country more bilingual.

INDIRECT INVOLVEMENT

Apart from rather small statutory grants to the provinces negotiated at the time of their entry into Confederation, the federal government did not become involved in unconditional monetary transfers to the provinces until 1941. In that war year all provinces entered into tax-rental agreements with Ottawa, whereby the federal government was given exclusive jurisdiction in the income, corporation and inheritance tax fields in return for rental payments based on the 1940 yield or other formula satisfactory to the province concerned. There was no true equalization involved; nor were these payments grants within the usual meaning of the term. These tax-rental agreements lasted with minor changes until 1951. The tax-rental agreements were continued for the 1952-1956 time period but with additional payments containing the germs of both the unconditional-grant and equalization-grant ideas. There were guaranteed minimum payments related to these figures in 1948. Some provinces, notably Quebec, but including Ontario for some purposes, opted out of some of these arrangements.

For the 1957-1962 Fiscal Arrangements Act, unconditional equalization and stabilization grants were spelled out for the first time. The tax rental payments were based on "standard tax rates" on three tax bases — income, corporation profits, and inheritance. The provinces received rentals at the rates of 10 per cent, 9 per cent and 50 per cent respectively of federal collections on the three bases in the provinces concerned but were provided also with an equalization grant to bring the per capita yield of these three taxes for each province up to the average per capita yield for the two provinces with the highest per capita yield (Ontario and British Columbia). In addition, there were to be stabilization grants which were either annually adjusted save-harmless provisions related to the previous arrangements, or a guarantee of 95 per cent of the average of the payments under the standard taxes and equalization grant for the two previous years. The true equalization principle in federal grants to the provinces began in 1957 with some foreshadowing in 1952-1956.

The standard taxes on which equalization and stabilization grants are based were increased from the three mentioned above to 16 provincial revenue sources in 1967, and to 23 sources in 1972 including one (school-purpose taxes) which, while a provincial revenue source in Prince Edward Island and New Brunswick, is a municipal revenue source in most.

Since these unconditional grants cannot be assumed to be subsidizing any particular aspect of provincial spending, they must be assumed to go to the support of all provincial services in the same proportion as total provincial or provincial-local revenues. Thus federal unconditional grants may be said to contribute indirectly to education. W. J. Brown, in his Ph.D. dissertation "Redistributive Implications of Federal-Provincial Fiscal Arrangements for Elementary and Secondary Education in Canada" (1974), has calculated the indirect federal assistance to elementary and secondary education from this source for the country as a whole and for each province for the years 1960, 1965 and 1970. Table 3.1 shows for each of those years the percentage contribution to total government spending (all levels) on elementary and secondary education in five of the provinces, made by:

a) Federal direct payments;
b) Federal indirect payments ; and
c) Federal direct and indirect payments.

In terms of a combination of educational and financial need (personal income per weighted child aged 5-19) these provinces had indices as shown in Table 3.2 compared with the Canadian average. A comparison of Tables 3.1 and 3.2 will show that the federal indirect aid to education was related inversely to relative fiscal capacity and need, and hence displayed a strong equalizing element.

Table 3-1. **Federal direct and indirect assistance for elementary and secondary education as a percentage of total government expenditures on elementary and secondary education 1960, 1965 and 1970**[a]

Province	Direct aid 1960	1965	1970	Indirect aid 1960	1965	1970	Direct and indirect aid 1960	1965	1970
Newfoundland	1.91	1.00	0.33	35.42	25.28	27.87	37.34	26.29	28.20
New Brunswick	2.48	1.94	8.96	19.48	21.56	17.79	21.96	23.50	26.75
Ontario	1.98	4.34	1.55	0.98	1.32	0.74	2.96	5.66	2.51
Manitoba	7.94	7.46	6.46	7.21	8.30	6.28	15.16	15.76	12.74
British Columbia	5.18	9.76	3.06	2.06	0.55	0.28	7.24	10.32	3.34
Canada	3.07	5.45	3.55	5.34	4.70	5.48	8.41	10.15	9.03

a) Derived from W. J. Brown, "Redistributive Implications of Federal-Provincial Fiscal Arrangements for Elementary and Secondary Education in Canada", unpublished Ph.D. dissertation, University of Toronto, 1974.

Table 3-2. **Indexes of five provinces for personal income per weighted person aged 5-19 years in 1960, 1965 and 1970**[a]

Province	Index of personal income per weighted[b] school age child 1960	1965	1970
Newfoundland	45	48	54
New Brunswick	58	59	65
Ontario	128	124	123
Manitoba	102	97	95
British Columbia	129	123	116
Canada	100	100	100

a) Adapted from W. J. Brown, *op. cit.*
b) Persons aged 5-14 were given a weight of 1.0 and those aged 15-19 a weight of 1.5.

The question: "What proportion of federal revenues is used for elementary and secondary education?" is a difficult one to answer. As was noted above, direct federal spending on education is only a part of total aid to education. The indirect aid is hard to measure over time because in 1950 it consisted of payments made under tax rental agreements and could be considered as provincial rather than federal money. Statistics Canada's *Survey of Educational Finance* gives figures for direct payments only back to 1953, and 1975 figures are not yet available. Brown's (1974) estimates of indirect aid to elementary and secondary education in 1960, 1965, and 1970 are used to arrive at estimates of both direct and combined direct and indirect assistance as percentages of total federal revenue. These figures are shown in Table 3.3.

Table 3-3. **Percent of federal revenues devoted to elementary and secondary education: 1960, 1965 and 1970**

Year	Direct aid	Indirect aid	Total aid
1960	0.59	1.03	1.62
1965	1.37	1.18	2.55
1970	1.08	1.66	2.74

Table 3-4. **Percentage of total government expenditures on education coming from federal sources in 1960, 1965 and 1970 (Canada)**

Year	Federal direct payments	Federal indirect payments	Total federal payments
1960	3.07	5.35	8.42
1965	5.45	4.70	10.15
1970	3.55	5.48	9.03

The same sources will be used to answer the question: "What proportion of total revenue for elementary and secondary education came from federal sources in selected years?" Table 3.4 shows the answer to this question for 1960, 1965, and 1970.

FEDERAL EDUCATION POLICY

From the standpoint of the provincial governments, talk of federal priorities in education is anathema because educational policy and administration are clearly defined as provincial responsibilities. Federal objectives in this area have always been justified on other than purely educational grounds. Thus as broad national interests have changed, federal priorities in education have changed, but have not been very wide-ranging. Since 1957 equalization has been a priority, not for education alone, but for all provincial government services. This concept has not been seriously challenged and the recent federal-provincial conference made no change in that aspect of federal-provincial fiscal arrangements. The most recent federal priority to change was that related to language teaching which is described in Chapter IV. This arrangement began in 1970 and may be intensified at the school level as a result of less-than-desired success with the program of language training for civil servants. The federal initiatives in the area of technical and vocational training have been limited largely to financial assistance for buildings and equipment and have been on-again-off-again affairs.

Chapter IV

FINANCIAL INSTRUMENTS USED TO CHANNEL FUNDS TO PRIMARY EDUCATION

There are three general financial instruments used to channel funds to schools in Ontario. These are provincial grants, municipal taxation, and borrowing, of which the characteristics and uses are set out in detail in provincial legislation and regulations. They all make use of the accounting structure outlined in the *Uniform Code of Accounts* and especially of the categorization of all expenditures into ordinary and extraordinary. The distinction was originally made between types of expenditures which all boards incurred (ordinary) and those which were not incurred by all boards (extraordinary). Ordinary expenditures are defined to include non-capital expenditures on business administration; computer services; instruction; educational services; attendance, health, and food services; plant operation, plant maintenance; tuition paid; transportation on field trips; and a small miscellaneous category for other operating expenses. Extraordinary expenditures include transportation (home to school, school to home, and school to school only), board, lodging, long term debt charges, captial expenditure (investment) from revenue, and the capital portion of tuition paid and of rental payments for facilities. Generally speaking, ordinary expenditures are borne by boards in proportion to the numbers of pupils, whereas extraordinary expenditures are related to other factors including the enrolment history and the pupil population density of the district. These two categories include all expenditures except capital investment financed by borrowing, which ultimately appears under extraordinary expenditures as part of the debt charge.

PROVINCIAL GRANTS

The Province of Ontario grants money to boards using two different formulae, one for ordinary expenditures and one for extraordinary expenditures. The provincial contribution is a much higher proportion of recognized expenditure for extraordinary expenditures than for ordinary expenditures.

Grant on ordinary expenditure

The present Ontario grant on ordinary expenditures takes the form of a percentage equalizing grant which, in effect, puts all boards on an equal footing with respect to providing equal dollars, up to a maximum or ceiling dollar amount, per unit of need. The unit of need is a "weighted pupil". Pupils are weighted in relation to the extra cost presumed to be incurred in educating them because of the characteristics of the pupils themselves, their socio-economic environment, their geographical location, the size of their school or school authority, or the program they are in. Where the distribution of a particular high-cost factor is assumed to be roughly proportional to enrolment among school authorities no weighting is needed or used. It is only where some authorities have the high-cost factor and others do not, or when some authorities have it to a greater extent than do others, that a weighting is used. Weightings for elementary pupils in use in Ontario in 1977 are as follows:

1. A weighting factor for special education which, in effect, counts each special education pupil in excess of 13 per 1 000 of enrolment as 3.5 weighted pupils.
2. A weighting factor to recognize the need to provide compensatory education for socially, economically, culturally or linguistically atypical children. The presence of large numbers of such children requires higher unit costs due chiefly to the need for lower pupil-teacher ratios. The factor, which can add 2 to 5 per cent to the enrolment used for grant purposes, is based on an authority's score on four measures:
    i) Percentage of population in receipt of general assistance and family welfare benefits;
    ii) Percentage of all income tax returns with taxable income less than $5 000 ;
    iii) Percentage of population with neither English nor French as the language of the home ; and
    iv) The number of public housing units per 1 000 persons adjusted to reflect the bedroom count of the units.
3. A weighting factor to recognize the higher cost of goods and services in the vast northern and northwestern part of the province. Authorities in these areas that do not include a city or town with a population in excess of 25 000 receive a weighting factor of 9 per cent, while those which do include such an urban municipality receive a factor of 6 per cent.
4. A weighting factor to recognize the higher costs of maintaining and operating older school buildings is provided for boards with more than 14.7 per cent of their pupil places provided before 1945. This factor is graded in steps of 0.1 per cent to a maximum of 2 per cent reached when more than 43.24 per cent of pupil places were provided before 1945.
5. All boards in excess of the median with regard to the percentage relationship of admissions to total enrolment, other than admissions during the month of September and admissions of students entered on the roll of an elementary school for the first time, receive a weighting factor ranging from 0.1 per cent to 2 per cent to reflect the additional costs experienced when the admissions rate during the year is high. A high admissions rate reflects either a highly mobile urban population or a rapid rate of new housing development.
6. Population sparsity is recognized as a factor causing higher unit costs in two ways:
    a) The higher costs of administrative and supervisory service in small jurisdictions are recognized by providing a factor of 0.1 per cent for each 100 pupils a board's elementary enrolment falls below 4 000 pupils, to a maximum of 2 per cent.
    b) The higher administrative and instructional costs of operating schools with fewer than 20 pupils per grade or per age-level are recognized for such schools when they are more than five miles by

road from another school operated in the same language, by allowing a weighting of two percent per pupil for each full pupil-per-grade, the school falls below 20.

7. Finally there is a weighting factor to recognize cost differences caused by higher proportions of highly qualified and experienced teachers. This factor, the computation of which is too complicated to report here, recognizes only a small part of the additional salary cost and is a carry-over from a period when limitations were placed on expenditure per weighted pupil. At that time it was very necessary to take salary differentials caused by qualifications and experience into account in setting spending limits for boards. The maximum weighting factor for teachers' salaries is now 1.5 per cent, and applies only to the top 75 per cent of boards in this dimension.

The weighting factor for a board, 1 000 (for the actual pupil) plus the sum of the individual factors calculated according to 1-7 above, is multiplied by the board's average daily enrolment (ADE) to obtain the number of weighted pupils (WP) for grant purposes. In 1977 the range in elementary-board weighting factors was from 1.0060 to 1.2526.

Each year the Minister of Education announces a dollar figure representing the maximum ordinary expenditure per weighted pupil that will be recognized for grant purposes. For 1977 this figure is $1197 for elementary pupils. To determine the maximum ordinary expenditure for which a grant may be obtained, the ADE in the above procedure is replaced by the full time equivalent enrolment on September 30 of the previous year which gives boards advance knowledge of the amount of their grantable expenditure. Expenditures above this figure must be financed entirely from the local property tax. Expenditures at or below the figure are financed by a combination of provincial grant and local taxation in such a way that recognized ordinary expenditure per weighted pupil (ROE/WP) is the sole determinant of differences in the property tax rate required to raise the local share of ROE on provincially equalized assessment of real property.

The formula by which this equalization is achieved is as follows:

$$G = \left[1 - 0.4 \left(\frac{LEA/WP}{PEA/WP}\right)\right] ROE$$

where G   = Provincial grant on ordinary expenditure payable to a board.
       LEA/WP = Local equalized assessment per weighted pupil.
       PEA/WP = Provincial equalized assessment per weighted pupil.
       ROE   = Recognized ordinary expenditure of the board the lesser of the actual ordinary expenditure and the ceiling amount which equalled weighted ADE x $1197 in 1977.
       0.4   = The proportion of the ROE of a board of average wealth that will be financed from local taxation.

The weighted pupils in the expressions LEA/WP and PEA/WP are determined by mutiplying the enrolment on the last school day of September of the year preceding the grant calendar year by the weighting factor for each board.

The fraction $\left(\frac{LEA/WP}{PEA/WP}\right)$ known in Ontario by the term "assessment index", measures a board's relative wealth in terms of equalized assessment per weighted pupil. When this fraction is multiplied by the 0.4 in the formula, the proportion of a board's ROE that must be borne locally is determined. Each board's local share of ROE is directly proportional to its LEA/WP — a board whose LEA/WP is 5 times that of another will be responsible for raising a percentage of its ROE

75

that is five times as great as that required of the second board. The balance of a board's ROE will be paid by the province as a general legislative grant, as indicated by the formula. Thus, up to the ROE ceiling, a board's rate of taxation is a function only of its ROE per weighted pupil of September enrolment and not of its assessment or pupil population. There is a simple one-to-one relationship between tax rate and ROE per weighted pupil which is unaffected by per-pupil assessment and which holds for all boards in a given year. Above the grant limit, boards must pay 100 per cent of costs, so that assessment per pupil becomes very important at that level. If there is to be effective equality of educational service levels, then the expenditure limit for grant purposes must be kept at a realistic figure, one at which most boards can operate satisfactorily. Otherwise it will operate as a foundation program level with some of the boards operating at that level, but with the wealthier boards greatly exceeding the foundation level at a low tax rate.

To encourage boards to provide instruction in the French language to non-Francophones, the general legislative grants provide for a stimulation grant at the board's percentage rate of grant of a sum equal to $54 per annum per elementary pupil taking instruction in oral French for an average of 20 minutes a day, five days a week. A similar grant is available for each pupil in a school or class conducted in the French language. There is a small per-pupil grant to help defray the costs of converting learning materials and equipment to the metric system. Apart from this the Ontario grants for ordinary expenditure are general-purpose grants, providing equalization and local tax relief to the various school jurisdictions.

But the weighting factor for special education may be considered as a stimulation grant, and a very effective one at that, since from an individual board's point of view, the extra pupils generated by the factor can be turned into extra dollars, and these extra dollars are paid entirely by the province. This is true, of course, of the other weighting factors as well, but none of them can be considered as a stimulation grant. There are two reasons for this. First, under a percentage equalizing formula the incremental cost of an increase in the number of pupils is borne entirely by the province. Second, the number of pupils for grant purposes can be increased by reclassifying pupils from normal to special, since this increases the weighting factor. The other weighting factors are based on measures external to the board and cannot be altered by the board in this way.

Grant on extraordinary expenditure

As was previously mentioned, extraordinary expenditure includes expenditure for debt charges, capital from revenue, transportation of pupils to and from school and from school to school, lodging and board for pupils, and the capital element in tuition fees paid to other boards and in rent paid for accommodation and equipment. It will be recalled that for ordinary expenditure there was a ceiling on the amount that was eligible for a provincial grant, an amount known as the ROE. In the area of extraordinary expenditure there is also a recognized extraordinary expenditure (REE). But owing to the nature of such expenditure, ceilings cannot be in terms of dollars per weighted pupil as in the case of ROE. Instead, there are various methods of determining that portion of the various types of extraordinary expenditure that will be recognized by the Minister for grant purposes.

Debt charges include the annual (usually for 20 years) instalments on the outstanding debt and the interest payments associated with them. Typically the annual payment (principal plus interest) is the same throughout the 20-year period on each particular building project. For many years there were few central controls on building projects, boards being legally free to build as far above the provincial standard as they wished, the determining factor usually being the tax-paying ability of the jurisdictions concerned. What the Ministry did do was determine what part of the cost of a new building project it would approve for grant purposes. The debt charges on the approved portion would form part of REE for the duration of the term while the remainder would be entirely the responsibility of the local rate-payers. More recently, the Ministry's approval formula has been made more sensitive to regional differences in building costs and to the secular increase in such costs. It is now possible actually to construct a building within the approval level of the Ministry, though most boards exceed the approvals by about 10 per cent. Another change has been the province's near absolute control over building projects since 1970 through its control of the major sources of capital borrowing. The part of REE that is composed of debt charges is very closely controlled centrally. The amounts that are recognized for various boards will vary with present and past building needs as assessed by the Ministry.

There is not as stringent a control on expenditures for the transportation of pupils. The Ministry has a formula, calculated for each bus route, related to bus seating capacity, weighted occupancy ratio, and geographical location, which determines for each board the maximum expenditure eligible for grant. Transportation expenditure that forms part of REE is the lesser of this maximum and the actual expenditure on transportation. Boards are free to determine which pupils are to be transported at board expense.

Capital expenditure from the revenue fund that is recognized for grant purposes is subject to very close Ministry control. A board is limited by the statutes from spending from current revenue in any year more than an amount equivalent to the yield of a tax rate of 0.1 per cent on the taxable assessment that supports it for the purchase of sites, the erection of buildings, the purchase of capital equipment, and contributions to a reserve fund. This permits larger dollar expenditures per pupil from the boards with above-average LEA/WP's. In order to ease the pressure on the capital market, the Ministry encourages such boards to finance as large a portion as possible of their capital needs for building and site purchase from current revenue. Capital from revenue of this type included in REE is, then, subject to the same central controls as are debt charges. Capital expenditures for furniture and equipment are recognized up to an amount equivalent to seven dollars per weighted pupil. The capital element in tuition fees paid to other boards and in rent are specified by the Ministry. The REE consists, then, of those portions of extraordinary expenditure approved by the Minister for grant purposes as noted above.

Because of a special set of circumstances, the province pays grants on REE at a considerably higher rate than it does on ROE. During the late 1950's and throughout the 60's, the Ministry was encouraging the centralization of rural schools, a process that often resulted in 75 to 100 per cent of rural pupils being bused to school, and in all pupils being in accommodation on which there were outstanding debentures, and hence debt charges. This resulted in the REE per WP for such boards being 400 to 700 per cent higher than was the case for urban boards where very few, if any, pupils were bused and where a large part of the pupils were in accommodation that was debt free.

Because the province wanted to encourage centralization, it devised a grant plan for extraordinary expenditure that made possible such centralization without drastic increases in the local tax rate. In other words, the province agreed to pay most of the additional cost of centralization. This was accomplished, beginning in 1958, by a growth-need grant which ensured that, as the unit recognized extraordinary expenditure increased, the rate of provincial grant would also increase. Thus between 1958 and the present (except for the year 1976) the rate of grant on REE went up (1) as LEA/WP went down and (2) as REE/WP went up.

In 1975 this was accomplished by paying boards a 75 per cent equalizing grant on the first $60 of REE/WP and a 95 per cent equalizing grant on the REE/WP in excess of $60.

For the year 1976, provincial policy with respect to transfer payments to local governments, including school boards, changed. For the first time, the cabinet decided beforehand the total amount by which transfer payments would increase over 1975, and the split between school boards and other local government authorities. This resulted in a fixed total sum of money for elementary and secondary school boards. Since school-based costs had risen by a higher percentage than the grants were to rise, and since, for the sake of equity, it was desirable to keep the ceiling on ROE at a realistic level, cuts had to be made elsewhere in the system. Grants to secondary boards were drastically reduced. For example, a 7.98 per cent increase in ROE/WP increased tax rates by 30.71 per cent. But some money had to be saved in elementary schools as well. The provincial share for elementary schools was cut from 62 to 60 per cent. In addition, the growth-need feature was dropped from the grant on recognized extraordinary expenditure at both levels. In 1976 all boards received their grant on REE according to the following formula:

$$\text{Grant on REE} = \left(1.00 - 0.25 \times \frac{\text{LEA/WP}}{\text{PEA/WP}}\right) \text{REE}.$$

Since this was a percentage equalizing grant it contained no inherent inequities, in that boards with the same REE/WP had the same REE tax rate. However, boards with very high levels of REE/WP, those with a high percentage of pupils bused and a high ratio of pupils in debt-laden buildings to those in debt-free buildings, had a greatly increased tax rate for REE. The percentage equalizing grant formula was designed to equalize in terms of expenditure per weighted pupil and tends to break down for expenditures that do not vary strictly according to the number of pupils. This is especially true if the expenditures are partly beyond the control of the board as is the case with busing in rural areas. Most of the wealthier boards are those which contain large urban areas or which are largely urban. These tend to have much lower REE/WP. On the other hand, boards with high transportation and debt expenditures tend to be more rural and hence lower in LEA/WP.

The dropping of the second-level rate of grant for boards with high REE created such dissatisfaction that it has been partially reinstated for 1977. REE has been divided into two levels.

Level 1 includes the sum of approved debt charges incurred prior to 1977 and approved transportation expenditures incurred in 1977 in excess of $172 per weighted pupil.

Level 2 includes all other REE, including all approved capital from revenue.

Level two expenditures are supported by a percentage equalizing grant paid at the rate of 75 per cent for a board of average wealth and level one expenditure at the rate of 95 per cent for such a board. This restores, though to a lesser degree than prior to 1976, the growth-need principle for boards in the upper half of the distribution of transportation expenditures and pre-1977 debt charges per weighted pupil.

MUNICIPAL TAX LEVIES

The valuation of property

As was explained in Chapter II, the local source of revenue for education is a locally imposed tax on real property and business assessment. A crucial element in this type of taxation is the process of placing a value on real property. Until 1970 this was a function of appointees of local governments and resulted in valuations among municipalities at widely different percentages of actual market value. This was not in itself bad for the purposes of the municipality concerned as long as all properties in the municipality were assessed at the same ratios. But it made use of these unadjusted local valuations useless for purposes of distribution of provincial aid. The province was forced, from 1958 on, when equalization became a major feature of provincial grants to schools, to adjust local valuations by centrally determined factors to bring the various local assessments to some common base. The factors, known as equalization factors, were computed for each municipality, first after spot-checks by central assessors on various parcels of the different types of real propery in each municipality, and later by comparing the selling prices of properties sold in the previous year with the local assessed valuation of these properties. The figure obtained by adjusting the local valuations by the equalization factors was known in Ontario as "provincial equalized assessment." This system provided a vehicle by means of which a fair amount of equity could be assured in the distribution of provincial funds to school boards, but did not ensure intertaxpayer equity either within or between municipalities. For these reasons the province in 1970 passed legislation removing the function of assessing the value of real property from the municipal level and placing it directly under provincial control. Since then, all real property in Ontario has been reassessed at market value by assessors employed and directed by the province. But for various reasons, use of the new valuations has been postponed several times. As of now, it is scheduled to come into universal use in 1978. Meanwhile, most municipalities are still using the old valuations made by local assessors and grants are based on "provincial equalized assessment."

The system proposed for 1978, subject to a special hearing being conducted by the Ontario Municipal Board, has somme interesting departures from former practice among which are the following:
1. All real property will be assessed at full market value.
2. All real property will be taxable except churches, cemeteries, and property held in trust for a band of Indians. This means that it is property to tax all provincial and municipal property including schools and school sites.
3. Residential property will be taxed at 50 per cent of assessed value and all other property at 100 per cent.
4. Taxes on farmland, non-residential farm buildings, and managed forests will be paid by the province.
5. All real property used for business purposes including government administrative facilities will be subject to an additional business assessment of 50 per cent of market value.

Local taxation for public schools

Public school boards are required to make estimates of the sums they will require to operate their school systems for the calendar year, and, after making due allowance for any surplus or deficit of the previous year, and after estimating receipt of grants from the province and other revenue, submit such estimates, together with a requisition of the amount required to be levied on the local tax base, to the councils of the municipalities concerned. The councils are required by law to levy and collect the sums requested on the property of public school supporters and pay them over at regular intervals to the board.

Since most school boards have jurisdiction in several municipalities, the requisition is required to be split among the municipalities in the same ratio as their equalized assessments bear to the total equalized assessment supporting the board.

Local taxation for separate schools

Separate school boards are empowered, after preparing estimates in the same manner as do public school boards, to set a tax rate to be levied on the taxable assessment of the separate school supporters within their jurisdictions. Although separate school boards have the power to levy and collect their own rates, municipal councils must do the levying and collecting if so requested by the board. This latter is the practice almost universally followed.

Limited power of boards to levy and collect taxes

All boards have the power to levy and collect taxes on real property in territory within their jurisdiction that is not organized municipally. In such cases the school board is performing a function of a municipal council and the separate school board is exercising its basic right as noted in the previous paragraph.

BORROWING

Long-term borrowing

All school boards, except those in Metropolitan Toronto, are empowered to issue long-term (20-25 year) debentures to finance the construction of schools and other buildings, and the purchase of school sites and school buses. The approval of the Ministry as to need and purpose, and the approval of the Ontario Municipal Board (OMB) must be obtained if a board wishes to have any portion of the debt recognized for grant purposes or if it seeks to market its debentures through provincial channels. Debentures receiving such approvals may be sold to the Ontario Education Capital Aid Corporation (OECAC), a special arm of the province. The advantages of such a sale are twofold:
1. it assures the existence of a market for the debentures, and
2. interest rates are lower than would be required if the debentures were sold on the open market, particularly for the smaller boards.

The OECAC rate is determined by the rate the province has to pay on borrowed funds at the time a debenture receives OMB approval.

Short-term borrowing

All boards are empowered to engage in short-term (one year or less) borrowing, usually from commercial banks, for the following purposes and subject to the following rules:
1. Boards may borrow to meet current expenditure requirements, including those for debt charges pending the receipt of revenue from the province

and municipalities. This need comes about because boards' needs for expenditure on a monthly or semi-monthly basis do not coincide with their intake of revenue which usually comes from the province and from the municipalities in quarterly instalments. The borrowing is subject to two major conditions:
   a) the interest rate paid must not exceed the minimum lending rate of the majority of chartered banks on the date of borrowing; and
   b) the total of such short-term borrowings must never exceed the unreceived balance of the estimated revenue of the board as set forth in the estimates adopted for the year.
2. Boards may borrow, pending the sale of debentures, but after their issue has been approved, such sums as are needed to meet capital expenditures incurred up to the total of the amount of the authorized debentures.

FEES AND OTHER USER CHARGES

1. Fees are outlawed in publicly supported elementary schools in Ontario, even to pay for textbooks and school supplies.
2. Fees are the chief instrument used by non-religious private schools. Fees are calculated in such a way as to meet the net costs of the school. Other income is from donations and endowments, particularly from former students of the school.
3. Religious private schools also use fees as a major source of income. Fees are based partly on costs but also on the perceived ability of parents as a group to pay. Besides some donations from former students, these schools usually receive subsidies from their parent religious bodies.

LIMITS PLACED ON INTERGOVERNMENTAL ALLOCATION OF FUNDS

Provincial

Earlier in the chapter, in the course of describing the provincial grants structure, limits on provincial allocation of funds for elementary education have been described. However, these limits will be summarized here.

Ordinary expenditures. The Minister determines the ordinary expenditure per weighted pupil that will be eligible for provincial grants. Any ordinary expenditure above this level falls entirely on the local property-tax base. The province thus knows in advance the maximum outlay it will need to make for this grant.

Extraordinary expenditures. The Minister has control over the total grant on extraordinary expenditure in the following ways:
1. Debt charges are eligible for grant only when the projects for which the debentures were issued were approved by the Minister and by the Ontario Municipal Board, and only at the same percentage as ministerial approval was given on the project. The Ministry thus knows in advance what its commitments will be each year. The total amount of future commitments is also controlled by the recent ministerial practice of allocating each year a maximum amount of new capital spending for elementary schools and apportioning this amount according to demonstrated need among the various elementary school boards.

2. Capital expenditure from revenue: when money is spent from current revenue for site or land purchase or for erection or renovation of a building, it is recognized for grant purposes only by a specific ministerial approval in each instance. Other capital expenditure from revenue is approved by formula, $7.00 per WP for furniture and equipment. All other capital expenditure from revenue must be financed entirely by local taxation. Here again the Ministry knows in advance what its maximum commitment in grants will be.
3. The capital element included in rent is subject to Ministry approval, and the capital element in tuition fees to another board is fixed by the Minister in the grant regulations ($70 per pupil of ADE in 1977).
4. Transportation expenditure is subject to Ministry approval but to a much lesser extent than are other extraordinary expenditures eligible for grants. Transportation of pupils is not mandatory in Ontario although most boards engage in it. This means that policies with respect to transporting pupils vary widely from board to board. Some boards transport pupils living less than one mile from the school and go to the farm gate to pick-up rural pupils. Others have minimum distances below which the board will not transport and require pupils to gather at pick-up points. Policy with respect to the use of extra-curricular activities also varies. The Ministry's control lies only in the area of "approved cost" which refers to a per diem cost per bus, based on seating capacity, weighted occupancy ratio and geographical location. It is crucial to a board that its operating costs for transportation be at or below the approval level since the rate of grant on approved transportation is higher than that on ROE and since unapproved transportation that cannot be included in ROE receives no grant at all. Thus by keeping a tight rein on the per diem approval levels for buses, which tend to rise as inflation rises, the Ministry can force boards to cut costs to keep within the approval limits. Unfortunately there is a counter pressure to keep the per diem rates high enough so that no board is forced to incur unapproved transportation expenditures if it cuts all the excess out of its operation. This whole area is a crucial one in Ontario at the present time, because of the inadequacy of the controls in this area and because of the energy shortage.

Municipal

Municipalities have no control over the current spending of education authorities. Between 1971 and 1975, however, the province controlled indirectly the growth of the local rate of property taxation for schools by setting expenditure ceilings for ordinary expenditure expressed in terms of dollars per weighted pupil. Since these controls have been removed, the only control on school tax rates is that exercised every two years by the ratepayers when they elect their public and separate school boards.

As mentioned earlier, there is control in the statutes over the annual expenditure school authorities can make from current revenue for capital purposes and contributions to reserve funds, limited to a sum equivalent to the yield of a tax rate of $1.00 per $1000 of taxable assessment.

In Metropolitan Toronto, where the six public school boards do not have the power to issue debentures for capital purposes, the Council of Metropolitan Toronto has some control over capital spending. The long-term borrowing needs of the six boards are rationalized on a series of priorities by the Metropolitan School Board and submitted for approval to the Metro Council. If the Council refuses to issue the debentures, the School Board has the right to appeal to the Ontario Municipal Board. If the latter so orders, the Council must issue the debentures. In practice, there is usually a prior agreement among the Metro Council, Metro School Board, Ministry of Education and the OMB as to the total amount of new school debt that will be available for Metropolitan Toronto for a given year and how it is to be partitioned. The Metro Council's influence, then, is limited to its bargaining power in this quadrumvirate.

MEETING RISING COSTS CAUSED BY INFLATION

The regulations governing provincial grants to boards are revised each year. Among other changes, the expenditure level eligible for grant is increased to compensate for cost inflation and teacher salary increases. Changes have been made in the French grant and in weighting factor limits for the same reason. Failure to keep the grant formulae in line with increases in board expenses tends to shift responsibility for these expenses to the local ratepayer and this necessarily discriminates against those boards with low per-pupil assessment. This is particularly serious when, as is often the case, the cost increases are beyond the control of the board.

So far, provincial policy has been to try to keep the limits on ROE/WP realistic in terms of actual rising costs but this causes two problems:
1. While the policy places great restraint on boards' spending at or in excess of the grant ceiling, it places very little restraint on the many boards that were spending well below the previous year's ceiling.
2. Since the province has been operating for several years with a deficit budget, it is adopting a policy of limiting percentage increases in transfers to local government to the percentage increase in the yield of provincial revenue. This means that if the ceilings are kept in line with proposed local expenditure increases, the provincial share will have to be decreased. This would mean that grant per pupil would increase at a lower percentage than would ROE per pupil. (Under this method, however, local tax rates to provide the ROE/WP level would all increase by the same percentage.)

The problem of inflationary costs is being partly met as a result of wage-and-price-control policy of the federal government. New wage settlements are subject to examination and often rolled back by the Anti-Inflation Board.

COST CHANGES ARISING FROM YEAR-TO-YEAR FLUCTUATIONS IN ENROLMENTS

The Ontario grant plan looks after year-to-year fluctuations in enrolments automatically. As previously pointed out, the local property tax rate for recognized ordinary expenditure depends on ROE/WP of the previous September enrolment. Thus any increase in enrolment for a board between one September and the next does not affect its local tax rate unless the board is spending above the ROE ceiling. The costs of educating the additional students are borne either by the province via an increase in grants or by all boards in the province through a decrease in the level of provincial support. The latter method applies in a period when the province is providing a fixed sum for grants to school boards. Likewise, a decline in enrolment is not reflected in a lower mill rate for the board experiencing it. It will mean either a lowering of the province's total grants to that board or an increase in the provincial level of support to all boards. Enrolment increases that result in higher pupil-teacher ratios will, of course, lower the tax rate, while enrolment decreases accompanied by decreases in pupil-teacher ratios will raise the tax rate.

Declining enrolment is proving to be a greater problem for school boards than increasing enrolment was. This is because of the following factors:
1. Boards find it difficult to reduce administrative, supervisory, and teaching personnel at the same rate as enrolment declines. This has the effect of increasing cost per pupil and hence the education tax rate.
2. Boards are faced with vacant school space and the costs of maintaining and operating it.
3. Boards find it difficult to adjust to a climate of contraction of service after so many decades of training and experience that was growth-oriented.

Because of these problems the province used a weighting for declining enrolments for the three years 1973, 1974 and 1975 which, for the grant and expenditure ceilings, counted half a pupil for each pupil by which the enrolment had declined from one September to the next. This factor was removed when the expenditure ceilings were discontinued in 1976 — a spur to force boards to keep staffing ratios constant even in the face of declining enrolments. Counter pressures are brought to bear to increase the staffing ratios, particularly by teachers, who have recently gained the right to bargain collectively for working conditions. In many cases this is being interpreted as including the number of teachers to be employed.

Chapter V

RATIONALE FOR PRESENT SYSTEM OF FINANCING AND THE DISPARITIES RELATED TO VARIOUS OBJECTIVES

The elementary education policy of the Ontario government has, since the 1969 school district reorganization, been based on the theme of equality of educational opportunity for all students in the province, and fiscal equalization of school boards to help attain this objective. The percentage equalizing grant plan, together with a system of weighting factors, was the financial instrument introduced to implement the latter. The basic philosophy of this plan is that the financial burden of each school board jurisdiction should be directly related to its level of expenditure, and that all jurisdictions, irrespective of local wealth, should have an identical tax rate for a comparable level of expenditure per weighted pupil. This system of financing education has not managed to achieve complete equity. Two studies, one by Humphreys (1972) and one by Humphreys and Rawkins (1974), show that rural-urban inequality among boards in provision of services declined between 1969 and 1971 but that it increased between 1971 and 1973. A study of per pupil expenditure inequality by Bezeau and Currie (1976) showed a significant decline in overall inequality among boards between 1965 and 1973 but a slight increase between 1973 and 1974. Inequality, after having been reduced for many years, now appears to be increasing. One exception has been continued decrease in inequality between public and separate elementary school boards. Separate school expenditure per pupil as a percentage of public-school expenditure per pupil has been as follows for selected years: 1963: 70.2; 1965: 80.3; 1967: 88.2; 1972: 95.2; and 1974: 97.1 per cent.

It has been difficult to translate fiscal equity into equalization of levels of service, particularly in relation to personnel. In Ontario, there is no centralized control of personnel recruitment. Teachers are hired and paid at the local school board level. While fiscal equalization and reorganization have reduced the disparities in salaries evident prior to the creation of larger administrative units, there has not been a corresponding redistribution of personnel. The urban and metropolitan centres, because of their social and cultural amenities, continue to hold a higher attraction for teachers and therefore highly qualified and highly motivated personnel are unequally distributed throughout the province. It seems unlikely that fiscal measures alone can compensate for this situation. In addition, the equalization of service levels depends on the decision-making of the local boards.

The province has made a further attempt at equalization in the areas of high-cost students. These students can be in groups, as in special-education classes, or they may be students in special situations which require extra finanical outlay. Under the present plan, the extra unit costs incurred in providing primary education to such students are met by the province. Thus, all high-cost students can be provided with the appropriate services. The majority of specialized services are, however, concentrated in the urban areas. In part, this is because such centres have already been identified as areas of high-cost student concentration. On the other hand, such high-cost students as those with aphasia and cerebral palsy are such a small percentage of the total population that it is only in the largest centres that enough can be gathered together to provide the necessary services.

Inadequacies and deficiencies in local property assessment have hindered the equalization process. The province presently calculates the amount of grant for which a school board is eligible, based on a provincial average equalized assessment. In terms of real value, however, much of the property in Ontario is under-assessed.

While all property has been reassessed at market value since the province assumed responsibility for all assessment, school grants are still based on the former municipal assessments, with all their inherent flaws, adjusted by provincial equalizing factors. The new market value assessment will not be used for purposes of local taxation and provincial subventions until next year (1978). It is the present intention of the government to permit municipalities, in the first few years after implementation, to cushion the increased burden on rate payers, who have for many years been undertaxed, by over-taxing for a few more years those who have for many years been over-taxed.

The adoption of the new assessment base in 1978 will eradicate the disparities among boards and among individuals caused by the former methods of assessment. Some problems will remain, such as those related to inflated property values in some localities, notably the major urban areas.

The original intention was to set grant ceilings per weighted pupil at about the 80th percentile on the scale of school board expenditures. In this way, most ordinary expenditure would become grantable and hence equalized. Grant ceilings have increased yearly with inflation and greater percentage increases have been made in the elementary than in the secondary ceilings. The main reason for this more rapid rise in elementary school ceilings was the introduction in 1973 of legislation requiring that new primary school teachers in Ontario hold a university degree or recognized equivalent. This legislation resulted in an increase in salaries which raised the per-pupil costs. In addition, there has been a desire to close the gap between the pupil-teacher ratios in the elementary and secondary school systems. The 1977 level of recognized ordinary expenditure is 1 197 dollars in the case of an elementary school pupil and 1 712 dollars for a secondary school pupil. One result of the difference in these levels is that separate school boards may encounter difficulties in supplying adequate service at the upper levels of elementary school. Separate school boards are allowed, but not required, to provide grades nine and ten as part of elementary education. If, however, a board does decide to offer these grades at the elementary level it may face difficulties in providing these services within the ceiling level. Public elementary school boards, on the other hand, offer education only to the grade eight level and therefore grade nine and ten students are treated fiscally as secondary school pupils.

Since the removal of expenditure ceilings, the grant ceilings, while keeping pace with inflaton, have not increased at the same rate as school costs. The result has been that almost 50 per cent of elementary boards have spent beyond the grant ceilings.

Prior to the 1969 reorganization of school districts, stimulation grants were utilized by the province. With the introduction of the percentage equalizing grant plan, such incentive grants were discontinued and replaced by general grants. To promote local decision-making, these grants were made unconditional, and therefore boards could follow their own priorities for spending the sums received. But the staff salary bill accounts for between 70 and 80 per cent of operating costs and this, together with other fixed costs, makes the actual area of decision-making small. Thus, a board can change its priorities in operating expenditures but its freedom is limited by prior budgetary and programming commitments. The present grant system, however, includes a special education weighting factor and some special grants that encourage school boards to invest in certain specific areas. The result has been a large expansion in the area of special education, and therefore this weighting factor effectively operates as an incentive grant. The present grant system, then, was designed to encourage and permit a greater measure of local autonomy. However, the power of local boards, particularly the more able ones, to decide on the level of service to be offered and on the levying or requisitioning of local funds, was severely restricted by the provincial expenditure ceilings. In effect, the only decision a school board could make was to spend below the provincially approved maximum level. Expenditure ceilings were, however, removed for 1976 and are unlikely to be reimposed.

There has also been some feeling that the administration of primary education is too far removed from parents and local communities. The province has reacted by instituting a special grant for community school development through which it hopes to encourage school boards to become more involved with their local communities.

Under the existing grant system, operating expenditure is eligible for provincial support up to a maximum outlay per weighted pupil. All expenditure in excess of this amount has to be met by the school board from local tax revenue. The province designed the grant system in this form to make school boards more accountable to the residents within their jurisdiction. Any expansion of services, therefore, results in an increased tax rate. In theory, then, a school board that desired to lower the tax rate in response to local demands could seriously curtail the program it offers. In practice, however, the large administrative units have tended to minimize this danger. There are, additionally, some mandatory factors in the Education Act which limit the types of cuts in service which can be made.

Education in Ontario is conceived of as more of a provincial function than are other municipal services, and therefore the school board is, in many respects the representative of the province in this area. The finance plan covering education supports this view by eliminating municipal control of education finance. That is, school boards plan their budgets and request the appropriate funds from the local municipality which is then required by law to levy the appropriate tax rate to collect the funds. In times of monetary restriction, this situation can lead to confrontation and lack of co-operation between school and municipal authorities. Since the school board has a prior claim to municipal revenue, a situation may arise, if the local tax pool is seen as limited, where needed municipal services are cut back. Separate school boards have the right to set the local tax rate for their funds whereas public boards may only requisition an amount of money. The separate school board usually waits until the public rate has been set by the municipal council and then sets the same rate.

During the period 1958-1975, provincial grants on extraordinary expenditure were designed to encourage the tendency towards centralized administrative units which reached a peak in the 1969 reorganization of school districts. There was also a parallel move towards centralization of schools within districts with the consequent transportation of students from rural areas to such schools. This trend resulted in the construction of many new schools, to replace rural one-room schoolhouses, and the development of a school busing system to transport the pupils. Most of the extra costs generated were borne by the province.

The creation of the larger county units of administration in 1969 was based on the rationale that they would eradicate small pockets of extremely high and extremely low tax-paying ability. While the range in tax-paying ability among both separate and public school boards was greatly lessened, the reorganization had little effect on the differences existing between the two groups. The disparity in taxable capacities of the public and separate school systems is related to the local tax base. In virtually every county or district with a dual elementary system, the separate school has a smaller fiscal capacity than the public school. This is chiefly because the taxes on property of corporations go almost entirely to the public system. Since the tax base for separate schools is smaller, it produces less revenue per pupil than it does in the public school system in the same community. The result is a chronic revenue deficiency for the separate schools which has to be compensated for by provincial grants. In 1974, 85.1 per cent of separate school expenditure was met through provincial grants, whereas the corresponding figure for public elementary school expenditure was 52.4 per cent. Separate schools are at a disadvantage only in respect to expenditures above the grant ceiling, but here the disadvantage is great.

Chapter VI

POLICY GOALS AND THEMES

There are three major, interconnected themes in Ontario's education policy:
1. Equality of educational opportunity;
2. Decentralization of decision-making; and
3. More equitable treatment of special populations.

Less prominent, but still of considerable importance, are four other policies:
4. The integration of educational services with other services;
5. Unlimited access to primary and secondary education;
6. Socialization for life in the general Canadian culture while maintaining aspects of minority-group culture; and
7. Innovation.

These will be discussed in turn.

1. EQUALITY OF EDUCATIONAL OPPORTUNITY

Ontario's stated policy aim is to reach a point where access to the kind of education needed by each student is available, regardless of geographical location, social class or economic conditions. A major stated aim of reorganization in 1969 was to make possible greater equality both within and among the county and district school boards. The cities and large towns often had more diversified programs, more highly-qualified teachers, better-paid teachers, and better-equipped schools than did rural areas within the same county. There were differences as well between counties, and particularly between the counties and the areas of northern Ontario not organized into counties. Reorganization created 46 enlarged public and separate school boards in this area. As well as more equality between urban, rural, northern, and southern students, there was and is concern about equality between public school and separate school pupils and between students in areas of high and low tax-paying ability. It is not provincial policy to force equality on local areas, but rather to encourage it and make it possible by removing administrative and fiscal barriers to its achievment. The former was felt to be achieved through reorganization of school administrative units and the latter by the implementation of the percentage equalizing grant, and later, by ceilings on the expenditure of wealthier boards.

2. DECENTRALIZATION OF DECISION-MAKING

Ontario traditionally had a very large measure of central control, particularly concerning the curriculum, texbooks, methods of teaching, and supervision of instruction. In addition, through extensive use of incentive grants, it sought to control the decision-making of boards by making spending money in some ways more attractive than in other ways. Except for the major cities, this centralization of power was almost necessitated by the smallness of the units of administration and their lack of competent personnel.

Some examples of the extent of decentralization under reorganization are the following.

a) Prior to reorganization, only cities and a few other units of administration with 2 000 or more pupils employed their own supervisory officers. For the rest, supervision of instruction was a function of school inspectors employed by the central authority. Since 1969, all but a few very small jurisdictions employ their own directors, superintendents, supervisors and consultants.

b) The decision as to level and type of services to be offered is left with the local school board (subject to certain mandated requirements in the Education Act).

c) Whether to transport pupils, which pupils, and how far, are all matters for local decision.

d) Whether or not to provide kindergartens for four- and five-year-olds is a local decision.

e) Textbooks are no longer authorized but may be selected from lists of books approved by the Ministry.

f) Boards are free either to adapt curriculum guidelines prepared by the Ministry or to draw up their own curricula and have them approved by the Ministry.

g) Boards are no longer subject to municipal councils for the making of long-term loans.

h) The new grant system placed all boards on an equal footing, fiscally, for most purposes, thus furthering real local decision-making power as opposed to mere legal power without adequate resources.

3. TREATMENT OF SPECIAL POPULATIONS

Considerable emphasis has been placed in recent years on the provision of educational services for the disadvantaged, whether mentally, physically, emotionally, culturally, geographically, or economically. Specifically, provincial policy in this field falls into several categories.

a) *Native population*

The education of the native Indian population of Ontario is the responsibility of the federal government if the persons concerned are treaty Indians living on "reserves", but a responsibility of the province otherwise. Within the past decade the policy of both governments has been to integrate the education of Indian children with those of their non-Indian neighbours. To this end, where distances make it possible, Indian children are bused from the reserves to schools operated by the public and separate school boards. In such cases, the gross cost of their education (defined as the average cost of educating a pupil at the board's schools) plus the cost of transportation are paid by the federal government to the board. Policy in this area is, however, somewhat fluid since there are counter- pressures by the native people to have more say in their own education. This often means more rather than less segregation.

b) *Special education*

This is a term used to encompass students with mental, physical, emotional, and social handicaps. The policy has been to avoid segregation of such pupils as much as posssible. According to policy, they should be educated with normal pupils and receive special help, both in the form of equipment and supplies and in the form of expert assistance and advice for the teacher. The new larger units of administration were seen as facilitating the education of such pupils, who in earlier times, either failed as normal students, withdrew from school, or were taken by their parents to larger centres where special education services were available. The financing of the extra costs of such pupils was to be ensured through the use of a special education weighting factor as described in Chapter IV.

One particular group of mentally handicapped children, now called "mentally retarded" (I.Q. below 50) though formerly excluded from school as ineducable, are not treated under the special education category. Instead, in order to avoid duplication of services between public and separate school boards, they are the responsibility of the secondary panels of boards of education. These pupils are trained in special schools with very low pupil-teacher ratios, although here, too, policy is to avoid complete segregation. Often such schools are wings or rooms in an elementary school. For grant purposes, each retarded pupil is counted as 1.6 secondary students.

The province would like to make mandatory on the boards the provision of an adequate education for all students classified as in need of special education, but is hesitant to do so at a time when it is finding it difficult to support present levels of service at previous levels of support.

c) *Franco-Ontarians*

The province endeavours to ensure that Francophone students have educational opportunities in their own language, equivalent to those provided for Anglophone students. The legislation, therefore, permits the establishment by a school board of classes or schools for the education of Francophones in their own language. When a minimum of 25 elementary students choose to be taught in French, a school board is required to provide such instruction. As of September 1975, Ontario had 305 French language elementary schools with an enrolment of 77 424 students or 5.6 per cent of the total provincial elementary enrolment. In order that any extra costs of providing education in French may be met and to encourage boards to provide adequate service levels, the special grant described in Chapter IV is provided.

In addition, start-up grants are available when a classroom is initially used for a full-time program in the French language and in a school in which previously all instruction was in English. These grants are chiefly to cover the costs of library, text and reference books in French, and any other supplies or equipment that would not normally be available in a classroom where English had been the language of instruction. At present the Ministry has let a research contract to determine the costs of French education and whether the present grant is at a reasonable level.

d) *Early childhood education*

Provincial policy is to expand services in early childhood education. To this end it has greatly encouraged the spread of kindergartens (K) to rural areas and the rapid growth of junior kindergartens (JK) for four-year-olds. The former was encouraged by the policy of centralization of rural schools and the reorganization of school administrative units. Both were encouraged by the grant structure under whch the ordinary expenditure on behalf of pre-school pupils did not increase local tax rates so long as the per-pupil cost could be kept within the ceiling limitations in ROE. If JK and K pupils can be educated at a lower cost per pupil than those in grades one to eight, then the expansion of services for such pupils can result in a lowering of the local tax rate from what it would be if the services were not supplied, except in the first year of operation, when a board must bear its percentage share of the cost of new or increased kindergarten services for the four-month period from September 1 to December 31. The operation of junior kindergartens and kindergartens at a per pupil expenditure level that is less than the average for a board results in a net subsidy flowing from the kindergarten level to the higher grades. Thus the net marginal cost (marginal expenditure minus marginal revenue from province) to a board of operating a kindergarten may be negative. There are two caveats to be considered.

1. Under the policy of a fixed sum to be distributed in grants, any increase in JK/K provision will result in lower overall levels of provincial support to all boards.
2. It is not always possible to provide JK/K programs at less than the average cost of pupils in grades 1-8, particularly where schools are small, making it difficult to keep pupil-teacher ratios for JK/K pupils high enough to provide the service economically. Despite the massive encouragement provided by this fiscal device, the province has not yet begun to question the advisability of continuing its policy of advocating more early chilhood education.

e) *Compensatory education*

The concept of compensatory education in Ontario is one which sees extra resources needed to provide adequate level of education going to pupils who are culturally, socially, and economically disadvantaged. A word of explanation may be needed to explain what is meant by these terms.

1. A culturally disadvantaged child is one who, while a member of a rich culture of his own, is disadvantaged by being forced to receive his education in the English language and (more particularly) in a different cultural environment from that of the home. It is provincial policy to encourage boards to provide more resources for the education of such pupils. In urban centres, where this problem chiefly occurs, certain schools are designated as "inner-city schools" and supplied with greater resources such as:
   a) a somewhat smaller average class size;
   b) teachers of English as a second language; and
   c) community workers and teachers' aides of the same cultural backgrounds as the students.
2. Socially disadvantaged pupils include those from broken homes and those with marked behavioural problems.
3. Economically disadvantaged pupils include those from families in receipt of welfare benefits as well as the children of the so-called working poor.

It is obvious that these categories overlap. The compensatory education weighting factor is the fiscal device used to encourage boards to make adequate provision for these types of pupils. This was described in Chapter IV. The "admissions" weighting factor also measures the prevalence of those disadvantaged children mentioned in (2) and (3) above.

f) *Geographically disadvantaged pupils*

Provincial policy has for many years been directed towards trying to equalize educational opportunities for geographically disadvantaged pupils, that is, those pupils who attend small rural schools, whose school-board jurisdiction is small, or who live in isolated settlements in Northern Ontario. The small-board and small-school weighting factors have already been described, as well as the weighting factors for students in Northern Ontario in general where most school costs tend to be from 8 to 10 per cent higher than in the south. In addition to the enlarged boards to which the percentage equalizing grant formula applies, there are in Ontario 39 small boards known as "isolate boards", each operating only one elementary school and all, except two Protestant separate schools, in remote areas of northern Ontario too far from other schools or major centres to be included in the reorganized district boards of education and district combined separate school boards. Of these boards, eight employ only one teacher each, 11 only two teachers, and only nine employ more than five teachers. A board is considered an isolate only if it has fewer than 300 pupils enrolled in January of a given year. Realizing that grant formulae devised for the new larger units would badly serve such small jurisdictions, the province provided for a very simple grant formula for such boards. All expenditures, both ordinary and extraordinary, incurred by the board and approved by the Minister through the Regional Office are payable as grants except for an amount equivalent to a yield of $8.00 per $1000 of provincial equalized assessment, which must be raised by local taxation. Thus the concepts of weighted pupils, ROE and REE do not apply to these boards. In effect they are fully funded by the province, since the $8/M tax levy is a provincial tax, locally collected. The Regional Office of the Ministry acts as a Budget Review Board which has the final say with respect to levels of service for these boards. Provincial policy also provides higher base salaries for teachers in these schools and has formed a Northern Corps of Teachers to recruit and retain teachers for the challenging but often isolated job of staffing these schools.

g) *Students from homes where neither English nor French is spoken*

Approximately 55 per cent of all immigrants arriving in Canada choose to settle in Ontario, and Toronto is the primary location of the majority of these. In recent years, there has been an increase in the proportion of immigrants from non-English speaking cultures. It is provincial policy to encourage the pupils to learn English as quickly as possible. Special ESL teachers are provided. It is part of official policy, also, that ethnic groups be permitted to retain their own culture. This of course, would not occur to any realistic extent if the language were lost. Some school systems provide the space in which ethnic organizations, sometimes supported by the governments of their native countries, can provide instruction in the native language and literature.

4. INTEGRATION OF PUBLIC EDUCATION WITH OTHER PUBLIC SERVICES

In recent years there has been a move to integrate education with other social services. The basis for this has been both economic, in that more efficient use can be made of the available facilities and resources, and social, where the attempt has been to make the school more responsive to, and part of, the community. With a few exceptions, this policy has been hindered by the separation of school and municipal government finance. One good example, however, is school board cooperation with municipal parks and recreation branches in urban areas. This usually takes the form of mutual use of athletic and recreation facilities. In addition, each regional office of the Ministry of Education has a community education officer on staff. This officer works with school boards in developing plans for the fuller use of school facilities by the community. To further encourage this, the province instituted, in 1975, a special grant of $ 10 000 (maximum) to any board submitting an approved community-school development proposal.

Some boards employ psychiatrists and psychologists for work in the school system while others cooperate with municipalities in providing these services. Schooling opportunities are offered in hospitals, children's homes, psychiatric facilities, detention and observation homes with the participation of the Ministry and local school boards. Provision is made in the legislative grants for the province to pay the salaries of teachers involved in such special education programmes, and this has allowed school boards to expand these services considerably. The existence of universal medicare for physicians' and hospital services has lessened the need for school involvement in health-care services, but municipally employed public-health nurses still operate through the school system.

5. ACCESS, SELECTION AND CERTIFICATION

School attendance is compulsory in Ontario from age six to sixteen years. Students pay no fees, and books and other materials are supplied free of charge. Where necessary, transportation to and from school is paid. Roman Catholics may choose a public or a separate school for their children to attend.

In most recent years, 91 per cent of the students entering grade one continue into grade eight. No standardized examinations are set in elementary school and promotion to some form of secondary education is based on age.

6. SOCIALIZATION

Socialization is a natural part of the school experience. In Ontario, no conscious efforts are made to integrate schools with given proportions of students from various ethnic backgrounds. In general, children attend their local public or separate school. Both Canadian and Ontario policy is basically opposed to the melting-pot theory and emphasis is placed on the multicultural character of the country. Thus, English as a second language is taught in schools where there are significant numbers of students with mother tongues other than English or French. This is particularly common in Toronto with its high proportion of immigrants from such diverse cultures as those of Italy, Portugal, Greece, India, Korea and Hong Kong. Attempts, however, are made for the students to retain a pride in and knowledge of their own background to maintain their own identity. This is viewed as healthy for the individual and also as contributing to Canada's cultural enrichment. In some cases support is given by the native country; for example, the Italian government currently contributes financially to Italian language education in Toronto.

There has recently been a strong move towards French language education for Francophones. Where a minimum of twenty-five elementary students requests such education, the school board must supply it. Where the numbers are justified, French language schools have been provided. In such schools, the principle objective is to enable the Francophone students to expand their knowledge and enjoyment of their native language and culture.

The Ministry of Education in some cases specifies the curriculum, a major tool in socialization, and in others issues general guidelines. The Ministry may also approve or disapprove curricula devised by local education authorities. Textbooks are chosen by schools, with the approval of their educational authority, from a list of books approved by the Ministry. Recently much research has been done on textbooks and at the present time there is an attempt to remove the class, race and sex biases evident in some of them.

The reorganisation of school districts had little effect on students in urban centres but the centralization of rural schools has contributed to the socialization of rural students by bringing them into contact with students from outside their rural home community.

7. INNOVATION

The central education authority has seen the encouragement of innovation as one of its major functions. In addition to its major influence in the area of curriculum, and in the employment of innovations officers in the Regional Office, the Ministry has in the past used incentive grants to encourage innovations it favoured such as the use of television, free milk distribution, industrial arts and home economics education, centralized schools, and larger units of administration. These were for the most part discontinued in 1969 as part of the attempt to foster local autonomy.

At the local level, innovation has traditionally been done by those boards that had the tax-paying ability and governing bodies interested in adapting their school systems to the changing needs of their communities. This type of board was handicapped during the 1970-1975 period because of provincial ceilings on expenditure per weighted pupil. Boards could not spend above the ceiling even if they had the desire and fiscal capacity. The removal of the expenditure ceilings in 1976 has restored innovative power to such boards. In general, though, innovation tends to suffer in periods of financial austerity as is presently the case.

Chapter VII

RELATIONSHIP BETWEEN POLICY GOALS AND FINANCIAL INSTRUMENTS

This chapter will attempt to show the ways in which the financial instruments used in Ontario have helped or hindered the attainment of primary education policy goals. The chapter is organized in the same way as was Chapter VI so that there is comparability between the two, thus avoiding any need to recapitulate the policy goals.

1. EQUALITY OF EDUCATIONAL OPPORTUNITY

Greater equality within the newly reorganized county and district units very quickly became apparent. A single salary schedule for each of the new boards brought salaries in rural and small town communities into line with those in the cities and larger towns. Pupil-teacher ratios became rationalized throughout the new jurisdiction and the new board's policy on staffing was implemented. Services that only the cities or large towns were previously large enough to provide economically now became available throughout the district: teachers of art, music, and physical education; kindergarten classes; special-education programs; and remedial-reading programs. In some cases the change resulted in a lowering of standards, particularly where a former small board was well above-average in tax-paying ability. In such cases the local school might have had a better pupil-teacher ratio than that which the new large board policy allowed. Sometimes the new boards tried to apply a uniform staffing policy regardless of school size.

There has also been greater equality achieved among the new larger jurisdictions. This was achieved particularly during the years 1969 to 1975 when the province was increasing its share of total school board expenditures from about 45 per cent to 60. During these years it was possible for many boards rapidly to increase their levels of service and expenditure per pupil while at the same time achieving a decrease in local tax rate. The combined effect of the percentage equalizing grant, annually rising levels of expenditures per weighted pupil eligible for grant, and an annually increasing provincial share of costs was to dramatically increase the levels of educational service in areas where service levels were previously low.

So successful was the new financial plan in stimulating expenditure, that the province felt impelled, after only two years' experience with it, to introduce limits in 1971 on the expenditure per weighted pupil that would be permitted. This act, in itself, contributed further to the equalization among boards since it was the wealthier, higher-spending boards that were chiefly affected by the limitations.

The high spenders were originally given three years to bring their expenditures down to the ceiling. In 1972 and 1973 limits were also placed on the percentage expenditure increases allowed by all boards. These were graduated so that the low spenders were allowed somewhat larger increases. In 1973 the ceiling was placed 5.9 per cent higher than in 1972. A board spending, for example, 4.2 per cent below the ceiling in 1972 was permitted to move to the ceiling in 1973. But a board spending 16 per cent below the ceiling in 1972 was permitted an increase of only 12 per cent which brought it to a level which was still 11 per cent below the ceiling. This extra restraint on the low spenders was removed in 1974.

In 1976 the province, faced with too many demands on its resources, abandoned its plan of meeting 60 per cent of the expenditures of all school boards from provincial revenue sources. It was the attempt to adhere to the plan which had initiated the expenditure ceilings. It was apparent that to pay 60 per cent of an uncontrollable expenditure amounted to granting blank cheques to the school boards. When the plan was abandoned in 1976, ceilings on expenditure were no longer needed. It was stated policy that in future the controls on expenditures would be the effect on the local tax rate of excess spending above the levels recognized for grant purposes. It remains to be seen whether expenditure-per-pupil levels of the wealthier boards will begin to pull away from those of average and below-average wealth. Ontario's experiment was a rare one — that of trying to bring the expenditure levels of all boards up to that of its wealthiest ones. The traditional approach in North America has been to use the mean or median expenditure level as the target for state equalization. A significant measure of success was achieved, at least in the short run. A major factor in the move away from this type of equalization was the uncertainty brought about by very high rates of inflation. Teachers in Ontario had recently won the right to strike and were using it and gaining large wage settlements. The federal government was pursuing a policy of rapid expansion of the money supply (40 per cent in two years) to finance its own deficit. The economy was unsettled and there was greater price uncertainty than in any period since the war. The need to control public expenditure in the face of considerable uncertainty led the Government to abandon its plan of meeting 60 per cent of school expenditures.

2. DECENTRALIZATION OF DECISION-MAKING

There have been counterbalancing results in the area of local autonomy. The large units of administration brought with them definite gains in the area of local supervision of instruction instead of central supervision. More boards began to develop their own curricula. Boards were completely freed from dependence on municipal councils and the traditional non-involvement of the public in budgetary decisions was continued.

For the boards in former low-spending areas, the new grant plan brought some real fiscal autonomy. They now had not only the legal right to spend at the same level as their wealthier neighbours, they had the resources as well. Such boards could now decide to employ more highly-qualified teachers, to expand the program downwards to the pre-school classes, to initiate or expand facilities for special education, or to decrease class size. But for boards spending at the ceilings on ordinary expenditure, the new plan represented a loss of autonomy formerly exercised. In effect the province decided, each year from 1971 to 1975, what these boards' budget totals would be. The only fiscal autonomy remaining to them was the determination of how the money allowed to be spent was to be spent. But even here the area of decision-making was small, since negotiated salaries made up about 80 per cent of the budget. Boards were loath to cut staff, the only effective way of freeing up money for new or improved services.

Another concern of school trustees is the locus of local control. Many of them feel that any increase in local control devolves on the professional staff and that the elected trustees have less power than they had in the days of small units of administration. It must be said, however, that concern about local autonomy has been weak except for a few of the highest-spending boards. This was particularly evident during the period of expenditure controls which were welcomed by most school trustees.

3. TREATMENT OF SPECIAL POPULATIONS

a) *Native population*

The policy of avoiding as much as possible the segregation of Indian children in schools of their own is meeting with some opposition from Indian groups who would prefer to have their children educated in their own cultural environment. This has some implications for the financial instruments used. For children on reserves, it would mean a shift from schools operated and paid for by the federal government through its Department of Indian Affairs to schools or educational processes administered by the native population and financed by Ottawa.

For those Indian bands that want to continue to have their children educated along with the majority population, the present fiscal arrangement poses some problems. Because of the great differences between the expectations and ambience of the Indian home and the public or separate school, a large proportion of Indian pupils tend to be classified as in need of some form of special education. In charging fees to Ottawa for such pupils, a local board must charge a fee that is the average cost to the board of educating all pupils in its schools. There is provision, however, for charging higher fees for "high-cost" pupils. Some boards seek to collect such fees for their Indian pupils. The federal government has a political objection on the grounds that it is discriminatory to claim that a higher percentage of Indian children need high-cost services than is the case with other children in the board's schools.

b) *Special education*

The effect of the financial instruments on policy with respect to special education has been almost too successful. As was shown earlier, the extra costs of a board for special education, in excess of that for two teachers per thousand pupils, is borne by the province rather than the individual board. During the period of central controls on expenditure per pupil, it was important that the weighting factor for special education be kept realistic, otherwise a board would be forced to cut other services to maintain the program. This is no longer the case since expenditure ceilings have been removed.

The form the weighting factor takes is strongly influenced by provincial policy with respect to atypical or handicapped children. It is keyed to the number of personnel dealing with these children rather than the number and type of children in need of special education. The province wants to avoid categorizing these pupils as problems, in line with its policy of integrating such pupils into the regular stream. This policy has made difficult the development of a really effective weighting factor that differentiates between special education programs requiring almost a one-to-one pupil-teacher ratio, and those requiring a ratio only slightly less than that for regular pupils.

It has already been mentioned that the weighting factor for special education represents a strong element of central control over local decision making, up to the point where the maximum weighting factor has been earned. This is not necessarily bad, however. An alternate way to exert central control in this area would be for the province to pass legislation making mandatory the provision of education suitable to the special needs of all pupils eligible to attend the publicly supported schools.

c) *Franco-Ontarians*

There is some doubt as to whether the grants for operating schools and classes in the French language for Francophones are straight incentive grants or whether they are related to the extra costs incurred in providing such education. The incentive principle is not theoretically needed since boards are required to provide such schools and classes when asked for by Francophone parents. Judgement on this point must be reserved until the outcome of a research study now under way is known. It is investigating the costs of education provided in the French language.

The relationship between the special grant for the teaching of French to non-Francophones to increased costs is more obvious, though also being studied in another research project. Boards are not required to teach French as a subject in elementary schools, so the grant could be justified as an incentive grant. But in many cases a board hires additional teachers who go from school to school teaching conversational French in 20-minute periods. This is obviously an increased cost.

The whole area of bilingualism and biculturalism is at present a sensitive one with serious political overtones. The reason the province has commissioned research in this area is that its policy is to provide the maximum opportunity for Francophones to be educated in their own language and for non-Francophones to have the opportunity to learn some French, and it wants its financial instruments to maximize the implementation of these policies.

d) *Early childhood education*

Financial instruments have been such that kindergarten classes for five-year-olds have become almost universal. It must be understood that boards are not required to provide these classes, nor are parents required to enrol pupils in them (compulsory attendance begins at age six, although the Education Act does specify that underage pupils who are enrolled — as for example in kindergarten — must comply with the attendance regulations). Despite these facts, kindergarten enrolment of five-year-olds in September 1975 was 96.1 per cent of the enrolment in the first year of the primary school proper. One would have to conclude that the financial instruments have been a strong contributor to this high participation rate.

The same financial incentives have contributed to the rapid increase in junior kindergartens for four-year-olds. Since these were first recognized for provincial aid in 1966, enrolment in them has increased 13- fold. In 1966, enrolment was only 1.89 per cent of the enrolment in year one of the primary school proper, whereas in 1975 it was 31.81 per cent.

A consideration from the province's point of view is its decision to provide each year a fixed sum for transfers to school boards. If junior kindergarten enrolments continue to mount, the general level of support for all students will have to go down. It is to no individual board's advantage to discontinue junior kindergartens nor to refrain from instituting them in schools that do not have them. The relative importance of the policy with respect to these classes, as opposed to other policies (expanded special education services, greater aid for the education of Francophones, etc.), will have to be made at the provincial level.

e) *Compensatory education*

In the area of compensatory education, the grants (via the weighting factor) are not in any way related to the provision of services. They merely recognize the probable existence of a high level of need for such programs. Boards may use the additional revenue provided to lower the local tax rate or to provide higher service levels to other types of students. The financial instrument used to encourage compensatory education, then, has neither the advantages nor the disadvantages of those used to encourage special education and early-childhood education. Neither an increase nor a decrease in actual service levels for students needing compensatory education will alter the maximum ROE/WP of the board, not its rate of grant. This instrument is clearly, then, not an incentive of stimulation grant. Instead it attempts to recognize the need for additional expenditure, and leave the decision as to how best to deal with the problem to the local boards. Unfortunately this means that a board faced with the need for financial cut-backs can make real savings by cutting back on its compensatory education programs. There is some evidence that urban boards were forced to cut back on programs in inner-city schools, especially during the period of expenditure ceilings.

f) *Geographically disadvantaged pupils*

There has been little complaint concerning the adequacy of the weighting factor to compensate for the higher cost of goods and services in Northern Ontario. There has been concern about the lack of refinement in the factors — either six or nine per cent. It is felt that the additional costs in the north are probably on some kind of continuum, from perhaps three per cent to 12 or more. But the hard data are not available on which to calculate such factors. In addition, there are probably differentials in the average cost of goods and services among the county boards of the south that are not recognized.

The small board factor applies chiefly to some northern public school boards and many separate school boards, both north and south. It is based on the extra cost per pupil of minimum administrative services in small units of administration and appears adequate. It is not high enough, however, to be a disincentive for the union of two or more smaller boards to create a larger administrative unit. The province always has to walk the tight-rope between recognizing the extra costs of a service and stimulating the service.

This is particularly evident in the case of the small school factor. The present factor is not large enough to compensate for all of the increased cost per pupil of small schools. If it were raised to that level (assuming it could be accurately determined) it could well become an incentive grant for the creation of small schools or a compensatory grant for declining enrolments, making it less necessary to release staff as enrolments declined.

This illustrates very well a major problem in the whole area under discussion. It is this: provincial policies are rarely clear-cut. There is a certain ambivalence about them. For instance, the commitment to large, centralized primary schools is not complete. In fact, the pendulum may well swing back towards smaller community schools as it has done in some countries. This movement may be hastened by the energy crisis, and hence the high economic and social cost of busing pupils long distances. At present, though, official provincial policy is still opposed to the small school where a larger one is possible, so financial instruments that bonus small schools, even necessary ones, are difficult to maintain for fear they will work counter to the basic policy on school size.

The financial instrument by which funds are made available for the isolate boards appears to be adequate. It will be even better, when in 1978, property assessments carried out by the province are used for the first time. Some will argue that there is not much local decision-making for isolate boards, and that is true. It is more important from the standpoint of provincial policy that these isolated schools have adequate resources than that they have local autonomy. They are considered as too small for their school boards to represent the interests of the state in determining educational levels to be offered.

One area of concern from the standpoint of overall policy is the local tax rate required to be levied by an isolate board. If it is kept lower than the rate in a district board there will be a disincentive for the isolate board to become part of an enlarged district board, if and when the possibility arises. This is not likely in the immediate future, however, especially with the energy shortage.

g) *Students from homes where neither English nor French is spoken*

The financial instrument in this situation bears little or no relation to services rendered. Language of the home is only one of four measures used in determining the compensatory education weighting factor. The policy of encouraging immigrants to retain their cultural identity is chiefly verbal. In order to make a real effort to assist various ethnic groups to maintain their cultural heritage, the province would probably need some form of earmarked grant tied to compliance provisions. In other words, it would probably require central, rather than purely local, decision-making. This has not been done. Some local boards have responded by providing language and literature classes other than in traditional English, French, German, Spanish and Italian for secondary pupils, but little public money has been spent at the primary level.

4. INTEGRATION OF PUBLIC EDUCATION WITH OTHER PUBLIC SERVICES

The existence of a separate school system for Roman Catholics, protected by constitutional provisions, militates against the integration of educational services with other municipal services. This could come about if the administration of separate and public elementary schools and secondary schools were operated under a single umbrella board. This has been suggested but there is little likelihood of its coming about in the near future.

The provision of educational services in hospitals, children's homes, psychiatric facilities, detention and observation homes, by local boards is related directly to the financial provisions provided for by the province. The development of community school special projects is always sufficient to use up the provincial funds allocated for this specific purpose ($500000) in 1976. Some boards are able to cooperate with municipalities without additional costs, and others have the local resources to provide for such extra costs if they arise. During the period of expenditure ceilings, the province backed up its policy pronouncements in this area by exempting expenditures clearly related to "community use of schools" from the limitations.

Now that ceilings have been removed and local school tax rates have begun to rise with per-pupil expenditures, there is a tendency for programs in this area to suffer for boards whose expenditure is above the amount recognized for grant.

There has been a demand on the part of boards for some assistance from other ministries when the boards provide services (such as psychiatrists, offices for public-health nurses, etc.) that do not normally fall under the jurisdiction of the Ministry of Education.

Policy with respect to library services has not been rationalized. Both school boards and public library boards have jurisdiction and their own libraries. There has been very little cooperation between the two.

5. ACCESS, SELECTION AND CERTIFICATION

There would seem to be no problems in these areas: that is, no indication the provincial policy is hampered by the financial instruments chosen to implement them. Indeed, there has been a recent trend to devote an increasing proportion of the provincial school-aid dollar to elementary as opposed to secondary education. This has been accomplished in two ways:

  a) By increasing the ROE/WP for an elementary board by a higher percentage each year (since 1970) than that for a secondary board; and
  b) By paying a larger percentage of the recognized ordinary expenditure of elementary boards than of secondary school boards from provincial sources.

This latter first occurred in 1976 and will continue in 1977. The province pays 54 per cent of secondary school costs as compared to 60 per cent of elementary school costs.

This trend indicates a shift in policy towards a strengthening, particularly of the primary education component, of elementary education. It is partly a follow-up of studies showing that expenditures at the secondary level may not be very effective if the education at the primary level has been poorly done. This is of particular importance in a society which attempts to provide a secondary education for all students, not just the intellectually elite. There is at present a move to have the pupil teacher ratio the same for elementary as for secondary schools.

Another relationship in this area is that of grants to growth in participation rates. The nature of the grant is such, as has been demonstrated, that there is little, if any, increased cost to a local board if it increases the participation rate of the age groups in the school program. For elementary boards, of course, this means chiefly increasing the participation rate in the two pre-school levels (JK and K), and this has already been discussed.

6. SOCIALIZATION

The three major concerns in the area of socialization in which financial instruments might be expected to exert an influence are:

  a) The socialization of immigrant children to life in Canadian society;
  b) The socialization of Franco-Ontarians to the French-Canadian culture; and
  c) The socialization of immigrant children into some of their ancestral cultural heritage.

In the first of these areas, it is felt that generally the financial instruments are not adequate. The federal government is annually asked by Metropolitan Toronto, for instance, for federal funds to assist in the process of socialization of immigrant children since immigration policy is under federal jurisdiction. As was indicated earlier, the compensatory weighting factor provides some funds, but these can be used in other ways and often are when boards are under financial pressures. No specific recognition is given by the province to classes in English as a second language.

In the second area, the relationship between the financial instruments and the policy of providing adequate French language schools is under investigation. It is possible that in some cases the extra grants are more than sufficient to meet the extra costs. If so, the grants operate as a very strong stimulation grant to continue and expand the program (in terms of pupils served).

In the third area, little has been done in a concrete way. But it has been only recently that the concept of developing the ethnic culture and language has come to the fore. This is an area for action in the future. The socialization of rural pupils through centralization of schools has been highly successful—too successful in the eyes of some communities who feel that these schools socialize the pupils away from farm life. This has been particularly true of the old-order Mennonite communities. Since 1969 these have opted out of the public school system and are operating their small community schools as private schools.

7. INNOVATION

The relationship between innovation policy and financial instruments was dealt with in Chapter VI.

8. A GENERAL COMMENT WITH RESPECT TO POLICY AND FORMS OF SCHOOL FINANCE

One gets the impression, after studying the situation, that there is no clear-cut distinction between policy making and decisions respecting forms of primary school finance. In many cases, decisions as to financial forms determine policy. One wonders if all the policy implications of changes in financial instruments are always fully understood by the policy-makers. Of course, both specific policy statements and changes in forms of financial support are approved by the Deputy Minister and Minister of Education. One is forced to conclude that if one wants to look at the effective policy in any area, one must not pay too much attention to paper policies, but must look instead at the implications and results of the ways in which primary education is financed.

Chapter VIII

PROPOSED CHANGES IN THE FINANCING SYSTEM

This brief chapter discusses some proposals for changes in the financial system for primary education in Ontario. Some have been under consideration by the Ministry; others are proposals by teachers' associations, special-interest groups, and academics.

Handicapped children

It has been suggested that all school boards be required to provide suitable educational experiences at provincial standards for all mentally, physically, emotionally and educationally handicapped children.

Such a move would substantially increase the costs of primary education, and would remove the need for the present type of funding, whereby, for the lower-spending boards, the entire cost of increased services in the area is borne procinvially. There would, theoretically, be no further need for a strong stimulation or incentive grant. However, there would still be a need to recognize the additional cost of such programs, particularly if it could be shown that the incidence of handicapped pupils varied significantly from board to board, either in terms of percentage of total enrolment or in terms of types of handicap and the relative cost of providing for them. If it could be shown that there was no significant difference among boards, then the ROE/WP could be raised enough to cover the additional cost to all boards.

If this were done there would be a fear on the part of those most concerned with special education that some boards would provide minimum services in order either to keep their tax rate low or to provide some other service which they felt had higher priority. Thus it is a question again of local autonomy versus central stimulation of certain types of action.

Provincial funding of primary education

It has been suggested that primary education be removed from the property-tax base as post-secondary education is at present. This would require full provincial funding, thus releasing more property-tax revenue to the municipalities for meeting the costs of municipal services, and the concomitant lowering of provincial grants to municipalities to make up for the increase in provincial education costs.

It is difficult to imagine the province paying the full cost of primary education while leaving significant control over spending levels to local boards. Almost inevitably the locus of control would shift to the provincial level. But under such a system it might be easier to attain nearly equal levels of service throughout the province.

Combined public-separate school administration

It has been suggested that the administration of public and separate elementary schools be placed under the same local education authority with separate committees to look after matters of concern to Roman Catholics and non-Catholics. This would greatly narrow the range of tax-paying ability among elementary boards, since all property would be taxed equally to support both types of schools. The greatest hindrance to this proposal is political. It might be felt by both groups that they would have to give up too much. This proposal would provide for more efficient use of resources than at present and would further the drive to equality of educational service.

Immigrant children

The cities have been urging the federal government to provide funds to help with the special problem of educating the children of immigrants, so that boards may begin to pay more than lip-service to the oft-stated national goal of a cultural mosaic, in which various groups, as well as learning English or French, keep their own language and develop those aspects of their own culture that they desire to keep. This is a politically sensitive area because educational policy is the sole prerogative of the provinces under the constitution, and all provinces may not wish to encourage multi-culturalism to the same extent. It would be difficult for the federal government to provide the funds with strings attached, or to provide more on a per capita basis to some provinces than to others. Yet the need is greater in some provinces than others. This problem may in time be worked out at federal-provincial negotiation sessions.

Weighting factors

The system of weighting factors is being re-examined. The need for exact measures of differential need was great during the period of expenditure ceilings on ordinary expenditure per WP, but no longer exists. The weighting factors are now applied in two ways:
1. to the September 30th enrolment of the previous year to determine the weighted pupils to be used in calculating LEA/WP, the local equalized assessment per weighted pupil, upon which rates of grant on both ordinary and extra-ordinary expenditure are determined and;
2. to the average daily enrolment (ADE) for the grant (calendar) year to determine the maximum ROE of the board for the year. It is the first operation that results in full provincial funding of the costs, up to the ROE/WP ceiling, of the additional pupils allowed by the use of the weighting factors. If only the second operation were in effect, the province and board would share in the additional expenditure according to their respective sharing ratios as determined by formula.

It is possible that a re-examination of the weighting factors would result in a decision to apply some of them to both September enrolment and ADE and others only to the ADE. Probably the latter would be most suitable for those factors, such as that for special education, that stimulate local spending.

Collective bargaining by teachers

Teachers in Ontario have recently gained the right to bargain collectively for salaries and working conditions. The bargaining is done, however, between the teachers of each board and the board administrators and trustees. But there is a strong tendency for teachers to want the same kind of settlement, particularly in similar types of situations, such as in the large cities, in the north and in other regions of the province. Thus a breakthrough by one board often results in teachers in other boards seeking the same settlement. In order that this "whip-saw" effect may be reduced or controlled, it has been suggested that teachers' salaries and perhaps even staffing ratios should be negotiated provincially. This would give the province a very strong measure of control over board expenditures — even stronger than was possible under the expenditure ceilings. But at the present time, the official positions of teachers, trustees and the Ministry are opposed to the proposal (such provincial negotiation is already in effect in the provinces of Saskatchewan, Quebec, New Brunswick, Nova Scotia, Prince Edward Island and Newfoundland).

Autonomy for individual schools

Some boards are granting greater autonomy in financial matters to individual schools. It has even been proposed that the total instructional budget for a school be allocated in a lump sum to the school. The principal, as administrator of the school, and perhaps with the assistance of his teachers or a school committee composed of parents and other local concerned citizens, would determine the number of teachers, teachers' aides, paid and volunteer community workers, and others needed, and would budget for the purchase of various types of needed outside expertise from other schools or from the central administration of the board. The lump sum would be enough to pay the salaries of all personnel, including the principal, as well as for school supplies, books, equipment, field trips, and office administration. In some situations, operation and maintenance costs might also be included. This system needs study before it is implemented on any large scale.

Federal equalization grants

The Canadian Teachers' Federation advocates federal equalization grants to the provinces specifically ear-marked for education and tied to compliance provisions related to provincial methods of distributing school grants and the percentage of provincial personal income that is directed to education. The conditions suggested are such that they would not be met by all provinces and hence the federal government would not act. In addition, until and unless the constitution is changed, it is difficult to imagine the federal government moving away from its policy of general purpose equalizing grants to the provinces in favour of specific grants, particularly for education. As long as the general purpose equalizing grants are sufficient to yield to the have-not provinces, provincial revenue per capita equal to the national average, if national average rates of taxation are levied on provincial tax bases, the decision as to what is to be spent on education should remain with the provinces, in the authors' view.

BIBLIOGRAPHY

Atherton, P. and Marsh, J., *Revenue Raising in Ontario,* Toronto: Ontario Secondary School Teachers' Federation, 1975.

Benson, R., "Towards Equity in School Finance", Toronto: Ontario Ministry of Education, School Finance Section, May 1976, unpublished paper.

Benson, R., *Educational Finance in Ontario: A Report Prepared for the Ontario Teachers' Federation,* Toronto: Ontario Teachers' Federation, 1971.

Bezeau, Lawrence M., "Equality of Educational Opportunity and Inequality of Per Pupil Expenditures in Ontario", unpublished paper, Toronto: The Ontario Institute for Studies in Education, 1976.

Bezeau, Lawrence M., "A Closer Look At the Weighted Pupil", *The Journal of Education Finance* (forthcoming), Vol. 3, No. 1, Summer 1977.

Bezeau, L. M. and A. B. Currie, "Per Pupil Expenditure Inequality Among Ontario Boards Over Time: A Preliminary Assessment", unpublished paper, Toronto: The Ontario Institute for Studies in Education, 1976.

Bird, R. M., *Who Pays the Property Tax?,* Toronto: Institute of Policy Analysis, University of Toronto, 1975.

Brown, Wilfred J., "Redistributive Implications of Federal-Provincial Fiscal Arrangements For Elementary and Secondary Education in Canada", unpublished doctoral thesis, The University of Toronto, 1974.

Cameron, D. M., *Schools for Ontario: Policy-Making, Administration and Finance in the 1960's,* Toronto: University of Toronto Press, 1972.

Canada, Government of, *Official Language Programmes,* Ottawa: Department of Secretary of State.

Canadian Tax Foundation, *Provincial and Municipal Finances 1975,* Toronto: CTF, 1975.

Canadian Tax Foundation, *The National Finances,* Toronto: Canadian Tax Foundation, 1976.

Clark, D. H., *Fiscal Need and Revenue Equalization Grants,* Toronto: Canadian Tax Foundation, 1969.

Finnis, F. H., *Real Property Assessment in Canada,* Toronto: Canadian Tax Foundation, 1966.

Fleming, W. G., *Ontario's Educative Society.* Volume 1: *The Expansion of the Educational System,* Toronto: University of Toronto Press, 1971.

Fleming, W. G., *Ontario's Educative Society.* Volume 2: *The Administrative Structure,* Toronto: University of Toronto Press, 1971.

Gayfer, M., *An Overview of Canadian Education,* Toronto: Canadian Education Association, 1974.

Hanson, E. J., *Provincial Municipal Finance in Ontario and the Four Western Provinces with Special Emphasis on Education: A Comparative Study,* Edmonton: Alberta Teachers' Federation, 1971.

Harris, R. S., *The Quiet Evolution: A Study of the Educational System of Ontario,* Toronto: University of Toronto Press, 1967.

Hettich, W., Lacombe, B. and Von Zur-Muehlen, M., *Basic Goals and the Financing of Education,* Ottawa: Canadian Teachers' Federation, 1972.

Humphreys, E. H., "Inequality and Rural Schools: Results of Survey in 1967 and 1969", *The Alberta Journal of Educational Research,* Vol. 18, No. 2, June 1972, pp. 111-23.

Humphreys, E. H. and V. J. Rawkins, *Equity and Ontario's Public Elementary Schools 1967-1973* (Educational Planning Occasional Paper No. 73/74-8), Toronto: The Ontario Institute for Studies in Education, 1974.

La Forest, G. V., *The Allocation of Taxing Power Under the Canadian Constitution,* Toronto: Canadian Tax Foundation, 1967.

Lawr, D. A. and Gidney, R. D. (Eds.), *Educating Canadians,* Toronto: Von Nostrand Reinhold Ltd., 1973.

Moffatt, H. P. and Brown, W. J., *New Goals, New Paths: The Search for a Rationale for the Financing of Education in Canada,* Ottawa: Canadian Teachers' Federation, 1973.

Munroe, D. *The Organization and Administration of Education in Canada,* Ottawa: Information Canada, 1974.

Ontario Committee on the Costs of Education, *Interim Report Number 7: Financing Education in Elementary and Secondary Schools,* Toronto, 1975.

Ontario Ministry of Education, *Annual Reports of the Minister of Education,* Toronto: Province of Ontario, issued annually.

Ontario Ministry of Education, *Regulations; General Legislative Grants,* Toronto: Province of Ontario, issued annually, 1976, 1977.

Ontario Ministry of Education, *Uniform Code of Accounts,* Toronto: Government of Ontario, 1969

Ontario Ministry of Treasury, Economics and Intergovernmental Affairs, *Municipal Finance Information,* Toronto, 1973.

Ontario Ministry of Education, *Education Statistics Ontario,* Toronto, issued annually, 1973, 1974, 1975.

Ontario Secondary School Teachers' Federation, *Financing Public Education in Ontario,* Toronto: Ontario Secondary School Teachers' Federation, 1970.

Robinson, A. J. and Cutt, J. (Eds.), *Public Finance in Canada: Selected Readings,* second edition, Toronto: Methuen, 1973.

Statistics Canada, Public Finance Division, *Provincial Government Finance,* Ottawa: Information Canada (Reference 68-209).

Statistics Canada, *Principal Taxes in Canada 1975,* Ottawa: Information Canada (Reference 68-201).

Statistics Canada, *Local Government Finance,* Ottawa: Information Canada (Reference 68-204).

Statistics Canada, Education, Science and Culture Division, "Minority and Second Language Education, Elementary and Secondary Levels", *Service Bulletin,* Vol. 4, No. 4, September 1975.

Wilson, R. A. P., *Financing Public Education in Ontario 1975,* Toronto: Ontario Secondary School Teachers' Federation, 1975.

FEDERAL REPUBLIC OF GERMANY

by

Peter SIEWERT
and
Helmut KÖHLER
*Max Planck Institut für Bildungsforschung
Berlin*

We should like to take this opportunity to thank all those whose willing co-operation in interviews and discussions helped make this report possible. Special acknowledgement should go to members of official and unofficial educational bodies and to our colleagues Beate Krais, Peter Matthias and Jens Naumann.

CONTENTS

INTRODUCTION 113

Chapter I
THE MAIN FEATURES OF THE CONTEMPORARY SYSTEM OF FINANCING PRIMARY EDUCATION AND ITS HISTORICAL AND CONSTITUTIONAL BACKGROUND 118
    Historical Development of the Volksschule and its Financing 118
    The Main Features of Organisational and Financial Responsibilities for Schooling in the Federal Republic of Germany 120
        Relationship between the Bund and the Länder 120
        Relationship between the Länder and their Local Governments 121
    Development, Distribution and Structure of Expenditure 124
    Sources of School Financing 130

Chapter II
FISCAL ADJUSTMENT IN THE FEDERAL REPUBLIC OF GERMANY 133
    Tax Apportionment and Legislation 133
    Fiscal Adjustment among the Länder 134
    Local Fiscal Adjustment 136

Chapter III
ORGANISATIONAL AND FINANCIAL RESPONSIBILITIES AT PRIMARY LEVEL AND CRITERIA FOR FUND ALLOCATION 141
    Staff 141
        Teaching Staff 141
        Other School Staff 144
    School Construction 145
        Länder Influence on School Building Plans 145
        Types of Länder Participation in Financing School Building 146
        Local Financing of School Building 149
    Other Non-personnel Expenditure 150
        Educational Materials 151
        Pupil Transportation 152
        Other Expenditure on Equipment, Maintenance and Administration 153

Chapter IV
EDUCATIONAL POLICY GOALS AND ASPECTS OF THEIR IMPLEMENTATION 155

Chapter V
ON PROPOSALS FOR RESTRUCTURING ORGANISATIONAL AND FINANCIAL RESPONSIBILITIES 165

REFERENCES 167

INTRODUCTION

Since the late 1960s discussions have been going on in the Federal Republic of Germany with a view to an overdue modernization of the educational system. This was referred to by the OECD Education Committee as long ago as 1972 in its country report on Germany[1]. A viewer from outside may, however, be surprised that the financial aspects of the intensely debated educational policy goals and reform measures have been considered with relative reluctance, and then only in general terms. In this area, the debate has been confined to more or less rough estimates of the financial requirements and how they might be met in view of predicted economic developments, possible changes in the State's share of the gross national product or national income, and the competition between education and other public services for available funds. Based on estimates of financial resources likely to be available to education, schemes have been devised for allocation between its various sectors, and some more or less specific proposals have been put forward on how the burden should be shared by the various territorial authorities.

This contrast between the detailed attention given to substantive structural and procedural aspects of reform and the comparatively superficial treatment of their financial dimension is not accidental. At the bottom of it is a fundamental difficulty that will be explored in the course of the present study.

Within the OECD comparative project, to which this paper affords a contribution, it is the purpose of the individual country studies to examine the influences financial arrangements have had on the conduct of primary education—or, more precisely, to analyse the effects specific financing instruments have had on the achievement of educational policy goals in this particular sector. The OECD project thus turns on a question that until now has not been explicity asked in the FRG. One of the main reasons for this (which has consequences for the present study also) is the peculiar administrative structure of the German educational system.

So far as matters of finance are concerned, the most important characteristics of this administrative system are these:

1. Education in the Federal Republic is treated as a public service, i.e. the structuring principles of the educational system and the mechanisms controlling it are not those of a competitive economy and open markets. The relative remoteness of the education system from social sectors that are primarily economically oriented and governed by direct economic mechanisms is reflected in the fact that it is financed, not by the sale of services nor by the collection of fees, but directly out of taxation, that is, out of general taxation, for no taxes are specifically labelled as being for educational purposes.

---

1. OECD, *Reviews of National Policies for Education, Germany.* Paris 1972, p. 43.

2. Education, as a public service, competes with or complements other public services (social security, health, transport, defence, etc.), all of which in their turn compete in the political market in parliaments, and in a broader sense also in councils, political parties and special lobbies and pressure groups. In order to make them subject to decision the various services competing in this "market" must, however, be made comparable, and by consequence their translation into general terms of required resources as, for example, number of staff posts and money, become of central importance. This is reflected in resource-requirement estimates in medium-term finance plans, and in the drawing up and passing of annual budget estimates. In this manner the various public services are "brought to a common denominator" in an aggregated, global form and thereby made amenable to decision.

3. The Federal Republic of Germany is a relatively large modern industrial country. This is reflected both in the size of its educational system in absolute terms—numbers of pupils, teachers, schools, etc.—and the variety of its differently specialized educational institutions (different levels and types of schools, teaching programmes, and so on). This size and internal differentiation necessarily demand a correspondingly diversified range of related administrative decision-making competences.

Whereas the Federal government's decision-making powers in education are generally limited (and this is particularly true when it comes to the school system), the Länder (individual States) have far-reaching overall responsibility for education. This responsibility has developed over time into a plethora of interrelated decision-making structures of various kinds. Thus, the Länder not only have the competence to decide on competences (i.e. the political and legal power to lay down general framework provisions that may be filled in by regulations of subordinate authorities on their own responsibility), but in many areas they themselves make these decisions for more specialized complexes right down to specific issues. That means that to a large extent the Länder carry out their decision-making function through specific instruments which also control the real structures: partly through very detailed legislation, partly through specialized orders and decrees that are carried out by subordinate authorities of the States' school supervisory systems. The result is that financial instruments play only a minor role as steering mechanisms. The main reasons for using monetary terms to express these structural and resource requirements is, rather, to enable:

a) Consolidation of the separate needs of the individual educational institutions and activities to allow for more effective decision making, and

b) translation of these overall decisions, once taken, into specific applications for the various sub-units of the system.

These processes take the form of public budgetary planning and accounting procedures.

As a result of the relative detailed structuring of the education system by the Land's education authorities, the decision-making competences left to local authorities are very restricted and entail practically no financing decisions at all.

In view of the foregoing, we have divided this study into five chapters. Chapter I reviews the historical development of primary education into a public service and the current division of organisational and financial responsibilities in the school system. These statements will be supplemented by relevant expenditure figures, an outline of sources of finance for primary education, and a survey on how these funds are apportioned down to the level of the individual school. Chapter II treats in more detail the general fiscal adjustment as it currently exists in the Federal Republic of Germany. As the educational system is financed from general taxation, the FRG's approach to fiscal jurisdiction, the tax pool, and so on, needs to be studied at the local, state, and federal levels if one is to understand the general framework of political and administrative activities in the FRG. Using this information as the background, Chapter III gives a detailed analysis of organisational and financial responsibilities at primary level.

The remaining topic of educational policy aims and their achievement is dealt with in Chapter IV, by which time it should have become clear that in the FRG there is no direct correspondence between educational targets, related measures, their financing and any attributable changes that may ensue. As a consequence, we shall be able to provide no more than a relatively general survey of the steering measures that seem to be important in this context. Finally, Chapter V will briefly take up some contemporary criticisms of the ways in which the Federal Republic organises the administrative and financial responsibilities for schools, and with a look at some proposals for change.

At this point, however, we should draw attention to a technical difficulty arising from exclusive concentration on primary education, while it is the German school system as a whole that is covered in the official statistics.

The traditional German school system, with its strong class-oriented selection processes, corresponds closely to the class structure of society itself. Compulsory education (from the age of 6-18 years) begins for all children with four years attendance at a Grundschule (four-year primary school)[2]. After this, children go on to the Hauptschule (up to the 9th or 10th year of schooling), or the Realschule (up to the 10th year of schooling), or enter the Gymnasium (up to the 13th year of schooling). In addition, special schools exist for mentally or physically handicapped children. All children leaving general education before the age of 18 must attend a vocational school for part-time instruction if they do not attend other vocational schools with full-time instruction (see Figure 1).

Proposed reforms call for this traditional structure to be replaced by a horizontally organised system of educational levels: the primary level, consisting of the 4-year Grundschule and the corresponding special schools; a 6-year secondary I level (comprising the Hauptschule, Realschule and Gymnasium up to the 10th school year, and the corresponding special schools); and a 2-3 year secondary II level to include academic streams—upper grades of the Gymnasium—and vocational schools. All educational tracks, according to the concept, should terminate with a leaving certificate giving access to the next highest step in the educational system.

The Länder have approached this reform in different ways[3]. Some are trying to achieve it by reorganising traditional schools; others have opted to establish comprehensive schools which generally combine the three types of school at secondary I level, though in some cases Grundschulen are also included.

Despite formal acceptance of this level-orientated-organisation in the Länder school laws, traditional structures still predominate.

As primary schools are sometimes organizationally linked with institutions of secondary I level (i.e. with Hauptschulen which, together with the Grundschulen, made up the former Volksschule), and official statistics in most cases lump together data for Grundschule and Hauptschule and sometimes even special schools, it has not always been possible to deal with primary education as a separate entity in the survey that follows.

---

2. In Berlin, Grundschule generally last six years and accordingly the duration of Hauptschule, Realschule and Gymnasium courses is two years less than in other Länder.
3. It should be noted that most proposals for educational policy reforms emphasize the reorganisation of the secondary levels, their leaving certificates and the right of access to streams leading upwards to academic, tertiary and other further education. Less emphasis has been placed on reform proposals for primary education.

Figure 1. STRUCTURE OF THE EDUCATION

PRESENT DAY STRUCTURE*

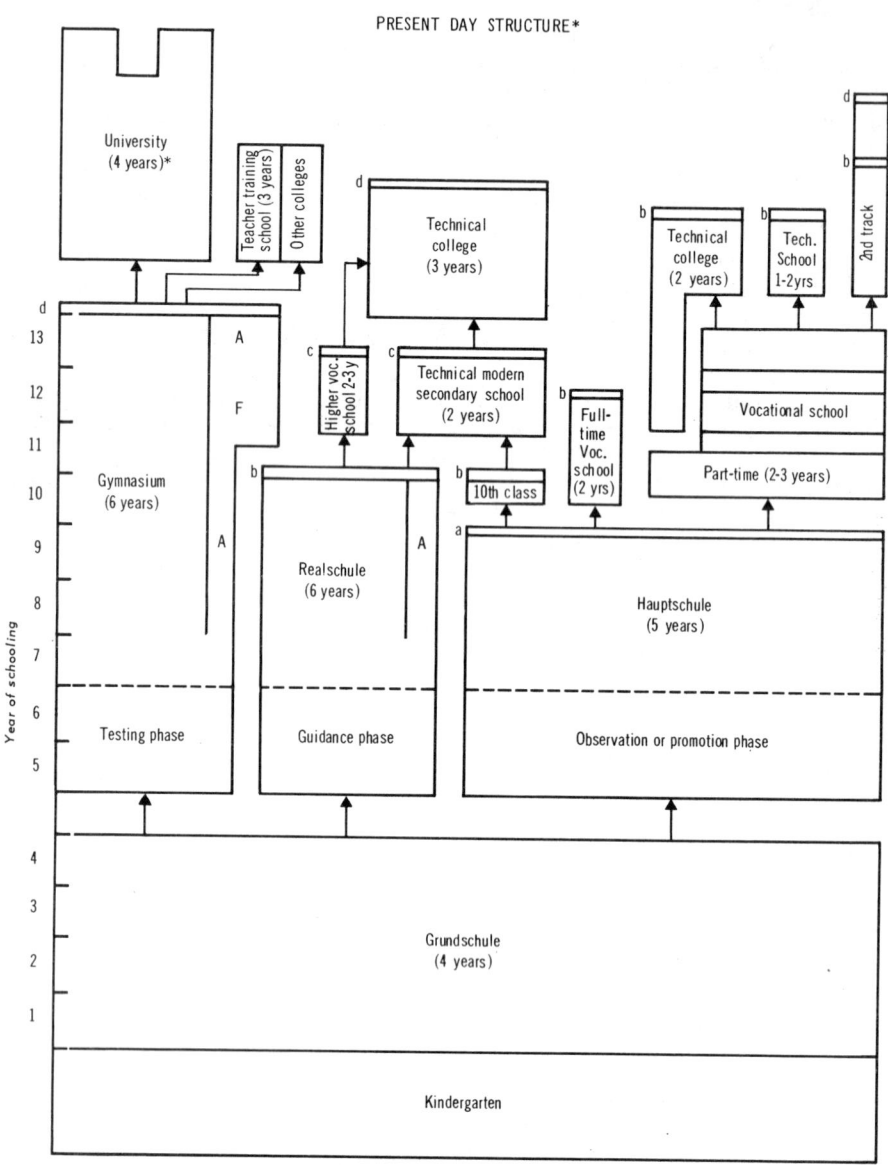

* Not included are special schools, types and arrangements peculiar to individual Länder. The observations concerning the 5th and 6th years - testing, guidance, observation or promotion phases - are not continued to that particular type of school.
Type of school :   A = preparatory type, F = F-Gymnasium.
School leaving certificate : *Present day structure* : a = completion of Hauptschule, b = completion of intermediate studies,
c = qualified for technical school, d = qualified for university.
in model of horizontal structure example : a = Abitur I, b = Abitur II (school-leaving certificates).
Source : Bildungsbericht 1970, pp. 73-74.

SYSTEM IN THE FEDERAL REPUBLIC OF GERMANY

MODEL OF HORIZONTAL STRUCTURE*

Preparatory and contact studies
Long study track
Short study track
COMPREHENSIVE UNIVERSITY

Further education

Technical school

(13) b
12
Main subjects, special courses, optional courses
11
SECONDARY LEVEL II (2-3 years)
inclusion of vocational education courses

practical vocational training

a
10
Main subjects, special courses, optional courses
9
8
SECONDARY I LEVEL (6 years)
7
6
Guidance phase
Internal differentiation, special courses
5

4
3
2
PRIMARY LEVEL (4 years)
1

ELEMENTARY LEVEL (kindergarten, pre-school) (2-3 years, voluntary)

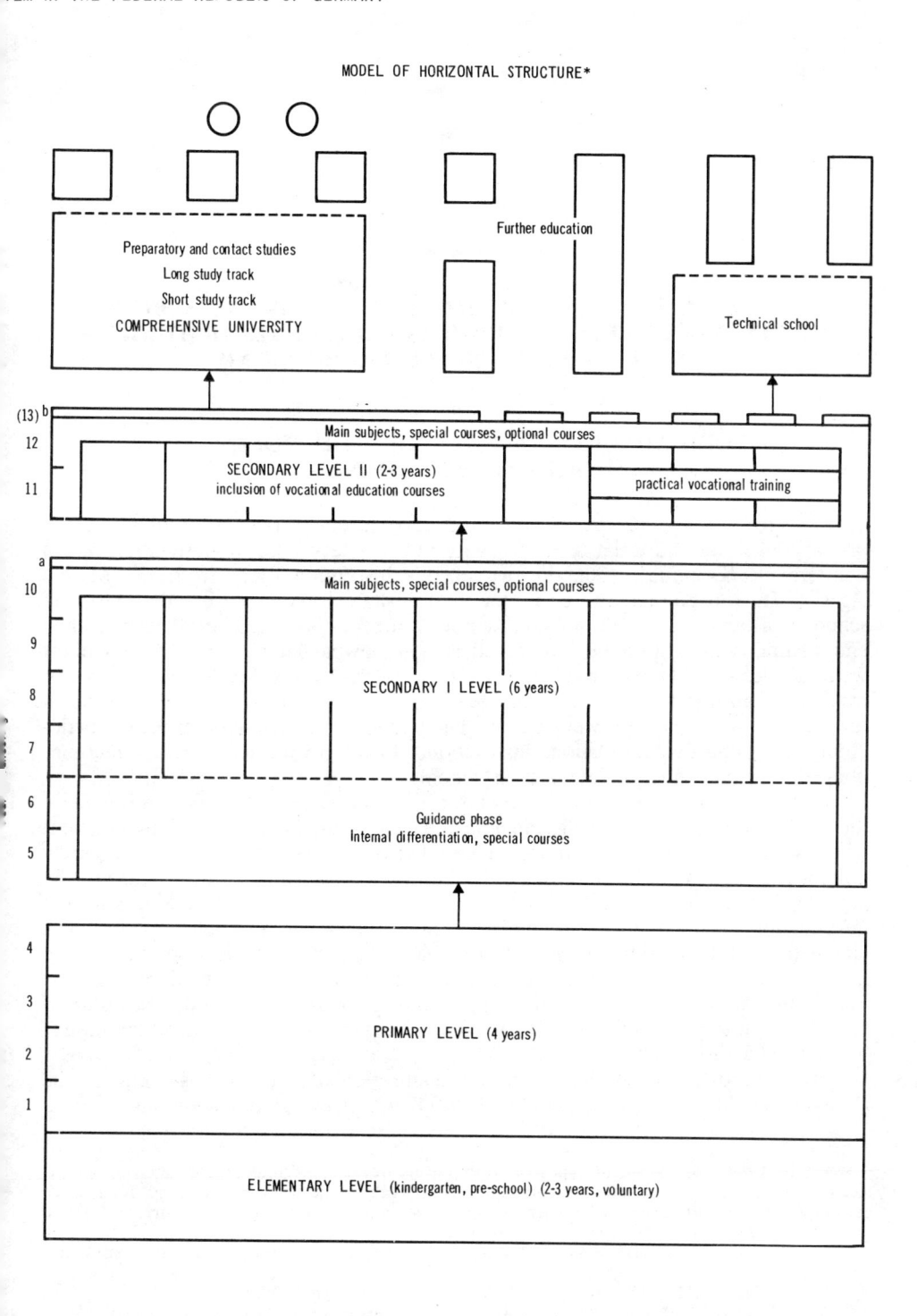

Chapter I

THE MAIN FEATURES OF THE CONTEMPORARY SYSTEM OF FINANCING PRIMARY EDUCATION AND ITS HISTORICAL AND CONSTITUTIONAL BACKGROUND

HISTORICAL DEVELOPMENT OF THE VOLKSSCHULE AND ITS FINANCING

Up to the mid-1960s, *Grund-* and *Hauptschulen* (i.e. institutions of the primary level and a special type of school at secondary I level) were embraced in the term *Volksschule*[1]. The history of this institution dates from the Middle Ages[2]. Its fore-runners were, in the first instance, the town-based "German" schools, as opposed to the more academic "Latin" schools. They taught reading and writing, with arithmetic introduced at a somewhat later date. These schools were financed partly by private individuals, partly by the local governments or by Church authorities[3]. During the Reformation, the Church also set up schools for the laity, the teachers were church personnel, mostly vergers, and the curriculum was primarily for religious instruction. Local governments were sometimes obliged to create and maintain such schools.

The concept of a general school for the lower social classes developed in the 17th century, and made gradual headway during the Age of Enlightenment when social and economic considerations began to take the place of a purely religious approach. The interest of the enlightened absolutist princes during the Age of Mercantilism fostered increased state influence on education, and the introduction of compulsory schooling. State financing as such still had not emerged[4]; Church, community and individual financing played the major role in funding, and school regulations remained part of church regulations. In the 18th and partly even in the early 19th century charities and industries started schools to combine instruction and work, so helping *inter alia* to produce money to keep education going.

One important legal step in the nationalisation of education is found in the Preussisches Allgemeines Landrecht of 1794, which declared schools and univer-

---

1. In 1964, the names of types of school were revised. While the term Grundschule had been in use since the 1920s to denote the lower Volksschule level, no accepted description existed for the upper level. The term Hauptschule, introduced in 1964, is borrowed from the Austrian designation of a type of Realschule.
2. Cf. Flitner, W.: *Die vier Quellen des Volksschulgedankens*, 3. Auflage, Stuttgart, 1954.
3. Cf. Heckel, H.: *Die Städte und ihre Schulen*, Stuttgart, 1959.
4. Leschinsky, A., and Roeder, P.M.: *Schule im historischen Prozess — Zum Wechselverhältnis von institutioneller Erziehung und gesellschaftlicher Entwicklung*, Stuttgart, 1976.

sities to be State institutions and set out regulations covering universal compulsory schooling[5]. But 19th century development of the school system was less influenced by this legislation than by the radical State and social reforms of Baron vom Stein in Prussia, the beginnings of local self-government, and the neo-Humanist reshaping of educational ideas connected with such names as Humboldt, Pestalozzi and Süvern. "Community responsibility formally centred on 'external school matters', i.e., the building and maintenance of schools, while 'internal school affairs', such as curricula and organisation, were regulated by the State. Despite this formal division of responsibilities, right up to the 19th century the efforts of the local governments in schooling emphasised equally both external and internal school affairs[6]."

With the expansion of the school system in the 19th century (especially, however, with the accomplishment of compulsory schooling) the sharing of responsibilities for organisational and financial matters began to change. While at the start, for example, the local governments for the most part selected and appointed the teachers and paid their salaries, they progressively had to leave these functions to the State. The massive financial outlay needed to build new schools could no longer be borne locally, and as a result the State involved itself increasingly in providing for these expenditures and thereby increased its influence on the development of schooling as such[7].

But to some extent, the 19th century German Länder continued to go their own ways, not least because the Constitution adopted at the founding of the Reich in 1871 contained no provisions for a central approach to education.

It was the Weimar Constitution of 1919 that first created legal grounds for greater uniformity in the German school system, but these, however, was hardly ever used. Only the Reichsgrundschulgesetz of 1920 contained the unifying paragraph: "The Volksschule shall be established in the lower four years of schooling as the common Grundschule for all pupils, on which also intermediate and higher schooling is based" (Art. 1, par. 1, sentence 1). No uniform provisions were laid down, either for financing of the Volksschule, or for the years following the fourth school year. Cooperation between Reich, Länder and local governments in school building matters was also envisaged in the Weimar Constitution, but this did not happen: the respective responsibility remained with the Länder and the communes, and the development of the school system was left to their initiative.

After the Nazi seizure of power, and the setting up of a Reich Ministry of Education in 1934, the educational system became increasingly centralized as local self-government was progressively dismantled. In order to unify schooling, for example, laws were passed on school authorities and maintenance (1937),

---

5. Spaniol states: *The Prussian Common Law of the Land* of 5 February 1794 (ALR) represents simultaneously the end and the high point of nationalisation of education in this period. Part. II, Clause 12, entitled Lower and Higher schools, is the first State law designed to lay down comprehensive regulations for the entire school system.
  Spaniol, O.: *Das Verhältnis zwischen Staat und Kommunen auf dem Gebiet des Schulwesens in der Bundesrepublik.* Diss., Marburg, 1960. Cf. also
  Bungardt, K.: *Die Odyssee der Lehrerschaft,* Hannover, 1965.
6. Boehm, U.: *Probleme der Planung und Finanzierung des Schulbaus in der Bundesrepublik Deutschland.* Diss. Berlin, 1971, p. 69.
7. It should be noted that even in the second half of the 19th century, as a result of the continuing shortage of public schools, there were still many private Volksschulen. By 1901 however, only about one per cent of the Volksschulen within the Reich's boundaries were still privately run, and that percentage is just as low for Grund- and Hauptschulen (Volksschulen) in the Federal Republic today. We shall not, therefore, go into the financing of private schools in this study.

compulsory education (1938), and the legal status of teachers of Volksschule and Mittelschule (1939). However, a centralised school policy covering all areas of schooling did not come into existence until after the war.

THE MAIN FEATURES OF ORGANISATIONAL AND FINANCIAL RESPONSIBILITIES FOR SCHOOLING IN THE FEDERAL REPUBLIC OF GERMANY

Relationship between the Bund and the Länder

The historical development just outlined has obviously had direct consequences on the division of responsibilities and the distribution of the financial burdens of the school system in the FRG. The Basic Law of the Federal Republic of Germany of 1949 handed the responsibility for structuring and financing the school system to the individual Länder (cultural sovereignty of the Länder), and competences for the Federal Government were not provided for. A constitutional amendment passed in 1969, when a Federal Ministry of Education and Science was created, of course laid down that—subject to agreement—the Federal Government and the Länder "may cooperate in educational planning and in furthering scientific research institutions and projects of supra-regional importance" (Art. 9 1 b GG), but independent Federal authority for the structuring and administration of the school system has so far not been granted. This division of responsibilities (cultural sovereignty of the Länder) naturally gave rise to problems in coordination between the individual Länder concerning the realization of the uniform social conditions in the educational field prescribed by the Constitution. For this reason, the Länder set up the Ständige Konferenz der Kultusminister der Länder in der Bundesrepublik Deutschland (KMK) (Permanent Conference of Ministers of Education of the Länder in the Federal Republic of Germany). This provides a forum in which the Länder can develop joint views and policies, and it works out agreements to unify regulations in the school system. The KMK has adopted a series of important standardising measures. Its decisions, however, must be unanimous, and proposals on which opinions differ as a result of different educational policy aims must be dropped.

At all events, educational planning and finance stay in the hands of the Länder and their local governments which, since the end of the 1960s, have set up an increasing number of planning committees to work out medium- to long-term school development plans for each Land and its regions and aims for the school system as a whole.

In addition to the KMK's coordinating efforts, a number of other organisations emerged to work out nation-wide recommendations and plans for the development of the German school system. Among them was the Deutscher Ausschuß für das Erziehungs- und Bildungswesen (German Committee for Educational and Cultural Matters), proposed in 1953 by the Federal Minister of the Interior and the Länder Ministers of Education, and established by the Federal President. Conceived as "a group of independent experts not subject to any official influence", the Committee completed 29 recommendations and reports from its founding to its dissolution in 1965. Its main contribution was the *Outline Plan for the Reform and Standardisation of the General Public School System*[8].

---

8. Cf.: *Empfehlungen und Gutachten des Deutschen Ausschusses für das Erziehungs- und Bildungswesen*, 1953-1965, Gesamtausgabe, Stuttgart, 1966.

Between 1965 and 1975 the Deutscher Bildungsrat (German Education Council, created in 1965 under an agreement between the Länder Governments and the Federal Government) also tabled a number of recommendations for the reform of the educational system. This Council, which brought together educational policy authorities, prominent laymen and members drawn from relevant academic disciplines, produced as one of its main proposals a long-term plan for structural changes in the educational system, published in 1970 as the *Strukturplan*[9].

One effect of the 1969 constitutional amendment was an agreement between the Bund and the Länder in 1970 to set up a joint committee for educational planning—the Bund-Länder-Kommission für Bildungsplanung (BLK). In 1973 this committee put forward a long-term overall plan for educational development in all the Länder, together with an estimate of how much it would cost (Bildungsgesamtplan)[10]. A long drawn-out controversy over the aims of the plan and alternative financing arrangement then started between educational professionals and representatives of other sectors (notably finance), and between education policy-makers in the different political parties. In this context, the educational strategies of the individual Länder had been carried out, it seems, relatively independently from the embattled overall plan, although it appears that by now there is a shared expectation of interdependence.

Relationship between the Länder and their local governments (see Figure 2)

In primary education (as for education generally) the basic relationships between the Länder and their subsidiary local authorities in matters concerning the school supervisory system, school administration, school maintenance and school financing are shaped by two constitutional provisions. The first is contained in Article 7 (1) GG, which states that "the entire educational system shall be subject to State supervision". This establishes the cultural sovereignty of the Länder, investing legislative authority in the Länder parliaments, and administrative authority in their governments and Ministries of Education. The Länder, as a result, are exclusively responsible for school supervision and the development of their educational systems. The second relevant provision appears in Article 28, par. 2, sentence 1 GG, which reads: "Local authorities must be granted the right to settle, in accordance with the law, all local community matters on their own responsibility". From these two constitutional rules (embodying two distinct principles of social regulation—one centralising, aimed at collective planning and uniform living-conditions, the other decentralising, aimed at taking into account specific community preferences)—there results a tension of acting in opposition and in union between the Länder and their communes and this has led to different applications of the principle of local self-government in the school system in the various Länder.

Despite differences of detail in regulations, in all Länder the traditional division of responsibilities between the Land and the local authorities in all school matters continues to hold good, in as far as the so-called internal school affairs remain the responsibility of the Land. They include school supervision, the establishment of teaching programmes, the determination of the school structure, the hiring and pay of teachers, and teacher training. The so-called external school affairs, however, such as the construction and maintenance of school

---

9. Deutscher Bildungsrat, *Empfehlungen der Bildungskommission, Strukturplan für das Bildungswesen*, Bonn, 1970.
10. Bund-Länder-Kommission für Bildungsplanung, *Bildungsgesamtplan*, Stuttgart, 1973.

Figure 2. REGIONAL ADMINISTRATIVE BREAKDOWN OF THE FEDERAL REPUBLIC OF GERMANY, 1975

Länder	Inhabitants mill.	Government/administrative Districts	Kreise	Communities
Schleswig-Holstein	2.6	1	11	1 170
Lower Saxony	7.3	8	48	1 035
North Rhine-Westph.	17.2	5	31	393
Hesse	5.6	2	24	598
Rhenish Palatinate	3.7	3	24	2 350
Baden-Württemberg	9.2	4	44	1 119
Bavaria	10.8	7	71	4 177
Saarland	1.1	1	5	50
City States				
Hamburg	1.7	1	—	1
Bremen	0.7	1	—	2
Berlin	2.0	1	—	1
Total	61.8	34	258	10 896

Communities and residential populations on the basis of size classification 1975

Communities with to less than... inhabitants	Communities Abs.	In %	Residential population Abs. (in 1 000)	In %
Under 100	249	2.3	16.9	0.0
100- 200	737	6.8	115.0	0.3
200- 500	2 193	20.1	743.8	1.2
500- 1 000	2 170	19.9	1 554.9	2.5
1 000- 2 000	1 883	17.3	2 676.6	4.3
2 000- 3 000	860	7.9	2 102.1	3.4
3 000- 5 000	811	7.7	3 275.1	5.3
5 000- 10 000	914	8.4	6 196.4	10.5
10 000- 20 000	588	5.4	8 070.1	13.1
20 000- 50 000	308	2.8	9 282.8	15.0
50 000-100 000	84	0.8	5 605.3	9.1
100 000-200 000	36	0.3	4 856.2	7.9
200 000-500 000	20	0.2	5 499.8	8.9
500 000 and above	13	0.1	11 537.1	18.7
Total	10 896	100	61 832.2	100

Source: Statistisches Bundesamt: Statistisches Jahrbuch 1976, pp. 51-54, 57.

buildings, the provision of teaching and educational materials, and the hiring of administrative staff are the responsibility of the local school authority. This local school authority may comprise the Land as well as individual communities, associations of local governments (e.g., Kreise) or school associations, especially set up for this purpose by several local authorities. But the local school authority for Grund- and Hauptschulen as for most public schools is usually the local authority. In Hesse school authority is in the hands of the Kreise, in Schleswig-Holstein and the Rhenish Palatinate it is relatively often held by community associations, and in Bavaria it lies mainly with associations of local school authorities specifically set up for the purpose. In the City State of Bremen, school authority is split between the local government sub-divisions of Bremen and Bremerhaven, and in Berlin and Hamburg, where local and State level are identical, the Land itself assumes the function of school auhority (see Table 1).

Table 1. **Grund- and Hauptschulen 1972 according to school authority**

Land	Total	Land	Kreis	Local authorities	Communities	School association	Other school authority
	1	2	3	4	5	6	7
Schleswig-Holstein	870	—	—	258	550	—	62
Hamburg	299	281	—	—	—	—	18
Lower Saxony	2 900	1	4	97	2 372	413	13
Bremen	143	—	—	—	139	—	4
North Rhine-Westph.	5 088	—	—	—	4 786	297	5
Hesse	1 645	—	1 363	—	276	—	6
Rhenish Palat.	1 558	3	—	—	1 128	—	19
Baden-Wurttemberg	3 343	—	—	408	3 158	171	14
Bavaria	3 042	—	—	—	1 231	1 763	48
Saarland	397	—	—	—	374	22	1
Berlin (West)	305	283	—	—	—	—	22
Federal Republic	19 590	568	1 367	763	14 014	2 666	212

Source: *Statistisches Bundesamt,* Fachserie A, Reihe 10, I. Allgemeinbildende Schulen, 1972, p. 14.

Thus a mixed system of State-local responsibility in education has grown up in the Federal Republic, in which the communities and local authorities constitute the school authority responsible for external school affairs. The school financing system, however, does not completely correspond to this theoretical division of responsibilities between Land and local authority. For example,
— the Länder share to some extent current material school costs and particularly costs of school building;
— the Länder partly make levies and impose contributions on the school authorities for financing purposes;
— communities pay contributions for school financing to other communities, as well as Kreise, local authorities and school-purpose associations.

These special school finance adjustment operations involve respectably large sums in terms of local government's school expenditure. A compilation of these monetary transactions between the territorial authorities in 1973 for Grund-,

Hauptschulen and special schools shows that, while the local government's own expenditure amounted to some 5 700 million DM, Länder allocations totalled about 1 000 million DM, and inter-community assignments raised more than 200 million DM (Table 2).

Apart from these earmarked financial allocations between the territorial authorities, the local governments also receive general allocations from the Länder in a general fiscal adjustment scheme. Although these sums do not direct'y serve for the financing of schools, they have an indirect effect by allowing the local authorities greater flexibility in decision-making.

All in all, this complex system of compartmentalised financial responsibility with each Land setting its own dividing lines (a matter that will be examined in detail below) involves a multifaceted exchange of operations to the point where its logic as well as its strain on, and easing of, school finance burdens become unintelligible.

DEVELOPMENT, DISTRIBUTION AND STRUCTURE OF EXPENDITURE

After this consideration of the development and patterns of school responsibilities at the primary level, a brief look at the following is necessary for further background information:
- the development of expenditures for Grund-, Hauptschule and special schools[11] and their importance in overall school expenditure, in educational and scientific spending, and in the budget;
- the distribution of expenditure to territorial authorities, and allocations for specific purposes.

A distinction should be made here between *net expenditure* and *direct expenditure*. *Net expenditure* consists of all the outgoing expenditures of an administration minus the ingoing payments of other administrations. They show, as a result, the amount of expenditure of one or more administrative level(s), financed from its (their) own receipts. These figures cannot be broken down into different types of expenditure; this can only be done with *direct expenditure*, which consists of funds directly disbursed by an administration (or an administrative level) in the course of performing its functions, i.e. without payments to other administrations.

Considering net public expenditure for education and science as a whole, for all schooling and for Grund-, Hauptschulen and special schools, we see that in nominal terms expenditures increased vastly in all three areas between 1952 and 1973 (Table 3). Increases in educational and scientific spending were relatively higher than those for the school system, which in its turn had increases relatively greater than those awarded to the Grund-, Hauptschulen and special schools. The proportionate increase from 1952-1973 in all three areas, however, was larger than the proportionate rise in budgetary expenditure and the gross national product, though for Grund-, Hauptschulen and special schools this difference is relatively small.

The figures in Table 3 clearly show that the gross national product, public budgets and the spending on education and science, the school system, and Grund-, Hauptschulen and special schools all grew at roughly the same rate until the beginning of the 1960s. In the mid-1960s, when education policy

---

11. As already touched on in the introduction, school organisation and techniques of data compilation sometimes make it impossible to deal exclusively with primary education.

Table 2. **Own expenditures of communities and local authorities, as well as allocations and loans for Grund- und Hauptschulen and special schools, 1973**

In 1 000 DM

Type of body, Land	Own expenditures	Allocations to		Loans given	Payments from			
					Communities		the Land	
		the Land	Communities		Allocations	Loans	Allocations	Loans
Cities without Kreise	1 574 104	13 113	2 370	50	6 321	—	200 880	4 102
Communities and offices belonging to Kreise	3 511 805	27 404	93 774	2 067	216 916	41 833	728 684	8 531
Rural Kreise	571 972	68	133 762	6 544	7 842	8 104	97 946	27 321
District bodies	84 972	—	2 632	23	543	—	15 440	123
Communities and local authorities combined	5 742 853	40 585	232 538	8 684[a]	231 622	49 937[a]	1 042 950	40 077
those in:								
Schleswig-Holstein	344 608	39 751	31 949	1 679	22 724	695	28 314	1 232
Lower Saxony	905 728	94	99 372	4 584	65 163	43 450	100 409	1 658
North Rhine-Westphalia	1 837 878	56	25 970	817	32 189	420	349 307	716
Hesse	369 940	167	8 787	—	7 372	—	53 413	31 413
Rhenish Palatinate	375 031	237	32 365	505	57 763	131	82 837	1 871
Baden-Württemberg	750 887	77	7 491	151	10 157	3 749	177 705	1 285
Bavaria	1 057 891	173	22 870	945	31 029	1 492	237 832	1 902
Saarland	100 890	30	3 734	3	5 225	—	13 133	—

a) The differences between payments made and received arise from various statistical delimitations which cannot be adjusted.

Source: *Statistisches Bundesamt*, Fachserie L, Reihe I, II. Jahresabschlüsse, Kommunalfinanzen, 1973, p. 56/57.

Table 3. **Net expenditures for education, 1952-1973**

Year	GNP (mill. DM)	All public budgets	Education and Science	School system alone	Grund-, Haupt- and special schools
			Net expenditures (mill. DM)		
		Absolute			
1952	141 700	40 411.6	3 821.9	3 099.3	1 839.7
1956	207 000	59 367.3	6 279.7	5 132.7	2 820.3
1961	326 200	98 518.9	11 354.4	8 254.3	4 642.9
1965	452 700	147 782.3	15 933.5	10 802.1	5 938.7
1970	685 600	211 869.5	28 071.7	17 826.0	8 867.8
1972	834 600	265 246.7	39 773.1	25 730.2	11 917.3
1973	930 330	277 191.1	45 104.2	28 064.0	13 407.5
		1952 = 100			
1952	100.0	100.0	100.0	100.0	100.0
1956	146.1	146.9	164.3	165.6	153.3
1961	230.2	243.8	297.1	266.3	252.4
1965	319.5	365.7	416.9	348.5	325.5
1970	483.8	524.3	734.5	575.2	482.0
1972	589.0	656.4	1 040.7	830.2	647.8
1973	656.5	685.9	1 180.2	905.5	728.8

Source: Albert, W. and Oehler, Ch.: *Die Kulturausgaben der Länder, des Bundes und der Gemeinden 1950-1967*, Weinheim, 1972. Albert, W. and Oehler, Ch.: *Die Kulturausgaben der Länder, des Bundes und der Gemeinden einschliesslich Strukturausgaben zum Bildungswesen.* Munich 1976: and our own calculation 1973 on the basis of official statistics.

became a major area of discussion in the Federal Republic, spending on education and science and the school system was considerably stepped up. This was not true, however, for the Grund-, Hauptschulen and special schools, where spending at first even lagged behind the expansion of the budget. Even cautiously interpreted the figures give an idea of the type of reform priorities discussed at that time: intensified expansion of the universities, and promotion of extra-university research on the one hand, the reform of the school system at secondary level on the other.

A brief consideration of how net expenditure was distributed over the various administrative levels in 1973 (Table 4) throws additional light on financial load-sharing in the school system. The financial contribution of the Federal Government, which accounted for almost 45 per cent of all public expenditure, was practically negligible in the field of schooling. The largest share of school finance was provided by the Länder (some 69 per cent), with 30 per cent drawn from the local authorities. School financing accounted for about 21 per cent of the Länder budgets, and 14 per cent of local authority budgets. The role of the Länder in financing Grund-, Hauptschulen and special schools was rather smaller (some 63 per cent), and the share of the local authorities proportionately higher (around 37 per cent). In both cases, the amount represented about 8 per cent of the respective territorial authorities' budgets.

The sharing of expenditure for Grund-, Hauptschulen and special schools between Länder[12] and local authorities has remained more or less static since 1968 as Table 5 shows.

---

12   We refer here only to the eight Länder of the FRG.

Table 4. **Net expenditures of public authorities, 1973**
In million DM

Net expenditure 1973

Field of activity	Total	Bund including special funds Absolute	In % of total	Länder Absolute	In % of total	Communities, local authorities Absolute	In % of total
All fields of activity (total budget)	277 191.1	123 517.3	44.6	93 689.3	33.8	59 984.6	21.6
Educational expenditures	45 104.2	6 276.1	13.9	30 250.0	67.1	8 578.0	19.0
Among them for the school system	28 064.0	261.3	0.9	19 333.5	68.9	8 469.1	30.2
thereof:							
Grund- and Hauptschulen	12 329.2	−17.3	—	7 754.4	62.9	4 592.0	37.2
Universities	12 513.7	2 669.2	21.3	9 844.5	78.7	—	—
Research	4 526.5	3 345.6	73.9	1 072.0	23.7	108.9	2.4
Share of total budget in % for							
Education	16.3	5.1	—	32.3	—	14.3	—
Schooling	10.1	0.2	—	20.6	—	14.1	—
Grund- and Hauptschulen	4.4	0.0	—	8.3	—	7.7	—

Source: Statistisches Bundesamt, Fachserie L, Reihe 1, II. *Jahresabschlüsse, öffentliche Finanzwirtschaft,* 1973, p. 74 and Fachserie L, Reihe 5, *Sonderbeiträge zur Finanzstatistik, Ausgaben der öffentlichen Haushalte für Bildung, Wissenschaft und Kultur,* 1973, pp. 44, 46, 82, 110.

Table 5. **Local authorities' share of net expenditure for Grund-, Haupt- and special schools in the Länder**
In percent

1951	38.5	1966	43.2
1956	39.3	1967	40.3
1959	39.7	1968	38.6
1961	42.0	1969	38.0
1962	43.3	1970	36.8
1963	45.5	1971	38.3
1964	46.8	1972	38.5
1965	45.0	1973	37.1

In the first half of the 1960s the local share certainly was considerably larger, but a clear trend towards shifting the financing burden on to the Länder, with their greater economic strength, as has often been stated, is not substantiated by the figures for Grund-, Hauptschulen and special schools.

The average percentages for the FRG are, however, deceptive insofar as the distribution of spending on Grund-, Hauptschulen and special schools in the eight Länder is by no means uniform. This is illustrated by the 1973 percentages shown in Table 6.

Table 6. **Net expenditures for Grund-, Haupt- and special schools 1973**
In percent

Land	Local authorities	Land
Baden-Württemberg	34.1	65.9
Bavaria	31.5	68.5
Hesse	30.1	69.9
Lower Saxony	39.5	60.5
North Rhine-Westphalia	43.5	56.5
Rhenish Palatinate	32.5	67.5
Saarland	33.5	66.5
Schleswig-Holstein	45.3	54.7
All Länder	37.1	62.9

While in Schleswig-Holstein, for example, the local authorities bore more than 45 per cent of the expenditures for Grund-, Hauptschulen and special schools, in Hesse they provided only some 30 per cent. These differences are, among others, influenced also by different arrangements of details for the division of responsibilities in various Länder, a topic we shall consider later.

For the reasons already stated, it is not possible to give a breakdown of net expenditure by types of school. Such statistics are only available for direct expenditure, i.e. without regard to the ultimate bearer of financial loads. Table 7 combines direct Land and local authority expenditure for Grund-, Hauptschulen and special schools in 1973. The total was some 13 000 million DM, with 10 000 million falling to the share of operating costs (76.3 per cent), and around 3 000 million DM on capital outlay (23.7 per cent). The largest share of the 13 000 million DM (some 61 per cent) went on staff, with construction costs (21 per cent) next, followed by current non-personnel costs (12 per cent). Certain

Table 7. **Direct Länder and local authority expenditures for Grund- and Hauptschulen, 1973**

Territorial authority	Direct expenditures					Expenditure from movement of assets			
	Total	Administrative and other designated expend.							
		Total	Staff expenditure	Expenditure on material	Allocations	Total	Building	Acquisition of movable property	Movement of assets

Absolute figures (in '000 DM)

Länder	6 364 388	6 364 285	6 327 736	13 398	23 151	103	—	—	103
Local authorities	5 619 923	2 790 749	894 678	1 495 275	400 796	2 829 174	2 464 158	137 408	227 608
Together	11 984 311	9 155 034	7 222 414	1 508 673	423 947	2 829 277	2 464 158	137 408	227 711
City States[a]	906 035	684 429	609 294	74 925	210	221 606	193 405	21 383	6 818
Total	12 890 346	9 839 463	7 831 708	1 583 598	424 157	3 050 883	2 657 563	158 791	234 529

In % (expenditure structure)

Länder	100	100.0	99.4	0.2	0.4	0.0	—	—	0.0
Local authorities	100	49.7	15.9	26.6	7.1	50.3	43.8	2.4	4.1
Together	100	76.4	60.3	12.6	3.5	23.6	20.6	1.1	1.9
City States[a]	100	75.5	67.2	8.3	0.0	24.5	21.3	2.4	0.8
Total	100	76.3	60.8	12.3	3.3	23.7	20.6	1.2	1.8

In % (distribution to territorial bodies)

Länder	49.4	64.7	80.8	0.8	5.5	0.0	—	—	—
Local authorities	43.6	28.4	11.4	94.4	94.5	92.7	92.7	86.5	97.0
Together	93.0	93.0	92.2	95.3	100.0	92.7	92.7	86.5	97.0
City States[a]	7.0	7.0	7.8	4.7	0.0	7.3	7.3	13.5	2.9
Total	100	100	100	100	100	100	100	100	100

Source: Statistisches Bundesamt, Fachserie 1, Reihe 5. Sonderbeiträge zur Finanzstatistik, Ausgaben der öffentlichen Haushalte, für Bildung, Wissenschaft und Kultur, 1973.

a) City States: Berlin, Hamburg and Bremen (large communities which are at the same time Federal States).

differences exist, however, between the City States and the Länder: in the City States Berlin, Bremen and Hamburg spending on staff was a slightly higher percentage of overall expenditure and spending on current material costs slightly lower than in the Länder.

A specific look at the structure of the Länder's expenditure and that of their local authorities shows that the Länder are exclusively financing current expenditures of which more than 99 per cent is allocated for teaching staff. Local authorities spent only around 16 per cent for staff, 27 per cent on current material costs, and 44 per cent on buildings. About half of their total spending went on current expenditure and the other half on capital outlays.

SOURCES OF SCHOOL FINANCING

Schools in the Federal Republic are financed almost entirely from public funds. School fees were abolished for Volksschulen, special and vocational schools in all the Länder of the Reich—by Article 145 of the Weimar Constitution (11.8.1919), and this is now true of all public schools in the Federal Republic. Levies or fees for other types of school play a very small part in educational financing; of some 28 469 million DM directed towards the school system in 1973, they contributed only 278 million DM. Since educational materials are largely free in most Länder, and pupil transport costs are borne largely by the public, pupils' families make only a minor contribution to educational expenses. The overwhelming source of educational finance is the general incomes of the various territorial authorities, because, as already mentioned, no taxes are levied specifically to finance education.

Table 8. **Bund, Länder and local authority revenue, 1972**
In million DM

Type of revenue	Bund Absolute	Bund In %	Länder Absolute	Länder In %	Local authorities Absolute	Local authorities In %
Tax and similar revenue	101 714	88.46	69 389	65.87	23 215	28.01
Loans	7 385	6.40	5 672	5.38	11 518	13.92
Revenue from reserves and capital assets	22	0.19	549	0.52	3 451	4.17
Other revenue	5 483	4.77	11 796	11.20	24 435	29.54
Allocations and loans from territorial authorities at other levels	373	0.32	17 938	17.03	20 098	24.29
Total revenue	114 977	100	105 344	100	82 717	100

Source: Own calculations based on: *Statistisches Bundesamt*, Fachserie L Reihe 1, II. *Jahresabschlüsse, Öffentliche Finanzwirtschaft*, 1972, Tabelle A.

Table 8 shows the several sources of income of the Bund, the Länder and the local authorities in 1972, and it can be seen there how widely the various territorial authorities may differ in their ability to finance activities from their own tax revenue. In fact, this source provides only 28 per cent of the communities' total revenue, while others (e.g. fees, charges, fines, rents, leases, sale of material assets, interest, returns on loans, and so on) account for 29.5 per cent. Allocations and loans from authorities at other levels (Bund/Land) make up a fairly high proportion of community receipts (24.3 per cent), as do borrowings (14 per cent) which help to explain the high capital budget of the communities. Despite the fact that the communities must defray a large part of public spending on health, education and transport, they are at least able to rely on an assured source of income that can be adjusted according to need.

This structure of revenue is reflected in local financing of the school system in general and the Grund-, Hauptschulen and special schools in particular (see Table 9). It is worth noting that the extent of credit financing in both the cases is higher than average.

Table 9. **Financing of direct local authority expenditures by borrowing and by allocations and loans from other levels, 1970 to 1973**

In million DM

Item		1970	1971	1972	1973
Total budgets					
Direct expenditure		55 759	66 545	73 834	82 325
financed by borrowing[a]	abs.	5 825	10 321	11 071	10 682
	in %	10.4	15.5	15.0	13.0
allocations and loans	abs.	15 533	17 542	20 098	24 090
	in %	27.9	26.4	27.2	29.3
Schooling					
Direct expenditure		6 958	8 938	10 003	11 192
financed by borrowing[a]	abs.	1 073	2 107	2 640	2 931
	in %	15.4	23.6	26.4	26.0
allocations and loans	abs.	1 705	2 167	2 362	2 835
	in %	24.5	24.2	23.6	25.3
Grund-, Haupt- and special schools					
Direct expenditure		3 796	4 782	5 239	5 684
financed by borrowing[a]	abs.	602	1 064	1 294	1 339
	in %	15.9	22.2	24.7	23.6
allocations and loans	abs.	809	963	1 016	1 083
	in %	21.3	20.1	19.4	19.1

a) From credit market funds.

Source: Our calculations based on: *Statisches Bundesamt,* Fachserie L, Reihe 1, II. *Jahresabschlüsse, Öffentliche Finanzwirtschaft,* 1970-1973; Reihe 1, II. *Jahresabschlüsse, Kommunalfinanzen,* 1970-1973, and Reihe 5. *Sonderbeiträge zur Finanzstatistik, Ausgaben der öffentlichen Haushalte für Bildung, Wissenschaft und Kultur,* 1970-1973.

These figures, being totals, do not reveal how allocations to the individual communities differ in amount according to their tax-raising power or financial capacity, nor how the division of functions between community and Land differs among the various Länder. Grants may be either general or earmarked and the apportionment of the latter is, by and large, at the discretion of the Länder. In some Länder, local school authorities are empowered to seek contributions from neighbouring communes whose children attend their schools.

It is now relevant to look at the allocation of funds for and within the school system. Since in practice no public revenue is specifically set aside for the school system (as is also usually true of other areas of public responsibility), territorial authorities establish the amount of school spending in the appropriate one- or two-year budgetary plan. A large portion of this expenditure and its allocation to specific areas of the school system has been committed by decisions taken previously or imposed by a higher level of authority. The remainder is allocated as a result of negotiations by the various Land or local authorities involved. Overall, the proportion of public money allocated for school expenditure shows a marked increase from 1950 to 1970 (see Table 10).

Table 10. **Proportions of public finances allocated to selected areas of expenditures, 1950-1973**

Percentages

Year	Defence	Public safety and protection of legal rights	School system	Universities, extra-university research	Social security	Health, sports, recreation	Housing regional developments	Economic promotion	Transport and Communications
1950	16.7	4.0	6.0	1.4	27.0	3.6	12.2	6.9	4.5
1953	12.5	4.5	6.8	1.6	28.5	3.5	10.5	5.5	4.7
1956	12.1	4.2	6.9	1.8	26.0	3.7	9.7	7.1	6.2
1959	12.4	4.0	7.0	2.3	26.3	3.8	9.4	6.4	7.0
1961	13.8	3.9	6.9	2.6	23.2	4.0	8.0	6.7	7.2
1962	15.9	3.7	6.7	2.8	22.3	4.1	8.3	6.8	7.8
1963	16.6	3.9	7.0	3.0	20.6	4.3	7.7	7.7	8.4
1964	14.8	3.8	7.3	3.4	21.7	4.5	7.8	7.5	8.5
1965	13.4	3.8	7.6	3.7	22.3	4.5	7.2	7.6	8.0
1966	13.3	3.9	8.0	3.8	22.1	4.7	6.7	6.7	7.9
1967	13.5	3.8	7.8	4.0	22.4	4.6	5.8	6.7	8.1
1968	11.0	4.0	8.2	4.2	22.6	4.8	5.7	7.6	8.2
1969	11.4	4.0	8.6	4.4	21.3	4.8	5.2	7.4	8.8
1970	10.1	4.0	9.1	5.0	20.6	5.2	5.5	7.3	9.0
1971	9.7	4.1	10.0	5.5	20.1	5.6	5.6	5.4	8.8
1972	9.9	4.1	10.1	5.7	20.0	5.9	5.6	5.2	8.3
1973	9.8	4.3	10.1	6.1	18.8	6.0	5.7	5.0	7.8

Source: Our calculation based on the *Statistisches Jahrbuch für die Bundesrepublik Deutschland*, 1976, p. 403.

Usually, school authorities' budgets do not show individual schools separately; instead, they are broken down into types of schools, and the expenditure appropriations, which are earmarked, are, in principle, binding. The earmarking results either from previous instructions from the Land, or from current regulations.

The actual amounts that go to individual schools from the sums earmarked depend on how far the instructions attached to subsidies are binding vis-à-vis the school. All schools of a given type are in competition for such funds as remain after prior claims for building and technical purposes have been satisfied. The commitments of principals and teachers, relations with the allocating authorities, political considerations and so on, must also be taken into account. In fact, individual schools get only relatively small amounts to use at their own discretion for such operational needs as teaching, educational materials, and minor repairs.

Individual schools receive some further financial help from parents' associations and other interest groups. It is not possible to gauge how important these sources are (though press reports indicate that they are sometimes quite sizeab.e); one can assume, however, that they are more common in secondary schools leading on to higher education than at the lower primary level.

Chapter II

FISCAL ADJUSTMENT IN THE FEDERAL REPUBLIC OF GERMANY

The decisive source of funds in the Federal Republic for the financing of public undertakings is tax revenue (see Table 8). Its apportionment among the various authorities (Bund, Länder and local) is, therefore, of paramount importance in bringing about uniformity of living conditions throughout the country—and educational facilities are, of course, a vital factor in this. It is relevant at this point, therefore, to review the fiscal adjustment in the FRG, in which the disbursement of tax revenue among the territorial authorities occupies the central place.

TAX APPORTIONMENT AND LEGISLATION

The apportionment of tax revenue among the Bund, the Länder and local authorities is regulated by the combination of a separating system and an interlinked system. In the separating system the revenue from a specific tax is entirely at the disposal of one of the territorial authorities. In an interlinked system tax revenues are consolidated and distributed to the territorial authorities according to specific formulae.

The legal authority for the separating system is Article 106 (par. 1, 2 and 6) of the Basic Law. In accordance with this, tax revenue is distributed between the territorial authorities as follows:

a) *Bund*

Customs and excise duties to which the Länder and communities are not entitled (e.g., petrol, tobacco and coffee taxes), road traffic tax on commercial goods, capital transfer taxes, insurance tax, bill tax and a supplement (not exceeding 10 per cent) to the income and corporation tax which the Bund has the power to levy. In addition there are one-off property levies and levies connected with the EEC.

b) *Länder*

Property taxes, inheritance tax, motor vehicle tax, tax on beer, levies on gambling establishments and racecourse betting taxes, lotteries and fire insurance taxes.

c) *Communities*

Non-personal taxes (e.g., tax on land), local excises and luxury taxes (on, for example, amusements, beverages, dogs and hunting).

Other local governments (the Kreise) are not, however, entitled to raise taxes except in a very few minor instances.

The *interlinked system* is established in Article 106 (par. 3, 7) of the Basic Law. This specifies that income tax should be made jointly available to Bund, Länder and local governments, with Bund and Länder each taking half of the revenue remaining after the deduction of the local government share (currently standing at 14 per cent). Bund and Länder also split the corporation tax (50 per cent each) and the value added tax. In addition, there is an interlinked tax-sharing arrangement between the Länder and the communes insofar as the communes receive a certain percentage (determined by the Land law) of the Land share of income taxes, corporation, and turnover taxes (VAT).

The apportionment of all Länders' share of income and corporation taxes to the individual Länder is based in principle on local revenue, i.e., each Land shares in the revenues proportionately to the taxes raised within its own territory.

In both 1975 and 1976, 62 per cent of turnover tax (VAT) went to the Bund, and 38 per cent to the Länder. Distribution to the individual Länder is determined (up to 75 per cent of the total) by need, reflected in population figures. The remaining 25 per cent serve for giving to the fiscally weaker Länder supplementary allocations. Thus Länder with per capita tax revenue below the Länders' overall average may come within 92 per cent of it.

The considerable regional variations in tax revenue through the separation system has given rise to a good deal of criticism of the system as such. Of principal concern in our context, however, is that, regardless of who receives the money, the economically crucial criterion of power to tax today lies almost exclusively with the Bund. Federal action is essential (and, indeed, required by law) whenever the legislation is needed on a national scale to further uniform social/living conditions, so little scope is left for the Länder. Local communities may alter the local rates as a percentage of the normal taxes levied in accordance with the law, but even here (as in arranging fees, contributions and loans) their freedom of movement is restricted by supervisory bodies, and by social constraints. On the other side there is also a slight brake on Federal power, since legislation regarding taxes the revenue of which goes wholly or partly to the Länder or the local authorities must be approved by the Bundesrat (Federal Council).

FISCAL ADJUSTMENT AMONG THE LÄNDER

The system as defined in the previous section does not in itself produce a uniform distribution of tax revenues among the Länder. In order to balance their differing tax-raising capacities more effectively a special fiscal adjustment mechanism has been set up. Under this, the Länder whose tax revenue (including community taxes) is above the average must turn over part of it to Länder with a lower tax capacity.

The basis for this horizontal fiscal adjustment is a comparison made between an adjustment index and a tax capacity index. The adjustment index is intended to show what the tax yield of a Land should be in order to reach the Federal average; the tax capacity index represents the tax-raising capacity of a Land, including the Land share of Federal taxes and the tax revenue of its communities.

Those Länder with a tax capacity below their adjustment index get financial allocations from the other Länder. The aim of this procedure—we will not go into its detailed operation—is to bring up the tax index of low-revenue Länder to at least 95 per cent of the average tax revenue.

In addition to this fiscal adjustment mechanism, the Bund may also allocate supplementary funds to low-revenue Länder. These are unearmarked fiscal allocations intended to cover the general financial needs of the Land. The Bund may also grant funds to the Länder for specific investments of Länder and local governments. Considering these allocations when calculating total Länder revenue of the Länder both before and after fiscal adjustment (and remembering that the Länder must contribute to the Equalisation of Burdens Fund[1]) Table 11 shows the order of magnitude of the net effects of these transactions for the Lowland States in 1970 and 1973 including total community revenue before and after these equalization and transfer operations.

Table 11. **Total Länder funds before and after financial adjustment, 1970 and 1973**[a]

Land	Total funds before fiscal adjustments in DM per capita	Total funds after fiscal adjustments in DM per capita	Deviation from federal average before fiscal adjustments In DM per capita	before In %	after fiscal adjustments In DM per capita	after In %
Fiscal year 1970						
High-revenue Länder						
Hesse	1 266.78	1 249.34	+129.45	+11.4	+74.38	+6.0
Baden-Württemberg	1 215.19	1 208.63	+77.86	+6.8	+33.67	+2.8
North Rhine-Westphalia	1 201.65	1 192.67	+64.32	+5.7	+17.71	+1.5
Low-revenue Länder						
Bavaria	1 096.55	1 149.94	−48.78	−4.3	−25.02	−2.2
Schleswig-Holstein	991.14	1 147.23	−146.19	−12.9	−27.73	−2.4
Rhenish Palatinate	1 030.11	1 139.02	−107.22	−9.4	−35.94	−3.2
Saarland	954.97	1 128.26	−182.36	−16.0	−46.70	−4.1
Lower Saxony	983.15	1 106.44	−154.18	−13.6	−68.52	−6.2
Federal average	1 137.33	1 174.96	—	—	—	—
Fiscal year 1973						
High-revenue Länder						
Hesse	1 907.94	1 924.79	+186.49	+10.8	+115.39	+6.4
Baden-Württemberg	1 850.70	1 854.04	+128.75	+7.5	+44.64	+2.5
North Rhine-Westphalia	1 791.05	1 804.81	+69.50	+4.0	−4.59	−0.3
Low-revenue Länder						
Bavaria	1 679.27	1 790.40	−42.80	−2.5	−19.00	−1.1
Schleswig-Holstein	1 505.59	1 784.20	−215.36	−12.5	−25.20	−1.4
Rhenish Palatinate	1 561.75	1 743.74	−159.70	−9.3	−65.66	−3.6
Saarland	1 434.89	1 716.36	−286.56	−16.6	−93.04	−5.1
Lower Saxony	1 514.34	1 760.16	−207.11	−12.0	−49.24	−2.7
Federal average	1 721.45	1 809.40	—	—	—	—

a) The calculations for 1973 are based in part on estimates.

Source: *Die Leistungen der Länder für den gemeindlichen Finanzausgleich,* Institut FSt, Vol. 105, pp. 22, 37, 49, 50, 63, 64 and our own calculations.

1. This is a fund set up by the Federal Government based on loans under an anticipated financing scheme to ensure an equal sharing of the cost of war damage and war-related damage.

A comparison of the total per capita revenue of the Länder with their respective net per capita school expenditure (Table 12) demonstrates that high total revenue is not inevitably matched by high expenditure of schools. The same holds true where the net Land spending per pupil in the area of Grund-, Hauptschulen and special schools is concerned: here the pattern differs from both that of total revenue and of per capita school spending. The figures as they stand fail, however, to provide any adequate foundation for a comparison of Länder performances in this field, though they are often used for that purpose. Assessments of performance would require comparison with an "objective" need, which in its turn depends on a host of other factors such as previous performance, population structure, and so on.

LOCAL FISCAL ADJUSTMENT

Just as at the Länder level, the aim of fiscal adjustment at the local level is to bring financial strength and financial need into equilibrium. This adjustment, however, is not carried out by the process of fiscally strong communities transferring funds to fiscally weak communities but it is connected with the vertical fiscal adjustment between the Länder and their communities. A horizontal effect is built in by the fact that the funds allocated by the Länder to their communities are graduated according to specific criteria.

As was shown in the previous section, the fiscal adjustments among Länder take the financial needs and revenue of the communities into account, and compensatory payments include shares designed to eliminate revenue capacity

Table 12. **Per capita net expenditures on the school system and net expenditures per pupil in Grund-, Hauptschulen and special schools in the Länder, 1970 and 1973**

Land	Schooling per capita 1970	Schooling per capita 1973	Grund-, Haupt- and special schools per pupil 1970	Grund-, Haupt- and special schools per pupil 1973
Länder				
Hesse	295.40	420.03	1 616	2 046
Baden-Württemberg	323.57	432.01	1 155	1 740
North Rhine-Westphalia	301.01	455.18	1 282	1 892
Bavaria	282.47	451.05	1 298	1 970
Schleswig-Holstein	285.64	437.75	1 497	2 215
Rhenish Palatinate	285.05	459.76	1 322	2 029
Saarland	263.11	398.42	1 192	1 846
Lower Saxony	282.99	452.96	1 291	2 075
Länder average	295.80	445.41	1 304	1 942
City States				
Hamburg	331.25	556.42	1 858	2 913
Bremen	328.71	510.91	1 677	2 408
Berlin	252.40	425.22	1 512	2 361
City State average	295.09	489.79	1 680	2 577
Federal average	295.75	448.67	1 330	1 978

Source: Our own calculations on basis of official statistics.

differences between them. However, there are no legal provisions governing these contributions to the communities. The Basic Law confines itself to stating that a specific percentage of the Land share of total revenue from income tax, corporation and turnover taxes shall be set aside for local authorities; it is left to the Land to decide exactly how much this shall be. As a result, all Länder have passed fiscal adjustment laws stipulating which tax revenues local authorities will receive and how the amounts so derived will be distributed among them.

Table 13 shows how much the Länder set aside for their communities in 1974. No uniform pattern emerges, either for taxes going into the collection pool, or for shares going to the communities and local authorities. Regulations also vary on the question of special tax pools, and how specific taxes should be channelled into them, or into the main pool. Shares of specific taxes in special pools passed on to the local authorities and associations are normally earmarked for predetermined current expenditure or investment. Allocations from the main pool, on the other hand, can be either specific or general; only and in the latter case their use is at the discretion of the communities.

Besides this tax-pool network, all Länder still transfer other funds to their local authorities. In some cases these special grants are considerable, exceeding even the appropriations drawn from the tax pool. In Lower Saxony in 1975, for example, tax-pool funds amounted to 1 821 million DM, while payments outside the tax-pool totalled 1 995 million DM[2].

The arrangements for local participation in the main tax pool vary considerably as a result of differences in the fiscal adjustment laws of the Länder. This is true, not only for the rules governing separation into specific and general allocations, but also for procedures of apportionment within both types of allocation. Clear distinctions between specific and general allocations are found in only a few fiscal adjustment laws. For the most part specific amounts or percentages are withdrawn beforehand for a number of previous'y agreed purposes, while the remainder forms a basic pool for general allocations. As a result, it is extremely difficult to draw useful comparisons between the various Länder with regard to the proportion of specific and general allocations. One can, however, hazard that the proportion of general allocations lies in the range 50-90 per cent, which means that communities and other local authorities are getting the major part of their share of the main tax pool as general receipts[3].

These general allocations consist almost entirely of "formula" allocations to communities and associations of local governments, with the total amount—differing from one Land to another—being first divided into partial "formula" funds for communities and rural Kreise or for specific types of communities.

The determination of these allocations based on indicators is in principle governed by the same provisions in all the Länder. The basis is a comparison of the *initial or requirements index,* designed to show the financial needs of community or local authority, with the *tax-revenue capacity index* of the community or the association of communes' *levy-capacity index*[4], which should reflect their financial strength.

All Länder turn to property tax and the community share of income tax (though in differing amounts) to calculate the *tax-revenue capacity index.* The *requirements index* is worked out on the basis of community population which,

---

2. *Haushaltsplan des Landes Niedersachsen,* 1975, Vol. 1, Vorbericht, p. 157.
3. Cf. Deutscher Städtetag: Kommunaler Finanzausgleich in den Bundesländern. *DST-Beiträge zur Finanzpolitik,* Reihe G, Vol. 1, Köln 1973, p. 7 et seq.
4. As associations of communes have no specific tax revenue, they are financed by a levy raised by their member communities. The *levy index* is thus determined on the basis of the tax revenue of the communal territorial authorities belonging to the association.

Table 13. **Pool and local participation percentage in fiscal adjustment between Länder and local authorities, 1974**

Source	Baden-Württemberg	Bavaria	Hesse	Lower Saxony	North Rhine Westphalia	Rhenish Palatinate	Saarland[b]	Schleswig-Holstein
Main pool								
Land share of joint taxes[a]								
Payments within the Länder fiscal adjustment scheme[c]	23.00	11.11	23.00	20.75	28.50	21.00	24.50[f]	21.00[g]
Supplementary share	—	—	—	20.75	—	—	24.50[f]	21.00
Supplementary allocations from the Bund	—	11.11	—	—	—	21.00	—	—
Trade tax share	23.00	—	23.00	20.75	28.50	—	—	21.00
Motor vehicle tax	—	—	—	—	—	21.00	—	—
Property tax	—	—	—	—	—	21.00[e]	—	—
Other Land taxes	—	—	—	—	—	—	—	21.00[h]
Fiscal adjustment levy	61.30	—	—	—	—	—	—	—
Special pools and relinquished taxes								
Motor vehicle tax	35.00	100.00	25.00	—	30.00	—	—	—
Property tax	—	—	61.50	—	—	—	—	—
Land transfer tax	100.00[d]	100.00[d]	100.00[d]	—	—	—	—	—
Fire protection tax	—	—	—	—	—	—	—	—

a) Income, corporation and turnover taxes.
b) Local authorities receive at least 19.64 % of all the Land tax revenue with the exception of fire protection and property taxes, and trade tax.
c) Total fiscal adjustment pool from these quotas increased by 15 million DM in 1974.
d) Available to communes in Bavaria, to city and rural Kreise, or cities not belonging to a Kreis in Baden-Württemberg and Hesse.
e) Of 75 % of property tax income.
f) Only 90 % of Land revenue from turnover tax and supplementary shares.
g) Adjustment allocations in the Land fiscal adjustment are only taken into account as far as they differ from 1955.
h) Except fire protection tax.
i) The amount remaining after certain deductions are apportioned to Kreise and cities not belonging to a Kreis.

Source: Own calculations on the basis of the fiscal adjustment laws of the Länder.

however, is modified according to the size of the community (main factor) and various other considerations (supplementary factors).

These supplementary factors are intended to meet the peculiar needs of a local territorial authority by the procedure of multiplying the population figure contained in the main factor. Supplementary factors take into account, for example, the central location of a community, its population growth-rate and composition, closeness to borders, any restructuring of local territorial authorities, the existence of military barracks, and any qualifications as a resort community. The type and weight of these supplementary factors vary from one Land to another, and within the Länder between communities and rural Kreise.

In Baden-Württemberg, Bavaria and Hesse, the number of pupils is also taken into consideration indirectly via the supplementary factor for population growth, and in Hesse and Saarland it is covered by the supplementary factor for population structure (children and youths under either 15 or 18 years old respectively). North Rhine-Westphalia, on the other hand, treats the number of pupils as a direct factor in assessment. The actual number of pupils is first weighted according to type of school attended; the sum of these modified figures is then included in the calculations with a specific percentage. It should, however, be noted that these in all cases are criteria for determining the general allocation for communities and local authorities which they can then dispose of autonomously. There is absolutely no guarantee that corresponding amounts will be channelled into the school system. Nor can it be assumed that the above formula will produce a distribution corresponding to requirements. Thus, index allocations of this kind can in no sense be considered as direct school financing. If, however, the tax-revenue capacity index of a community is lower than its requirements index, it will receive general allocations from the Länder in an amount worked out by reference to the difference between the two indices. This does not produce a complete adjustment, but it does result in an improved financial position up to certain thresholds which vary from one Land to another.

As mentioned earlier, besides these general allocations local authorities still receive earmarked grants from the Länder both within the tax-pool system and outside it. These have also to be taken into consideration when assessing the effects of fiscal adjustment operations. On the other hand, some Länder also raise levies among their communities and local authorities, or involve them in the financing of certain scopes of activity. One such example is the fiscal adjustment level of Baden-Württemberg (see Table 13), of which 37.5 per cent stays with the Land. Such transfers to the Land have the effect of again diminishing funds of the communities and local authorities.

It should be noted, when comparing the effects of local fiscal adjustment in the various Länder, that the laws governing the division of functions between the Land and local authorities differ from one Land to another. An attempt to eliminate the resultant influences on fiscal adjustment has produced the figures in Table 14 which show the order of magnitude of the net effects of local fiscal adjustment on local total funds for 1970 and 1973.

It should finally be borne in mind that local authorities depend heavily on their Länder for finance. This is not only because a major part of Land allocations are more or less earmarked but also because the Land can alter the amount of allocations, as well as the way in which they are broken down into general and specific funds.

Besides the above sketched vertical fiscal adjustment which has a horizontal effect, there is also a purely horizontal fiscal adjustment between the local territorial authorities of the Länder. As far as it is relevant for school financing this will be dealt with in the following chapter.

Table 14. **Total local revenues, before and after local fiscal adjustment, 1970-1973**[a]

1970	Schleswig-Holstein	Lower Saxony	North Rhine-Westphalia	Hesse	Rhenish Palatinate	Baden-Württemberg	Bavaria	Saarland	Combined
					DM per capita				
Total local revenue									
— before adjustment	247.49	265.38	339.96	368.95	297.37	340.06	305.22	226.78	317.69
— after adjustment	475.19	481.78	534.85	547.69	471.57	531.43	470.51	471.31	507.97
Deviation from federal average									
— before adjustment	−70.20	−52.31	+22.27	+51.26	−20.32	+22.37	−12.47	−90.11	—
— after adjustment	−32.78	−26.19	+26.88	+39.72	−36.40	+23.46	−37.46	−36.66	—
					in %				
Share of total revenue									
— before adjustment	21.6	24.0	28.5	29.5	26.1	28.1	26.5	20.1	27.0
— after adjustment	41.4	43.5	44.8	43.8	41.4	44.0	40.9	41.8	43.2
1973									
					DM per capita				
Total local revenue									
— before adjustment	411.38	418.72	523.47	575.09	457.86	538.67	484.90	344.35	497.71
— after adjustment	817.30	796.99	815.81	872.51	785.62	811.95	785.23	736.09	804.63
Deviation from federal average									
— before adjustment	−86.33	−78.99	+25.76	+77.38	−39.85	+40.96	−12.81	−153.36	—
— after adjustment	+12.67	−7.64	+11.18	+67.88	−19.01	+7.32	−19.40	−68.54	—
					in %				
Share of total revenue									
— before adjustment	23.0	23.8	29.0	29.9	26.3	29.1	27.1	20.1	27.5
— after adjustment	45.8	45.3	45.2	45.3	45.1	43.8	43.9	42.9	44.5

a) Some of the calculations for 1973 involve estimates.

Source: *Die Leistungen der Länder für den gemeindlichen Finanzausgleich*, Institut FST, Vol. 105, pp. 61, 62, 64, 66, 37 and our own calculations.

Chapter III

ORGANISATIONAL AND FINANCIAL RESPONSIBILITIES AT PRIMARY LEVEL AND CRITERIA FOR FUND ALLOCATION

The preceding chapters gave a general survey of the ways in which functions and financial responsibilities are divided at primary level, together with the sources of school financing and the apportionment of public revenue to the various territorial authorities. Against this background, we now propose to go into greater detail on school-related material and financial links between State and local authorities. Albers[1] states that this complex structure "has more in common with a patchwork composed of venerable traditions than with a system worked out on rational principles", a view also expressed in the Education Council's statement in 1968 that the system is "more shaped by tradition than by rational principles"[2]. Although this judgement may not apply equally to all sectors of the school system, it is still probably true of the present situation, although they have been some improvements in the meantime.

In the following discussion we shall concentrate (as required by the project) on primary education. We would stress that our findings should not automatically be applied to other levels of the school system. The results of our enquiry are presented in the three sections: staff, school building, and other non-personnel expenditure. This represents a reasonable demarcation of resources of varying importance and different organisational and financial responsibilities, while, at the same time, we felt that the other possible division—into current and investment spending—would have led to certain unnecessary difficulties in differentiating between the two elements.

STAFF

Teaching staff

The rules on fiscal adjustment between Länder and communities (local authorities) laid down on 10th December, 1937[3], called for the Länder to cover at least 25 per cent of Volksschule staff costs. This principle of joint Land/local

---

1. Quoted from Boehm, U. and Rudolph, H.: *Kompetenz- und Lastenverteilung im Schulsystem. Analyse und Ansätze zur Reform.* Deutscher Bildungsrat, Gutachten und Studien der Bildungskommission, Vol. 20, Stuttgart, 1971, p. 12.
2. Deutscher Bildungsrat: *Empfehlungen der Bildungskommission. Sicherung der öffentlichen Ausgaben für Schulen und Hochschulen bis 1975,* Bonn 1968, p. 47.
3. RGB1 1, p. 1352.

authority financing of staff, which was still applied after the war in a number of ways to meet the cost of teaching staff, is no longer used. Today the Länder meet all the expenditures on teachers of Grund-, Hauptschulen and special schools and they are also their employers, being responsible for hiring, promoting and dismissing them, and for their professional and curricular supervision[4]. The principal reasons for this change were probably a desire to reduce the financial burden of local authorities and the idea that this would be the best way to secure the prompt introduction and implementation of reforms and to ensure (as a contribution to the realization of equal educational opportunity) a quantitatively and qualitatively even spread of teacher supply over the various regions.

When considering the options for financing and financial control of teaching staff, it should be remembered that a young teacher beginning his career usually becomes a graded member of the civil service after two years' practical experience in the school system. This means, inter alia, that he has a post for life, appears on the general civil service payroll, and that his salary is fixed according to his educational qualifications when starting, and will increase automatically by a fixed amount as he gains seniority. The result is that the possibility of using the salary mechanism to rectify quantitative and qualitative imbalance in the teaching force is considerably restricted, especially in the short and medium term. For instance, the linking of salary to educational level at entry, and automatic increases that are independent of the acquisition of new teaching qualifications, makes it extremely difficult to motivate teachers financially to seek new qualifications other than those that can open the doors to teaching in another type of school or at a higher level. Nor can higher rates of pay be used as a short-term instrument to redress teaching staff imbalances between the regions, since the Länder have now co-ordinated regulations on pay, and differences in teachers' salary ranges are no longer permitted under the recently extended Federal legislative power over salaries. Nor can financial incentives be adopted as a tool to overcome teacher shortages in specific fields because all teachers with the same training can expect the same pay, and a general teacher shortage cannot be adjusted by salary increases unless such increases are extended to all other civil servants—and this would require a considerable increase in expenditures.

These problems an exacerbated by the fact that in principle a teacher holds his post for life. This can create severe difficulties in adapting to short- and medium-term fluctuations in personnel requirements while avoiding long-term financial commitments. In the long-term perspective it also implies that if the number of pupils steadily diminishes, excess staff and the costs they represent must also be gradually reduced. This provides an opportunity for implementing reforms aimed at improving the supply of teachers.

All in all, in the case of short- and medium-term imbalance in teacher supply, this situation leads either to a passive acceptance of certain inadequacies or to the introduction of administrative orders—such as teacher transfers—as regulatory mechanisms. Some flexibility is built in by special regulations relating to overtime, the continued employment of teachers beyond the official retirement age, the part-time employment of people outside the school system, and the recruitment of teachers as employees. Whether such measures are possible depends on a constellation of different factors, including, for example, the situation in the general labour market for teachers and in specific sub-divisions of the market.

---

4. Hesse is an exception in so far as the school authority (usually the Kreise) is empowered to create additional posts at its own expense, which it then administers. In practice, though, this rarely happens.

In the medium- to long-term context, the recruitment regulations act as the main regulatory mechanism in establishing the desired quantity and quality of the teacher supply. To establish recruitment criteria is a fundamental duty of the Länder's school authorities, though the Ministries of Education are subject to several constraints in exercising this right. The Bund, as has been pointed out, enjoys specific legislative power over civil service salaries; the decisions of the Permanent Conference of Ministers of Education must also be respected, and—since the constitutions of some Länder contain statements of principle concerning teacher training—even the Parliaments are involved. Civil service laws and career regulations are the province of the Ministries of the Interior; teacher's associations make their weight felt when they collaborate in the organisation of teacher training and qualifying exams; and finally the churches have in many cases obtained participant status under concordats and church treaties[5].

In order to regulate supply, the first step is to assess the desired provision of schools with teachers, in other words, to predict demand patterns (requirement planning). Such planning is based on indicators—such as the pupil/teacher ratio—that are normative postulates, taking into account not only didactic and pedagogical considerations but also feasibility, including financial feasibility. In primary education continuous efforts have been made to improve the pupil/teacher ratio, which is relatively high in comparison with other levels, and this has had corresponding effect on teaching staff requirements. Whereas in the past targets could not, in part, be reached because of an inadequate supply of teachers, today it is a real or alleged scarcity of resources that typically prevents desired targets from being achieved.

The number of teachers assigned to individual school authorities or schools is based on teaching hour requirements, determined by the number of pupils and classes, the number of classroom hours scheduled, and the teaching load obligations for teachers, taking into account specific replacement reserves[6]. School authorities and schools have no formal influence on this procedure, although there may be a certain amount of back-door lobbying. When it comes to filling teaching posts, however, school authorities and, on occasion, schools and authorities together are allowed a more or less extensive voice in the matter in all Länder except Bavaria. This can be exercised in one of two ways, sometimes both:

— through the right to propose candidates for teaching posts and/or the office of principal;
— through expressing a choice as between the various competing candidates proposed by the appointing authority.

These co-managerial rights as a rule do not, however, extend to all posts. In Baden-Württemberg, Hesse, the Rhenish Palatinate, Saarland and Schleswig-Holstein, they apply only to the recruitment of principals. In the Rhenish Palatinate and Saarland, agreement is required only with the school authority before the appointment is made, although in Saarland the school must also be informed and can at that point put forward its own proposals. If these are rejected by the Ministry of Education, an explanation must be given to the school. In Baden-Württemberg and Hesse, the school authority has the right to choose from among the candidates put forward by the State, or to submit an opinion. In Schleswig-Holstein a selection committee composed of the school authority,

---

5. Cf. Boehm, O. and Rudolph, H.: *Kompetenz- und Lastenverteilung in Schulsystem,* loc. cit. p. 56.
6. Indicators whose determination may be used to influence teaching staff requirements as a whole.

teachers and parents makes its choice from the various candidates submitted by the school supervisory board.

The Grund-, Hauptschulen and special school authorities in North Rhine-Westphalia have the right, depending on the size of the school, either to propose or select candidates for 75 per cent of all teaching posts. In Lower Saxony, the school authorities may propose candidates for all posts, but proposals for the post of principal in large schools can only be made with the school's participation.

Increased participation by school authorities and schools in staff matters has been widely discussed in recent years. The protagonists of the idea point out the central role played by teachers in the success of educational policy, which makes it seem advisable to have as many viewpoints as possible represented in staff policy decisions. They also urge local authorities to work closely with teaching staff, and argue that the structure of a school's teaching staff has a great bearing on the work it carries out. These arguments have achieved some initial changes in the laws governing participation over the last few years. Critics are, however, still warning that teachers may fail to grasp the broader issues involved, that educationally obstructive cliques could well emerge, and that the decision-making process will become less effective.

Other school staff

Non-teaching school staff are mainly employees whose recruitment and working conditions are based on the provisions of the Bundesangestelltentarif (BAT) (Federal Employees' Collective Salary Agreement). Although this component of school staffing creates fewer problems of salary entitlement than the teachers themselves with their civil servant status, a broader range of employment opportunities is available to this category of staff. As a result the schools are competing directly with other categories of employer, whose salary offers are such that the Länder and local authorities, committed as they are to BAT, have sometimes been unable to match them—especially in the years of full employment. In addition, other considerations such as organisational and financial responsibilities in this area (which will be described below) have created difficulties for the proposed stepped-up employment of non-teaching staff in order to achieve a better division of labour. It is hoped that such staff increase will result in improved teacher performance by releasing teachers from certain duties, a point which is particularly important for secondary schools.

The employer of non-teaching staff is generally the school authority or office responsible for non-personnel expenditure[7]. For certain categories of staff, however, the Land remains the employer. This is true, for example, of welfare and/or medico-pedagogical workers in special schools in Bavaria, Schleswig-Holstein and Lower Saxony, where the same ruling applies to pedagogical collaborators in whole-day schools, and to technical and/or pedagogical teacher assistants in Lower Saxony, Bavaria, the Rhenish Palatinate and Saarland, and to educators in Hesse. In Bavaria, the Land is also the employer of school administrative staff. In these cases, as far as can be established, the school authority has no right to take part in the recruitment of such staff.

The rule governing financial responsibility for auxiliary staff in schools is the same in all Länder: costs must be borne entirely by the employer. Such staff expenditure is thus mainly met by the local authority.

---

7. Some Länder, however, have reserved the right in their school laws to issue directives covering the recruitment of administrative staff for schools.

As an exception to this basic pattern special regulations concerning school experiments are possible whereby the Länder pay some of the costs caused by the experiment.

SCHOOL CONSTRUCTION

The fundamental principle of combined State-communal school maintenance in the Länder is that the communal territorial authorities, as the school authority, are responsible for exterior school matters; in other words, for all facilities and activities constituting the infrastructure and means for teaching and learning processes. Consequently, it would be the job of the school authority to initiate school building investments by ascertaining the "needs", establishing suitable buildings, and meeting their construction. However, the diminishing financial resources of local authorities and a growing realisation on the part of the Länder that education policy decisions are an important determinant of what is to be regarded as need, has meant a greater involvement of the Land in school construction planning, and procedures have emerged for their participation in the financing of school construction investments. In the following section, therefore, Länder control over planning and construction of school buildings will be examined first, followed by a look at the various types of Länder participation in financing school construction, and finally the financing of such construction by the local authorities.

Länder influence on school building plans

The planning of school development is an important instrument for regulating school building investment. In general terms, this concerns decisions on what desired structural, quantitative or qualitative changes in the school system should be achieved by a specified deadline based on specific structural data drawn from the existing school situation and the projection or postulation of future developments and objectives. In the present context, this means the determination and statement of school building requirements necessary to establish criteria for the allocation of scarce public financial resources to the various building projects.

Both local and Land authorities are concerned with school development planning, although at Land level a different terminology is often used and the objectives and programmes worked out are not always submitted as school development plans, as was first done in Bavaria in the autumn of 1963. The school development plans of the Länder—in some cases being part of or aligned with Land development plans and programmes (e.g. Hesse, North Rhine-Westphalia, Rhenish Palatinate)—differ, however, in projection and planning factors, planning deadlines, intervals for revision and amendment, regional breakdown (Land, government district, Kreise and communities), as well as in the consideration given to education policy reforms. Only the school development plan released in 1970 by Hesse contained, right from the beginning, the basis for a step-by-step transformation of the vertically structured school system into a horizontally structured one. It should also be noted that in some Länder, general education policy developments have resulted in school development plans already obsolete by the time they were first published, or badly outdated while they were being put into effect. This situation was dealt with in a variety of ways: in some cases a hasty revision was carried out, in others the plan was more or less shelved. In yet others it was pushed through as it stood, doing no service to the cause of reform.

Town and local authorities have not generally been involved in the overall definition of objectives and work on the guidelines of the Länder's school development plans, although in some Länder the communal central associations have participated. In certain Länder, specific school development planning remains fairly well established at Land level. This limits the scope of the local authorities to plan independently, although they participate to varying degrees in Land (regional) planning. This applies to Bavaria and Baden-Württemberg. In a number of Länder, however, this type of planning is entirely the province of the local authorities, but subject to Land approval (e.g. Lower Saxony and North Rhine-Westphalia).

The Länder are able to exercise further influence on the implementation of school development plans either by granting or withholding building permission, or by the allocation of Land subsidies. Local authorities are able to assert their authority when it comes to finance—that is, they can either produce or withhold their own share of the expenditure called for under the financing regulations. The result is that the implementation of a school development plan depends on how far the Land's planning on school building and financing can be brought into line with the plans of the local authorities. Some Länder have tried to draw up more or less detailed priority programmes in concert with local authorities; others, daunted by the difficulties, have abandoned similar attempts.

Other important instruments for shaping school construction in the Länder, apart from Saarland, are school construction directives, room standards and school building models centrally fixed by the Land[8]. The German Education Council noted in connection with school building directives (which now govern construction, though originally intended merely to fix technical and hygiene standards) that "in the Länder of the Federal Republic of Germany they are of confusing variety. The one characteristic they have in common is their going too far into details and fixing them to an extent that hinders or even prevents the identification of optimum solutions"[9]. This description remains accurate today. Regional development programmes centred on specific concepts of education and school organisation also differ in type, number and scope from one Land to another—another limit on project possibilities. According to Boehm, school authorities are mainly critical of the detail and inflexibility of such school building provisions, though planning assistance in this area is felt to be very useful and in some cases absolutely necessary[10].

Types of Länder participation in financing school building

The school authority, as we have already pointed out, is in principle responsible for meeting the costs of school construction. The Länder contribute nonetheless to these costs of their local authorities, though to varying degrees. The necessary funds are drawn in part from the local revenue available for local fiscal adjustment, and in part from the Land budget. Apart from Baden-Württemberg and partly Schleswig-Holstein, the repeal of the one-third refund

---

8. The absence of school building directives in the City States can be attributed to the fact that Land and local authorities are one and the same thing, as well as to the reduced size of these Länder—an aspect which also may lie behind the lack of such directives in Saarland.

9. Deutscher Bildungsrat: *Empfehlungen der Bildungskommission. Zum Schulbau.* Bonn, 1969, p. 16. One good example is the "Richtlinien für die Planung von Schul- und Hochschulbauten", issued as a circular by the North Rhine-Westphalia Minister for Residential Building and Public Works on February 23, 1967. It states that deviations in the building plans from rectangular forms must be approved by the Minister.

10. Boehm, U.: *Probleme der Planung und Finanzierung des Schulbaus in der Bundesrepublik Deutschland.* Diss., Berlin, 1971, p. 143.

of the cost of school building, mandatory by law in Länder formerly in Prussian territory[11], has left school authorities with no legal claims to specific financial assistance; the Länder rather may allocate funds as they see fit in accordance with commitments undertaken in directives.

The past and present forms of State participation in the financing of local authority school buildings are the granting of debt service assistance, loans, allocations and subsidies. The interest-free loans previously available from a number of Länder for the purpose of building schools were abolished in the beginning of the 1970s, except in Lower Saxony where the current regulations stipulate that these should amount to 15 per cent of the funds set aside for allocations. Faced with a shortage of financial resources and consequent restrictions on school building, some Länder (Bavaria, Lower Saxony and Baden-Württemberg) attempted to shore up local credit financing in the 1960s by taking over a large part of the interest or amortisation payments.

These Länder participation schemes were abolished in Baden-Württemberg and Lower Saxony after one and four years respectively, Lower Saxony giving as its reason the overall burden on the Land budget, and the fact that the system encouraged the local school authorities to incur debts. Today, only Bavaria provides assistance in debt servicing. In order to make them comparable with Land subsidies and eliminate disadvantages as compared with subsidies, the contributions are discounted on the basis of their current value. In Hesse, the Land takes part in a State/local authorities investment fund, to be built up within 15 years from 1970, in which 600 million DM will come from the Land budget, and 1 800 million DM from local fiscal adjustment funds. Further details will be given below.

Apart from these Länder-specific pecularities, all Länder grant subsidies or assistance for school building to their local authorities. The allocation ratio and calculation basis are important in determining amounts.

In Baden-Württemberg, where school authorities are entitled by law to claim school building subsidies, a ratio of between 20 and 45 per cent is legally fixed. In normal circumstances, the proportion should be 30 per cent but in exceptional cases more than 45 per cent can be obtained. If the number of out-of-town pupils is greater than 10 per cent of the total, an additional subsidy is usually granted, amounting to about 70 per cent of the building cost share involved. Subsidy rates in Bavaria range between 10 and 80 per cent, in Hesse between 30 and 70, in Lower Saxony between 10 and 50, and in North Rhine-Westphalia, where the authorities must finance 25 per cent themselves, between 30 and 70 per cent. The Land average resulting from these arrangements is about 50 per cent in Hesse, 22 in Lower Saxony, and 60 in North Rhine-Westphalia. The ratio of subsidy for Grund- and special schools can reach 45 per cent in Saarland, and in Schleswig-Holstein a rate of 33.3 per cent has been established, though school authorities which meet certain requirements may get from 40 to 45 per cent. Ratios may also be higher for model experimental schools that comply with the proposals of the German Education Council. In addition to these voluntary subsidies, Schleswig-Holstein has legally committed itself to meeting 50 per cent of the Kreis subsidy for local school buildings.

---

11. Under this provision, Lower Saxony, North Rhine-Westphalia, the Saarland and Schleswig-Holstein refunded one-third of Volksschule building costs—not including the cost of land—to school authorities in areas where the population figures or number of teaching posts were under a given threshold. This regulation encouraged requests for small Volksschule buildings, which—under educational policy aspects—soon came to be seen as a bad investment, as well as interfering with priority allocation of school building funds. With North Rhine-Westphalia leading the way in 1969, these provisions have now been repealed.

When it comes to a calculation basis, either the actual building cost of the school may be used, or standard values of cost worked out by the Land. Bavaria is the only Land still using the former approach, site costs—as in the other Länder—not being included. In all other Länder, standard cost values are in operation which are mostly based on one square metre of an intensive-use area, and correspond either to school types or levels (Baden-Württemberg, Hesse, Lower Saxony, Rhenish Palatinate and Saarland), or on the nature of the area (North Rhine-Westphalia). These differing criteria and differing cost classifications make it extremely difficult to compare standard cost values, and for this reason we will not reproduce them here. Similar discrepancies can be found among the Länder when it comes to aligning standard cost values with actual building costs; on occasion these can differ strikingly. It is by no means unusual to come across adjustment intervals of two or three years.

The trend among the Länder is to treat their standard cost values as cost limits, which means that excess amounts can only qualify for subsidies if they can be justified. To some extent, building projects that greatly exceed standard cost values are no more encouraged (e.g. Rhenish Palatinate), or subsidies are reduced by the amount in excess of the standard cost estimates. Subsidies are also sometimes reduced when costs fall short of the estimates (Saarland). However, in North Rhine-Westphalia subsidies are increased if costs fall short.

In spite of the controversy that surrounded the original idea, the concept of standard cost estimates is now generally accepted as being viable. As well as improving and stream-lining the procedure, it imposes economy at the drawing-board level, as well as at project management level, helps to stabilise costs, and makes planning easier for the school authorities involved.

Subsidy ratios and calculation criteria are not the only important factors in shaping State school construction in the Länder; placing criteria and the terms of promised aid (i.e., financing flexibility in terms of deadlines) also play a major role. These elements will be examined in the following paragraphs.

In all Länder, State participation in school building financing and the level of subsidy ratios are conditioned not only by the financial position of the Land, but also by that of the school authority and considerations of education policy. subsidies to be granted only for school centres; in Saarland, on the other hand, For example, in North Rhine-Westphalia, it is the general practice now for the dwindling number of pupils in the Grundschule and growing financial needs in other education sectors has caused the construction of Grundschulen to be discontinued. The financial situation of the school authority in each Land is supposed to be taken into account by assessing subsidies on the basis of "capacity for performance", "capacity for performance and scope of functions", and "financial capacity", though it is neither readily apparent nor clearly established what criteria are to be used in arriving at such an assessment. Depending on the Land, the result is a greater or lesser degree of flexibility in granting subsidies and this may, of course, have either positive or negative effects. On the one hand, it can mean that the allocation of scarce Land resources can be closer aligned with education policy objectives; on the other, it can complicate the school authority's planning. It should be noted that there are no Länder where the Ministry of Education alone takes the decision on subsidies. In some cases the Ministry of Finance is involved, in others the Ministry of the Interior including communal supervisory boards are brought in, and in yet others all three Ministries collaborate. The Länder also vary greatly in the degree of responsibility they assign to these authorities and departments for examining and assessing allocation criteria and determining subsidy quotas.

As to the timing of subsidies, the Bund, Länder and local authorities accept as a fundamental principle in their budgeting that payment commitments shall only be undertaken within the limits of the current budget. The same applies to the approval of Land subsidies for local school building. In order to reduce the resultant obstacles to planning and school building, some Länder have turned to the instrument of writing self-binding financial commitments for some future years into the present annual budget (so-called "Verpflichtungsermächtigung")[12] specifically to permit or at least to tolerate financing by local authorities in anticipation of the Land contribution. One effect of this was that in some cases later actual budget resources remained considerably lower than the advance authorisations, thereby limiting new authorisations. The result has been that in some cases the rule that buildings would only be approved if the Land's financial cooperation was assured was re-adopted.

Local financing of school building

The relations between Land and school authority in school building and school building financing having been defined, we shall now examine the role of local authorities in this matter.

The Hesse Investment Fund, mentioned above, is one type of local financing that lends to a load adjustment at Land level. Three-quarters of the total fund has to be raised by the local authorities within 15 years, their share being taken in advance out of the local fiscal adjustment fund. General fiscal adjustment resources are thus earmarked for a specific purpose[13]. The remaining 25 per cent has to be drawn from the Land budget. The Minister of Finance may also borrow for the Fund from the capital market, with the Fund then becoming responsible for interest payments and amortisation. Interest-free debt certificates may be issued on 75 per cent of the Fund (Heading A) by the Minister of Finance in agreement with the Ministers of the Interior and Education to local authorities for purposes set out annually in an economic plan. The remaining 25 per cent of the Fund (Heading B) is organised as a type of building society for local territorial authorities. They can receive interest-free loans of previously agreed amounts provided they have saved 20 per cent of such amounts with the Fund from their own resources. Loans in any case have to be repaid within 20 years.

These stipulations show clearly that the burden adjustment involved is mainly a temporary one, since the school authority must repay the loan from its own funds. The real burden adjustment exists only with respect to the interest-free nature of the loan, the main result of the Fund is to free the local authorities from the direct capital market and its fluctuations.

In Lower Saxony, the Rhenish Palatinate and Schleswig-Holstein burden adjustment takes place at the level of the Kreise, though to varying extents. In Schleswig-Holstein the only provision imposed is that the Kreise shall grant subsidies to their local authorities for school building if the cost exceeds an amount officially fixed by the Ministry of Education (the current figure is 50 000 DM). The authorisation of these subsidies, which are determined by the Kreise, must be endorsed by the superior school supervisory authority. In the Rhenish Palatinate, the Kreise must provide 10 per cent of the acknowledged school building costs incurred by their communes, and in Lower Saxony the share attributable to the Kreise is set at a minimum of one-third of the building costs. These allocations may consist of subsidies, interest-free loans, or a combination

---

12. In this way, the budget estimates may authorise measures that commit the Land to expenditure in subsequent fiscal years.
13. The same principle underlies the Land aid mentioned above, inasmuch as the Länder draw school building subsidies from the general fiscal adjustment fund.

of both. Irrespective of the type and amount of the Kreise participation, adjustment effects depend on the source of funds. While in Schleswig-Holstein and the Rhenish Palatinate they are drawn from the Kreis budget, in Lower Saxony they are provided by a Kreis school building fund financed jointly by the Kreise and the communes. Inasmuch as the resources of this fund do not represent returns on loans two-thirds of the funds have to be provided by the Kreis and one-third by its communities, based on the number of resident 1-4 year Grundschule pupils. The amount of the contribution is determined by the Kreis.

Where the financing of school building is not covered by these forms of local financing and State allocations, the majority of school authorities turn to loans from the capital market to finance their projects through credit. How dependent local school building finance is on local borrowing emerges from a comparison of overall expenditure on school building with loans for schools—although such loans are not used exclusively to finance building, this is their main purpose. Local loans for Grund-. Hauptschulen and special schools increased between 1970 to 1973 from 34 to 54 per cent of school building expenditures. This situation is a clear indication of the shortage of resources with which the local authorities are confronted; nor, as pointed out previously, do they have much chance of increasing their revenue, for example by raising additional taxes[14].

This reliance in the past on local borrowing to finance school building has meant that development has largely kept in step with general economic cycles, since in the main local authorities did not pursue an anti-cyclical financial policy—nor, indeed, did they really have the strength to do so on their own. The adjustment of school building expenditures to current revenue and the cyclically fluctuating borrowings had the further adverse effect that investments were made when the cost of capital goods and wages were relatively high. The fact remains, however, that the cyclical investment policy of local authorities was also caused by the strict application of the loan limit by supervisory local authorities, particularly in periods of economic recession, while the loan limit itself was also linked to current revenue and consequently also at the mercy of cyclical changes.

In addition, debt service aid paid in some Länder was not used anticyclically, and in some Länder the maximum interest rate for local borrowings was pegged so low that it became equivalent to a ban on borrowing.

OTHER NON-PERSONNEL EXPENDITURE

Other non-personnel expenditure, which accounts for some 15 per cent of school expenditure, includes outlay on school administration and maintenance, equipment, teaching and educational material and the transportation of pupils. These items are relatively small against the cost of staff and building, but their importance in the teaching and learning process is far greater than the relative or absolute amounts involved would imply.

Federal financial statistics, unfortunately, do not allow us to break down this category of spending into comparable sub-headings for the variety of measures and purposes covered. The differences between the Länder in burden sharing, and the different definitions and delimitations of specific spending from budgets which also vary from one Land to another, as well as from one local authority to another, preclude any such detailed analysis. Bearing this restriction in mind,

---

14. At the same time, public finance concepts such as the "pay-as-you-use principle" and "intergeneration equity" were scarcely applied during these borrowing operations.

we shall look separately at "educational materials", "pupil transportation" and "other plan expenditure".

Educational materials

Free educational materials are in principle available in all the Länder of the Federal Republic for primary grades, with the exception of Lower Saxony as as whole, and the Grundschule sector in the Rhenish Palatinate, where all supplies must be provided by parents[15]. This means that pupils are supplied with books and a specific quantity of materials free of charge from public funds; in most Länder this takes the form of a lending system. In some Länder operating this system (e.g. Hesse and Schleswig-Holstein), Grundschule pupils in the first grade are assigned educational materials gratis. Completely gratis assignment of educational materials is only provided for in North Rhine-Westphalia, the Saarland and—for special schools only—in the Rhenish Palatinate. Berlin has a semi-transfer system: pupils receive certain educational materials free, others are on loan.

This practice was current up to 1975, when financial pressure on public budgets forced cutbacks. In the Saarland, for instance, the budget allocation for free educational materials was reduced by 90 per cent in 1976, which meant that the provision of free materials was virtually abolished only two years after it was introduced. Free supplies are now reserved for children whose parents get either unemployment benefit or national assistance. In Hamburg, budget appropriations for teaching and educational materials were reduced by 12.3 per cent, which meant that "minor" supplies were no longer free. Berlin has limited transfer of textbooks, and in North Rhine-Westphalia educational materials should be lent "to the utmost extent still compatible with educational goals". A target figure of 20 per cent was fixed for the proportion of materials lent in primary schools and special schools for the mentally handicapped in 1975-1976.

In Berlin, Hamburg, and the Länder of Hesse, the Rhenish Palatinate and Saarland, the State bears the entire cost of free educational materials. In Baden-Württemberg, North Rhine-Westphalia and Schleswig-Holstein costs are defrayed by the local school authority. In Bavaria, the local school authorities finance free materials in advance, and on request the Land reimburses two-thirds of the amount involved.

Quite apart from these various financing patterns, all the Länder reserve the right to take important decisions concerning the procurement of educational materials. One major matter is the books approved for use in the classroom where decisions are taken by the Ministries of Education. In addition, specific spending limits per pupil are laid down, mainly at Land level, to determine either the maximum outlay (e.g. Hesse, North Rhine-Westphalia), or minimum outlay (e.g. Schleswig-Holstein) for free educational materials on an annual basis[16]. There are, too, provisions stipulating, for example, that the same books should be used for similar classes in a given school, in the schools of a particular type or district, and so on.

Within these decision parameters, the educational materials actually used in the individual schools depend on the outcome of a so-called "introduction" procedure and on the purchasing decision. The introduction procedure in fact selects

---

15. Some help is given to less well-off families through the provision of school textbook libraries and contributions for educational assistance.
16. The per capita rates established in North Rhine-Westphalia as average amounts according to type of school and grade may be exceeded if there is an adjustment within the school, and the total burden on the school authority is no greater than the total average amounts in all classes.

items from the catalogue of educational materials approved for use in schools that are to be bought with public funds or paid for by parents. In most Länder, up to three textbook titles are chosen for each subject by intermediary-level school supervisory authorities for schools of a particular type in a particular district, and the schools may then make their own final selection from among them[17]. Within these very limited choices, the purchasing decision for the individual school is then normally taken by the general conference. As will have become evident from the foregoing explanations the importance of these purchasing decisions for the educational and economic freedom of action in schools varies from one Land to another, depending on whether:

— parents are under a financing obligation without implications for other school decisions;
— educational materials are, or are not, free in the Land;
— decisions can be taken in connection with an overall budget, since the standard per-pupil ratio for various grades helps determine the overall budget, but not how it will be used;
— application of the standard per-school and grade-level ratios is also mandatory where the use of funds is concerned.

On purchasing procedure, it should also be noted that, where Länder have a transfer system, Land or school authority vouchers may be distributed to pupils who exchange them on the open market for the required books.

Pupil transportation

As a result of rural school reform that consolidated small and one-room schools into larger, more economic units, the distance pupils had to travel often increased to such an extent that the use of public or private transport became almost indispensable. Nearly all Länder coped with the situation by providing free pupil transportation at public expense.

The Land, however, is responsible for pupil transportation only in the Rhenish Palatinate. There the school authority merely has to provide and finance garage facilities for the vehicles. In the other Länder, pupil transportation financing is the duty of the school authorities, though the Länder participate with more or less substantial subsidies. The only exception is North Rhine-Westphalia, where the school authority must bear all the costs[18].

In Schleswig-Holstein, State support is offered in the form of supplementary subsidies in accordance with funds made available in the State budget. In Bavaria, the State makes an 80 per cent subsidy of the required amounts, and if the financial situation of the school authority is particularly weak, this figure can be increased to 100 per cent. Local school authorities in Lower Saxony receive subsidies covering 75 per cent of the costs: the amounts may be calculated as a fixed sum based on the number of pupils combined with overall population and traffic density. Only in Saarland, Hesse and Baden-Württemberg are State subsidies intended to cover all costs, but in Hesse and Baden-Württemberg this applies only in the case of pupils attending a school outside the commune where they live. Baden-Württemberg also sets a ceiling on the amounts reimbursable annually (in 1975 this was 4 000 DM per capita for special school pupils, and

---

17. Cf. Naumann, J.: *Medien-Märkte und Curriculumrevision in der Bundesrepublik Deutschland*. Studien und Berichte, Vol. 30. Max-Planck-Institut für Bildungsforschung, Berlin, 1974, p. 45 et seq.
18. Since 1970, when a revision of burden sharing between Land and school authorities took place. The simultaneous raising of the pupil ratio in the general fiscal adjustment may be considered as a partial compensation of the burden placed on the school authority.

1 500 DM for others). In the case of the authority's own pupil-transport vehicles in Baden-Württemberg, a lump sum reimbursement is made per kilometre of annual traffic performance, graded according to the passenger capacity of the vehicles.

The responsibility for operating pupil transport systems lies with the school authority which, however, must respect Land directives concerning the need and suitability for such transportation. Pupil transport must be provided if a defined home-school distance has been exceeded. In most Länder the relevant figure is two kilometres, in Baden-Württemberg it stands at three kilometres, and in Schleswig-Holstein at four. In almost all Länder these limits may be lowered in the case of special school pupils and for schools in hazardous locations, with the approval of the school supervisory authority. Where possible, use of regular public transport services is generally recommended to school authorities as the preferred solution. In Hesse, however, school authorities have been advised to set up a special school bus service.

Other expenditure on equipment, maintenance and administration

Expenditure incurred primarily for the equipping, maintenance and administration of schools is in principle the responsibility of the school authority in its capacity as plant expenditure agent. In this task school authorities are subject to comparatively few legal constraints, although in some Länder the Minister of Education (either alone or in cooperation with other Ministers) is legally empowered to issue directives on how they go about it—as is the case in North Rhine-Westphalia. There are, however, certain limits on decision-making flexibility when it comes to the type and scope of school upkeep and administration, as certain requirements arise more or less directly from the design and constructional characteristics of school buildings. The apparently logical step of including in school building plans not only non-recurrent (subsidized) costs in calculations for decision-making but also recurrent expenditure gives rise, however, to practical difficulties. One major stumbling-block is that there is no effective and simple way of calculating these costs; another, at the political level, is that the construction planning authorities who have already seen their freedom of action eroded by school building directives are not eager to accept further limitations.

The relative flexibility of the system is such that, apart from specific basic requirements, the equipping of schools depends on a range of incidental factors such as the involvement of the school authority, the commitment and interest of the school principal and teaching body, and the generosity of parents[19]. One danger inherent in this is the under-use of specially installed equipment, due to teacher turnover and consequent changes in the interests and specialties of the teaching body.

With regard to finding the money for such expenditure the same conditions obtain as for the other areas so far examined: in principle, responsibility lies with the school authority, but a great variety of forms of Land and local authority support exist, some of which are governed by law, and others left to the discretion of the authorities.

Baden-Württemberg meets about 85 per cent of the equipment expenditure for special school pupils. In 1974, this sum varied between 241 DM for mentally handicapped pupils, and 835 DM for those who were physically handicapped. The funds needed were drawn in advance from the local fiscal adjustment budget.

---

19. Cf. Siewert, P.: *Ausgabenberechnung für Ganztagsschulen, Ausgabenanalyse bestehender Ganztagsschulen im Vergleich mit Halbtagsschulen.* Deutscher Bildungsrat: Gutachten und Studien der Bildungskommission, Vol. 6, 2nd Edition, Stuttgart, 1972, p. 13.

The State budget also set aside funds for providing schools with films, slides and sound apparatus. However, in accordance with the fiscal adjustment law, these amounts—based on the number of pupils—must be reimbursed to the Land by the local territorial authorities out of the total local share of income tax and corporate taxes.

In Hesse, the Land may provide help for the construction of schools and classrooms, as well as for language teaching and television sets, depending on the state of the Land budget. The Land also meets the cost of audio-visual aids temporarily lent to schools by public audio-visual centres, but it charges the school authority 2 DM per pupil to help cover costs. Optical and acoustical aids that remain permanently in the school must be financed by the school authority itself.

In Saarland, contributions are made towards material costs for out-of-town special school pupils (350 DM per pupil in 1974). These, too, consist of amounts drawn in advance from the fiscal adjustment fund.

Lower Saxony provides help for initial equipment and special installations; it may also make contributions to school experiments, as is the case also in the Rhenish Palatinate and North Rhine-Westphalia. In Schleswig-Holstein, too, supplementary subsidies may be granted if the state of the budget permits.

The Land of Bavaria does not participate in this type of expenditure. Government districts, however, must supply aid to needy local authorities, and an annual Land-wide fixed amount per teaching post in the district must therefore be set aside for this purpose.

Town and local territorial authorities also have obligations. Lower Saxony Kreise are required to assist school authorities in procuring audio-visual apparatus, and for Baden-Württemberg, Bavaria, Hesse, Saarland and Schleswig-Holstein there is an inter-community fiscal adjustment between school authorities and the pupils' home community, and/or between school authorities that release and those that receive out-of-town pupils through so-called Gastschulbeiträge (contributions for out-of-town pupils). The authorisation and amount of these contributions are generally covered in Land legislation. In some Länder the contribution consists of a fixed sum for the entire Land, but it is broken down according to type of school (Baden-Württemberg and Hesse)[20]; in others the amount is determined by actual current maintenance costs per pupil and type of school in the locality (e.g., Bavaria). In both cases, however, special agreements can be negotiated. Land legislation must be respected by school associations in charging their costs to member local authorities.

The final picture is a blurred one, with an infinite amount of detail. It must also be noted that, as a rule, the term "current plant expenditure" used to determine out-of-town pupil contributions does not only include the type of expenditure discussed in this chapter but—according to terminology in use at Land level—all current school expenditure of school authorities, including that allocated for non-teaching staff. As a result, by such contributions a certain inter-community fiscal adjustment is effected too for the expenditure categories described above. Nor are the general equipment costs granted in some Länder ncessarily put to defraying the cost of what we have called here "other expenditure on equipment".

---

20. Out-of-town pupil contributions cannot be levied in Hesse unless a minimum of 10 per cent of the pupils in a particular type of school in a school authority's district fall into this category.

Chapter IV

EDUCATIONAL POLICY GOALS AND ASPECTS OF THEIR IMPLEMENTATION

So far we have concentrated on a broad survey of organisational and financial responsibilities at primary school level in the Federal Republic of Germany, backed by a more general examination of existing regulations. It will already have been noticed, however, that we have so far avoided discussion of the relationship between specific educational goals and financing instruments—a matter implicit in the purpose of the OECD enquiry. The reasons for this are not far to seek. As we have seen, a multifaceted system of different general and interrelated decision-making structures have developed in the FRG, offering abundant opportunities for interventions and regulations; but so far no direct correspondence between educational objectives and financial measures have become apparent. We shall now attempt to explore this in specific relation to the content of the foregoing section.

In general terms, the aims for primary level education—as for the education system as a whole—may be summarized as "improved performance". This is a twofold goal. On the one hand it aspires, through reforms in course content and teaching methods, to prepare students to be more effective in meeting the challenges of further education up to the standards of modern democratic society; on the other, it implies a commitment to equality of opportunity by identifying every individual's learning ability and developing it to maximise his or her chances of entering the next higher level of education. The determining factor in the latter respect is the realisation that the mere provision of formal equal opportunity, and the same instruction for children of all social strata during the four years of Grundschule, does not necessarily prevent socially determined selection taking place, and that, by itself, it fails to guarantee equal educational opportunity for all.

This definition of primary level objectives is undoubtedly too general for our present purposes; however, before going into further detail, we must first examine those measures and aims that are mainly concerned with pre- and post-primary education, but have a marked effect on the primary level. As a start, it should be mentioned that intensive efforts have already been made to extend facilities at the elementary level (kindergarten, pre-school) in order to improve equality of opportunity. In keeping with this underlying purpose, discussions have recently taken place on the possibility of introducing general compulsory education from the age of five in order to achieve the earliest equalization of different learning conditions, rather than depending on parental decisions to send their children to elementary-level institutions as was common in the past. The argument runs that lowering the compulsory school age would increase the chances of joint education of children from different social levels at an age when they are highly malleable. At the centre of this debate is the concept of a proposed 5-year primary school (age 5-10)[1], consisting of a two-year introductory stage and a three-year basic stage. During the introductory phase, pupils would gradually be guided from the various types of more playful learning at the elementary level towards more systematic types of school work, which would begin in earnest at the basic level. While the pros and cons of lowering the school-entrance age are still being debated[2], measures taken at secondary I level are already giving greater scope for individual pupil advancement. The introduction of a two-year guidance phase after the primary grades has to some extent relieved selection pressures on primary schools.

Returning now to the education policy goals at primary level: among their specific aims, in addition to changes in course content, is the introduction of thinking and working patterns that lead pupils to learn by discovery, to work independently as well as in cooperation with others, and give them practice in problem-solving. Secondly, there is the adaptation of form and content of curricula to the individual's educational aptitudes, experience and background, thus combining the principle of integration (children of all social classes attend the same type of school) with the principle of differentiation (each child should be individually encouraged). Many things are necessary before these aims are met, one of which is the qualitative and quantitative improvement in the allocation resources at primary level. Here mention must be made, for example, of the introduction of new teaching and learning materials, the abandonment of the concept of "magisterial" teaching, which forces pupils into the role of passive learners, and the differentiation of instruction so that it even includes special remedial courses for slow learners.

The long-standing demand for more financial support for primary education has to be seen in this context. A point worth underlining again is that the financial outlay per pupil in Grund- and Hauptschulen is considerably below that for Realschule and Gymnasium, even though there has been some relative improvement lately, the figures are set out in Table 15.

A rather more exact idea of the development of Grund- and Hauptschulen, however, can be gained if the overall financial picture is left aside for a moment and attention is focused instead on the actual amounts and their correlative figures for 1955-1974 as they appear in Table 16.

Looked at from this somewhat less generalised viewpoint, meeting the aims for the primary level requires in the first instance an improved teaching force for these schools in both quantitative and qualitative terms. Quantitative improvement implies a reduction in the pupil/teacher ratio and a rise in the teacher/class ratio—in other words reducing the size of classes. It is these constants therefore that are now used generally to describe the achieved or desired quality of schooling. As Table 16 shows, the situation for Grund- and Hauptschulen has visibly improved in this respect. However, when interpreting these figures, allowance must be made for the high probability that classes at the primary level (Grundschule) will be larger than those in Hauptschulen. Thus, the target figure of "a maximum of 25 pupils per class" in primary schools set by the German Education Council in 1970 has probably not yet been reached.

---

1. For various organisational models, see: Deutscher Bildungsrat, *Die Bildungskommission: Bericht '75, Entwicklungen im Bildungswesen,* Bonn, 1975.
2. In an attempt to clarify these points, model experiments (half financed by the Bund and half by the Länder) have been created. A first report on their evaluation has been submitted by the BLK in 1976, cf.: Bund-Länder-Kommission für Bildungsplanung: *Fünfjährige in Kindergärten, Vorklassen und Eingangsstufen.* Stuttgart, 1976.

Table 15. **Public outlay per pupil, 1952-1972**
1961=100

	Public outlay per pupil in					
Year	Grund-, Haupt- and special schools		Realschulen		Gymnasien	
	Absolute	Index	Absolute	Index	Absolute	Index
1952	307	36	400	36	756	41
1956	556	65	752	68	1 202	65
1961	860	100	1 110	100	1 850	100
1965	1 034	120	1 390	125	1 965	106
1970	1 330	155	1 692	152	2 391	129
1972	1 734	202	2 025	182	2 731	148

Source: Albert, W. and Oehler, Ch.: *Die Kulturausgaben der Länder, des Bundes und der Gemeinden 1950-1967,* Weinheim 1972. Albert, W. and Oehler, Ch.: *Die Kulturausgaben der Länder, des Bundes und der Gemeinden einschließlich Strukturausgaben zum Bildungswesen,* München 1976; as well as our own calculations.

One obstacle to reducing the size of classes in the past was the acute teacher shortage, which peaked in the 1960s. Initial attempts to plan teaching staff requirements at the beginning of the decade showed that it would be impossible to achieve the desired increase in the number of teachers, since, for demographic and other reasons, too few pupils were enrolled in courses of study that would qualify them for teacher training courses. Simultaneously, the age pattern of the teaching force was accelerating the need for replacements[3]. Under these

Table 16. **Pupils, classes and teachers in Grund- and Hauptschulen, 1955-1974**

Item	1955[a]	1960	1965	1970	1974
Number of Grund- and Hauptschulen	29 465	31 109	30 048	21 504	18 094
	Absolute number (in 1 000)				
Total number of pupils	4 636	5 219	5 556	6 347	6 504
grades 1-4	—	3 097	3 453	3 978	4 093
grades 5-10	—	2 122	2 113	2 369	2 411
Classes	127	143	160	187	211
Full-time teachers	126	142	161	188	226
Part-time teachers	32	31	38	61	50
	Correlative figures				
Pupils per school	157.4	167.8	185.2	295.2	349.6
Pupils per full-time teacher	36.9	37.2	34.8	33.9	28.8
Pupils per class	36.5	36.6	34.7	33.9	30.8

a) Omitting Hamburg, Bremen and Berlin.
Source: Statistisches Bundesamt, Bildung im Zahlenspiegel, 1975 Edition. Der Bundesminister für Bildung und Wissenschaft, Grund- und Strukturdaten 1976, and our own calculations.

3. Cf. Köhler, H.: *Lehrer in der Bundesrepublik Deutschland. Eine kritische Analyse statistischer Daten über das Lehrpersonal an allgemeinbildenden Schulen.* Max-Planck-Institut für Bildungsforschung, Studien und Berichte, Vol. 33, Berlin, 1975.

conditions, teacher training courses were abbreviated, retired teachers were employed again, and part-time teaching as well as overtime arrangements were introduced in an attempt to meet some of the need. At the same time efforts were made to increase Gymnasium enrolment, and teacher training colleges—the institutions where most teachers for Grund- and Hauptschulen get their training—. were expanded. Thus, during the period of expansion 1965-1970, teacher training colleges almost doubled their intake. At the same time the courses themselves were given more academic substance, bringing the curriculum nearer to university level. This not only raised training standards, but brought in its train the possibility for salary increase according to current regulations, since the salary status of teachers (as already observed) is strictly linked to their level of training. It can be assumed from this that the higher academic level offered was an automatic financial incentive for school-leavers to join the teaching profession.

In recent years, the picture has changed considerably. Although the supply of teachers is still felt to be far from satisfactory, the expansion of teacher training college facilities has been curtailed if not halted and strict limits have been imposed on the increase of teaching posts in public budgets, even making allowance for a certain level of teacher unemployment. Behind these cutbacks lies the fact that the growing scarcity of public funds has made it more difficult to obtain further funding for educational purposes in the political bargaining process. In addition, the sharp fall in the number of pupils resulting from the continued decline in birth-rate, is already showing up at primary level (see Table 17).

Table 17. **Children 6 years of age**
in thousands

Population figures (German and foreign)		Forecast (German only)	
1960	797	1975	829
1965	925	1976	724
1970	1 036	1977	682
1971	1 020	1978	597
1972	1 023	1979	525
1973	999	1980	508
1974	965	1983	495
		1985	507

Here we should refer to a relatively recent measure that has had a definite effect on teaching staff requirements and corresponding expenditure. This was the specific exclusion of teachers from the official shortening in 1974 of the working day for public service employees—in spite of the fact that they are themselves public servants.

The implementation of the education policy aims just outlined requires not only an adequately staffed teaching force, but sets new standards for their qualification. As a result, teacher training and in-service training have been receiving more attention. In the initial training phase offered in teacher training colleges, the Länder may exert influence on the courses of study and the conduct of examinations, and—by the way of their right of participation—on the recruitment of teaching staff. They may play an even more active role during the second training phase, which consists of practice teaching outside the training college. This period ends with the teacher sitting for the second State examination on which depends full qualification as a teacher. In the area of in-service training those who are already professionally active are being offered more opportunities to pursue further education and being given more free time (fewer class-contact hours).

As Table 16 shows, within the general increase in pupil numbers, the number of those in Grund- and Hauptschulen has decreased, thereby raising the number of pupils per school. This development should be considered in light of the goals for primary education. As well as it having been obvious for many years that small rural schools (*Zwergschulen*), in which often several or even all grades sat together, fell far below the standards for acceptable teaching and learning, the building of larger school units was seen as an organisational prerequisite for the provision of differentiated education[4]. Consequently, since the 1960s, more and more small schools have been shut down and larger units have been built to replace them. The Länder played their own part in this trend through their school development planning function, determining the size of the area serviced by one school, by regulating its minimum capacity, together with other directives and procedures we have already touched upon. They also pursued the same policy when allocating school construction subsidies. Some of the Länder, in the interests of greater flexibility, have cancelled the specific legal claim of local authorities to a Land contribution towards school construction investment (i.e., one-third of the construction cost). Another important move in this context has been the provision of necessary pupil transport at public expense.

These examples demonstrate how the Land by combining various measures (changes in legal provisions, offers of special aid in return for compliance with specific directives, the obligation to carry out additional services, sometimes with financial assistance from the Land) is able to influence the teaching and learning conditions even in areas where the main responsibility lies with the local authorities. Finally, it should be mentioned that the sharp decline in pupil numbers in the coming years will create new problems of school size which will call for increased cooperation among educational authorities.

The examples that have enabled us to give this outline of how education policy goals are implemented are all measures affecting teaching and learning conditions based on the objective of equal opportunity. The currently prevailing view is that the principle of equal opportunity is best served when the children receive optimal individual advancement in a common Grundschule. On the other hand, it is by no means contrary to this principle that children who need particular attention and surroundings on account of mental or physical handicaps or severe behavioural disturbance, should receive such special care outside the normal Grundschule.

In Germany, the compulsory schooling laws provided at an early date for the public education of handicapped children. Children with the same or a similar handicap were assigned to particular types of school, which became independent within the general school system. The expansion of the special school system, with its nine types of schools[5], has been substantially re-enforced in the Federal Republic over the last decade. Since the beginning of the 1960s the number of special schools has more than doubled, the number of pupils has almost trebled, the number of teachers has nearly quintupled while the

---

4. The Bildungsgesamtplan states that double—or multiple—track school systems should be introduced wherever possible, taking into account regional conditions.

5. Schools for the blind, deaf, mentally handicapped, physically handicapped, slow learners, the hard of hearing, the visually handicapped, those with speech impediments and the behaviourally disturbed.

Table 18. **Pupils and teachers in special schools, 1960-1974**

Year	Pupils	Full-time teachers	Part-time teachers	Pupils per School	Pupils per Class	Full-time teacher
1960	142 945	6 237	1 045	129.2	20.4	21.3
1965	192 323	9 599	2 492	130.9	18.5	19.0
1970	322 037	19 399	6 033	135.3	16.4	16.5
1974	384 952	30 540	5 920	146.1	14.8	12.7

Source: *Bildung im Zahlenspiegel*, 1975 Edition.

average pupil/teacher ratio and the average class size have become more favourable than in any other type of school. The figures are set out in Table 18. They include both primary and secondary levels.

Nevertheless, the situation in general is felt to be unsatisfactory because there is still not enough space in special schools to cater adequately for all children requiring such care[6]. The existing pupil/teacher ratio is viewed as demanding further improvement, and there is a long-standing shortage of specially trained school teachers, even though in the past Grund- and Hauptschule teachers could in principle attend the required supplementary courses and thereby reach higher salaries.

Recently, the idea that handicapped children are best provided for in schools specially designed for them has been fiercely contested on the grounds that separate education would jeopardise the general social integration of the handicapped. In 1973, the German Education Council—and more recently the Deutscher Städtetag (German Municipalities Congress)[7]—issued statements to the effect that a graduated system, which would progressively bring handicapped and normal children into closer contact, should be set up. It would range from visual contact to the integration of the handicapped children into the general school. Among the recommendations put forward, one argued that, in addition to better detection, treatment and help at an early stage, "openness, improved possibilities for differentiation and transfer, the appropriate class sizes and pupil/teacher ratios should enable the Grundschule in future to receive a proportion of those children who at present are sent to special schools"[8].

A host of measures may well prove necessary if this proposal for the further expansion and increased integration of special education into the general school system is to be implemented. Among them is the creation of more opportunities for study and training for special teaching staff, leading to an introduction of elements of special teacher training into the study courses of all teachers in training (a) by giving consideration to these special subjects in the courses of study and in regulations for examinations, and (b) by providing the necessary training for college staff. In addition, school development plans will need to be re-designed or supplemented with regard to this kind of integration, and State

---

6. The gap differs according to the various types of handicap. While there are enough places for blind and deaf children, and the increasing number of establishments in the 1960s mainly were for the benefit of slow learners, there is a 50 per cent shortfall of places in special schools for other types of handicapped children. The Conference of Ministers of Education has estimated that in 1970 some 230 000 children were unable to enter the special school appropriate to their handicap.

7. Cf. Deutscher Bildungsrat: *Zur pädagogischen Förderung behinderter und von Behinderung bedrohter Kinder und Jugendlicher*. Bonn, 1973; Deutscher Städtetag: *Hinweise zur schulischen Förderung Behinderter und von Behinderung Bedrohter*. Cyclostyled reproduction, Köln, April 29, 1976.

8. Deutscher Städtetag: *Hinweise*, etc. loc. cit. p. 4.

school construction directives, room standards, and so on, will have to be revised accordingly. In this connexion local authorities emphasize the desire for more flexibility to allow them to cope more effectively with local needs and options. Furthermore, it has, for example, been realized that an adequate supply of special teaching and learning materials can only be assured by developing publicly financed media, since the number of children in each handicapped group is too low to constitute an attractive market for producers of educational materials. Although this is by no means an exhaustive list, it contains some of the measures necessary to implement education policy aims in the special school sector; on the financial side a shift of staff and equipment funds to the general school system is called for, in conjunction with a corresponding transfer of functions. Local authorities have already requested that the additional equipment needed to fit out general schools to take handicapped children should be subsidised by appropriate fiscal adjustments.

Also within this province of education for special social groups is the increasing problem of schooling for the children of immigrant foreign workers, for whom education is also compulsory. This is mainly a matter of their long-term integration. Although it was supposed in some quarters up to quite recently that these foreign workers would eventually return to their homelands, it is now becoming clear that a large number of such families already in the Federal Republic will remain there, and must be integrated. During the recession strict limits were placed on the immigration of foreign workers, but the number of foreign children has continued to increase. This is due in part to the fact that the birth-rate for south European and south-east European immigrants is considerably higher than that of the German population, and in part to male immigrant workers continuing to bring in their families to live with them in Germany.

Table 19 shows the figures for foreign pupils attending Grund- and Hauptschulen up to 1974. Together with the rapid numerical increase, it should also be noted that age groups containing a large proportion of foreign children are only now reaching primary school age.

Table 19. **Foreign pupils in Grund- and Hauptschulen, 1965-1974**

Land	1965 Actual	1965 In %	1970 Actual	1970 In %	1974 Actual	1974 In %
Schleswig-Holstein	400	0.2	1 746	0.7	4 351	1.7
Hamburg	457	0.3	3 190	2.2	7 037	5.0
Lower Saxony	1 521	0.2	8 031	1.0	19 773	2.6
Bremen	108	0.2	1 037	1.5	3 707	5.5
North Rhine-Westphalia	10 574	0.7	39 806	2.3	97 387	5.5
Hesse	3 767	0.8	15 550	3.1	33 998	7.6
Rhenish Palatinate	173	0.0	4 988	1.2	10 380	2.5
Baden-Württemberg	8 793	1.1	36 559	3.9	68 141	7.2
Bavaria	4 662	0.5	18 825	1.6	42 077	3.4
Saarland	1 173	0.9	2 322	1.7	3 623	3.0
Berlin	604	0.5	5 652	3.7	15 259	9.0
Total	32 232	0.6	137 706	2.2	305 733	4.8

Source: CME (KMK), *Der Schulbesuch ausländischer Schüler in der BRD 1965/66-1974/75 - Allgemein-bildende Schulen.* Results of an evaluation of official school statistics.

Table 19 also shows that from the quantitative point of view the problem of educating foreign pupils varies markedly from one Land to another. But even the Land averages conceal within themselves sizeable regional differences, in that foreigners are more concentrated in particular sectors in congested industrial centres. For instance, the percentage of foreign pupils attending Grundschulen in Berlin in 1975 was an average of 9.6 per cent for the Land. However, in one Berlin district (Kreuzberg), about 36 per cent of the children attending Grundschule and even more than half the children under six years old had foreign nationality. It can therefore be assumed with reason that in many schools the percentage limit for successful integration of foreign children adopted by the Permanent Conference of Ministers of Education—20 per cent of the total—has already been considerably exceeded. It is also likely that in areas with a substantial foreign population the teaching conditions for staff without special training, and the learning conditions for both German and foreign children, fall well below generally accepted standards.

No general and comprehensive measures for tackling this problem have as yet been evolved, though an increasing sensitivity to the difficulty in official circles is witnessed by a number of individually issued administrative provisions. These deal with experiments in using the children's mother tongue for the first phase of instruction, the recruitment of teachers with foreign language qualifications, the opening of posts to foreign teachers, the stepping-up of staff numbers, the creation of special classes for foreign children in areas where the problem is acute, or the public subsidy of transport for these children to courses organised centrally.

Table 20. **Average school size and accommodation of pupils in schools of general education, 1972 (ratios)**

Type of school, Land	Pupils per School	Pupils per Class	Pupils per Full-time teacher	Full-time teachers per class
Grund- and Hauptschulen (FRG)	332	33	32	1.03
Schleswig-Holstein	286	29	34	0.85
Hamburg	489	32	27	1.16
Lower Saxony	283	29	29	1.01
Bremen	477	31	26	1.18
North Rhine-Westphalia	351	34	35	0.96
Hesse	323	31	33	0.93
Rhenisch Palatinate	272	33	28	1.17
Baden-Württemberg	284	33	33	0.99
Bavaria	408	36	32	1.14
Saarland	323	31	29	1.06
Berlin	548	32	25	1.27
Special schools (FRG)	144	16	15	1.09
Realschulen (FRG)	421	32	25	1.29
Gymnasien (FRG)	691	29	21	1.41

Source: *Statistisches Bundesamt*, Fachserie A, Reihe 10 I. Allgemeinbildende Schulen, 1972.

An education policy aimed at equality of opportunity cannot confine itself to achieving its targets on an average basis. But uniformity of living conditions on a regional basis is also an aspect of the principle of equal opportunity. This does not necessarily mean absolutely identical conditions but rather that recognised

Table 21. Classes in Grund- and Hauptschulen according to class size, 1972

| Land | Total | Grund- and Hauptschule classes with ... to ... pupils |||||||
		20 or less	21-25	26-30	31-35	36-40	41-45	46 or more
				Absolute				
Schleswig-Holstein	8 610	661	1 572	2 769	2 627	901	75	5
Hamburg	4 617	68	256	1 145	2 524	619	5	—
Lower Saxony	28 146	1 269	5 465	10 197	8 232	2 579	354	50
Bremen	2 233	39	200	777	1 029	181	7	—
North Rhine-Westphalia	52 662	739	3 048	9 952	18 001	14 764	5 552	636
Hesse	17 269	409	2 085	5 817	6 005	2 369	479	105
Rhenish Palatinate	12 972	243	1 375	2 846	4 299	3 135	969	105
Baden-Württemberg	28 856	524	2 863	7 261	8 620	6 004	2 657	927
Bavaria	34 123	76	762	4 332	9 587	11 780	5 761	1 825
Saarland	4 110	27	548	1 282	1 461	652	124	16
Berlin (West)	5 300	167	236	1 394	2 602	895	5	1
FRG	98 898	4 222	18 410	47 772	64 987	43 879	15 958	3 670
				In %				
Schleswig-Holstein	100	7.7	18.3	32.2	30.5	10.5	0.9	0.1
Hamburg	100	1.5	5.5	24.8	54.7	13.4	0.1	—
Lower Saxony	100	4.5	19.4	36.2	29.2	9.2	1.3	0.2
Bremen	100	1.7	9.0	34.8	46.1	8.1	0.3	—
North Rhine-Westphalia	100	1.4	5.8	18.9	34.2	28.0	10.5	1.2
Hesse	100	2.4	12.1	33.7	34.8	13.7	2.8	0.6
Rhenish Palatinate	100	1.9	10.6	21.9	33.1	24.2	7.5	0.8
Baden-Württemberg	100	1.8	9.9	25.2	29.9	20.8	9.2	3.2
Bavaria	100	0.2	2.2	12.7	28.1	34.5	16.9	5.3
Saarland	100	0.7	13.3	31.2	35.5	15.9	3.0	0.4
Berlin (West)	100	3.2	4.5	26.3	49.1	16.9	0.1	0.0
FRG	100	2.1	9.3	24.0	32.7	22.1	8.0	1.8

Source: *Statistisches Bundesamt*, Fachserie A, Reihe 10 I. Allgemeinbildende Schulen, 1972.

minimum standards must be maintained everywhere. In view of the Federal Republic's administrative structure this must be looked at in terms of conditions within a Land, and comparative conditions between Länder. Tables 20 and 21 give a clearer picture of the situation. They show that in 1972 considerable differences existed, for example, in class size, both within the Länder and between them, differences that can hardly be less even today.

To some extent regulatory mechanisms maintain balance of regional discrepancies within a Land, e.g. school development planning, the establishment of Land-wide pupil/teacher ratios, maximum pupil-per-class limits, and threshold limits for class divisions, as well as school construction directives and classroom standards, the establishment of specific equipment standards, outline teaching directives, admission and introduction procedures for educational materials, and the determination of maximum/minimum amounts for the provision of free educational materials. All these measures can be adopted to apply more directly to special problems arising locally. Another important factor is the widely differing economic and financial capacity of the various local authorities on which depend the implementation of directives, orders and decrees concerning the supply of real resources for school purposes. In this respect the financial contributions of the Länder play an important part. On these the German Education Council has, however, remarked: "even there, where Land subsidies are weighted according to the financial resources of the communities, general differences between them may occasionally be eliminated; for the most part, however, they probably are only alleviated. Taken as a whole, neither the local fiscal adjustment nor any other fiscal adjustment arrangements affecting school financing are the appropriate means for bringing differences in the financial resources of local authorities within acceptable bounds"[9].

In relations between the Länder themselves, the purpose of the Länder fiscal adjustment is to enable the States to fulfil their obligations, although it by no means eliminates financial imbalances between them. Each Land is free to dispose of these funds as it sees fit, and this makes it impossible to assess the effects of this fiscal adjustment on its school situation. It can be assumed, however, that an improved financial endowment as part of the political bargaining process also benefits the education system. Following the Constitution's stipulation on the uniformity of living conditions in the Federal Republic, the activities of the Permanent Conference of Ministers of Education have a direct effect on the establishment of uniform education conditions in the Länder. The Conference has adopted something like 1000 decisions since it was first set up. These include among others: agreements concerning uniform teacher training, free schooling and educational materials, the starting age and duration of compulsory education, the implementation of school experiments, and recommendations on work in the Grundschule, organisation of the special school system, and instruction for the children of foreign workers[10].

But as we pointed out earlier, the competence of the KMK is limited to decisions adopted unanimously by the Länder. Further unifying pressures result from the work of the Bund-Länder Commission for Educational Planning, the German Education Council and the nation-wide organisations of parties, trade unions and interest groups, against the background of a nation-wide debate on education policy.

9. Deutscher Bildungsrat: *Bericht '75, Entwicklungen im Bildungswesen*. Bonn, 1975, p. 307.
10. Cf. Ständige Konferenz der Kultusminister der Länder in der Bundesrepublik Deutschland (Hrsg.): *Sammlung der Beschlüsse der Ständigen Konferenz der Kultusminister der Länder in der Bundesrepublik Deutschland*. Loseblatt-Sammlung. Luchterhand-Verlag.

Chapter V

ON PROPOSALS FOR RESTRUCTURING ORGANISATIONAL AND FINANCIAL RESPONSIBILITIES

As we have already made clear, the Federal Republic has developed a complicated system of substantive and financial responsibility for the administration of school affairs. In this the basic separation of powers is constantly counteracted by various patterns of participation. As the German Education Council has stressed, this leads to conflicts between legal principles and actual development, and to an inadequate structuring of organisational and financial responsibilities that acts as a brake on the implementation of modified education policies. The Council, as a result, commissioned a report that made proposals for a new regime, including local administrative and district reforms as well as financial ones. So far, this remains the only attempt to deal fundamentally with problems related to the financing system and its reorganisation with a view to education policy objectives being achieved[1].

After analysis of the existing regulations, the authors of this report came to the opinion that, because of the fragmentation of organisational and financial responsibilities between the Länder and local authorities, the present position was highly unsatisfactory so far as concerned flexibility for structural reforms, planning adequacy, administrative efficiency and certain conceptions of organizing participation.

In the light of these findings, a radical, far-reaching separation of organisational and financial responsibility was proposed. In principle, the financial burden would be shouldered by the Länder, and fund apportionment would correspond to the directives of State regional planning, in which local authorities would take part. This would ensure uniform minimum (basic) school financing, irrespective of the varying financial resources of individual school authorities. At the same time, since allocations would not be tied to any instructions other than those contained in outline plans, subordinate levels would enjoy greater freedom of action down to the individual school (the smallest decision-making unit) which—according to the proposal—would have an enlarged responsibility for routine practical decisions, and would be guaranteed the appropriate financial allocations to carry them through. School authorities would retain the right to further the development of their schools with their own funds (supplementary financing) in addition to the State's basic financing.

In addition to this proposal, the report contains some less ambitious suggestions for reform in the existing system of combined State/local authority school maintenance in case political considerations (a possibility the authors are prepared

---

1. Boehm, U.; Rudolph, H.: loc. cit.

to admit) cause the idea of State financing in this rigorous form to be stillborn. Indeed, none of the Länder has taken up the proposal as it exists, and even the German Education Council chose more reserved words in a subsequent recommendation[2]. The reason for this, no doubt, is that such a separation of organisational and financial responsibilities politically has hardly any chances of becoming realized. The problems such a reshuffle would generate are difficult to assess and the focus of education policy has now shifted, in any case, to other problems deemed to be more urgent.

---

2. Cf. Deutscher Bildungsrat: *Zur Reform von Organisation und Verwaltung im Bildungswesen.* Teil I: *Verstärkte Selbständigkeit der Schule und Partizipation der Lehrer, Schüler und Eltern.* Bonn, 1973, p. A 85 et. seq.

REFERENCES

Albert, W. und Oehler, Ch.: Die Kulturausgaben der Länder, des Bundes und der Gemeinden 1950-1967. Weinheim 1972.

Albert, W. und Oehler, Ch.: Die Kulturausgaben der Länder, des Bundes und der Gemeinden einschließlich Strukturausgaben zum Bildungswesen. München 1976.

Boehm, U.: Probleme der Planung und Finanzierung des Schulbaus in der Bundesrepublik Deutschland. Diss., Berlin 1971.

Boehm, U. und Rudolph, H.: Kompetenz- und Lastenverteilung im Schulsystem. Analyse und Ansätze zur Reform. Deutscher Bildungsrat, Gutachten und Studien der Bildungskommission, Bd. 20. Stuttgart 1971.

Bundesminister für Bildung und Wissenschaft: Bildungsbericht '70. Bonn 1970.

Bund-Länder-Kommission für Bildungsplanung: Bildungsgesamtplan. Stuttgart 1973.

Bund-Länder-Kommission für Bildungsplanung: Fünfjährige in Kindergärten, Vorklassen und Eingangsstufen. Stuttgart 1976.

Bungardt, K.: Die Odyssee der Lehrerschaft. Hannover 1965.

Deutscher Bildungsrat: Empfehlungen der Bildungskommission. Sicherung der öffentlichen Ausgaben für Schulen und Hochschulen bis 1975. Bonn 1968.

Deutscher Bildungsrat: Empfehlungen der Bildungskommission. Zum Schulbau. Bonn 1969.

Deutscher Bildungsrat: Empfehlungen der Bildungskommission. Strukturplan für das Bildungswesen. Bonn 1970.

Deutscher Bildungsrat: Zur Reform von Organisation und Verwaltung im Bildungswesen. Teil I: Verstärkte Selbständigkeit der Schule und Partizipation der Lehrer, Schüler und Eltern. Bonn 1973.

Deutscher Bildungsrat: Zur pädagogischen Förderung behinderter und von Behinderung bedrohter Kinder und Jugendlicher. Bonn 1973.

Deutscher Bildungsrat: Die Bildungskommission: Bericht '75. Entwicklungen im Bildungswesen. Bonn 1975.

Deutscher Städtetag: Kommunaler Finanzausgleich in den Bundesländern. DST-Beiträge zur Finanzpolitik, Reihe G, Heft 1. Köln 1973.

Deutscher Städtetag: Hinweise zur schulischen Förderung Behinderter oder von Behinderung Bedrohter. Hektographierter Umdruck, Köln 29.4.1976.

Empfehlungen und Gutachten des Deutschen Ausschusses für das Erziehungs- und Bildungswesen 1953-1965, Gesamtausgabe. Stuttgart 1966.

Flitner, W.: Die vier Quellen des Volksschulgedankens. 3. Aufl., Stuttgart 1954.

Haushaltsplan des Landes Niedersachsen, 1975, Bd. I.

Heckel, H.: Die Städte und ihre Schulen. Stuttgart 1959.

Heckt, W. (Bearbeiter): Die Leistungen der Länder für den gemeindlichen Finanzausgleich. Institut "Finanzen und Steuern", Heft 105. Bonn 1974.

Köhler, H.: Lehrer in der Bundesrepublik Deutschland. Eine kritische Analyse statistischer Daten über das Lehrpersonal an allgemeinbildenden Schulen. Max-Planck-Institut für Bildungsforschung, Studien und Berichte, Bd. 33. Berlin 1975.

Leschinsky, P. und Roeder, P.M.: Schule im historischen Prozeß - Zum Wechselverhältnis von institutioneller Erziehung und gesellschaftlicher Entwicklung. Stuttgart 1976.

Naumann, J.: Medien-Märkte und Curriculumrevision in der Bundesrepublik Deutschland. Max-Planck-Institut für Bildungsforschung, Studien und Berichte, Bd. 30. Berlin 1974.

OECD: Reviews of National Policies for Education: Germany. Paris 1972.

Seipp, P. (Hrsg.): Schulrecht. Loseblatt-Sammlung. Neuwied und Berlin.

Siewert, P.: Ausgabenberechnung für Ganztagsschulen, Ausgabenanalyse bestehender Ganztagsschulen im Vergleich mit Halbtagsschulen. Deutscher Bildungsrat, Gutachten und Studien der Bildungskommission, Bd. 6. 2. Aufl., Stuttgart 1972.

Spaniol, O.: Das Verhältnis zwischen Staat und Kommunen auf dem Gebiet des Schulwesens in der Bundesrepublik. Diss., Marburg 1960.

Ständige Konferenz der Kultusminister der Länder in der Bundesrepublik Deutschland: Der Schulbesuch ausländischer Schüler in der BRD 1965-66/1974-75 - Allgemeinbildende Schulen. Ergebnisse einer Auswertung der amtlichen Schulstatistik. Bonn (o.J.).

Ständige Konferenz der Kultusminister der Länder in der Bundesrepublik Deutschland (Hrsg.): Sammlung der Beschlüsse der Ständigen Konferenz der Kultusminister der Länder in der Bundesrepublik Deutschland. Loseblatt-Sammlung. Luchterhand-Verlag.

Statistisches Bundesamt: Statistisches Jahrbuch für die Bundesrepublik Deutschland, 1976.

Statistisches Bundesamt: Fachserie A, Bevölkerung und Kultur, Reihe 10, Bildungswesen, I. Allgemeinbildende Schulen.

Statistisches Bundesamt: Fachserie L, Finanzen und Steuern, Reihe 1, Haushaltswirtschaft von Bund, Ländern und Gemeinden, II. Jahresabschlüsse, Kommunalfinanzen.

Statistisches Bundesamt: Fachserie L, Finanzen und Steuern, Reihe 1, Haushaltswirtschaft von Bund, Ländern und Gemeinden, II. Jahresabschlüsse, Öffentliche Finanzwirtschaft.

Statistisches Bundesamt: Fachserie L, Reihe 5, Sonderbeiträge zur Finanzstatistik, Ausgaben der öffentlichen Haushalte für Bildung, Wissenschaft und Kultur.

OECD SALES AGENTS
DÉPOSITAIRES DES PUBLICATIONS DE L'OCDE

ARGENTINA – ARGENTINE
Carlos Hirsch S.R.L., Florida 165,
BUENOS-AIRES, Tel. 33-1787-2391 Y 30-7122

AUSTRALIA – AUSTRALIE
Australia & New Zealand Book Company Pty Ltd.,
23 Cross Street, (P.O.B. 459)
BROOKVALE NSW 2100 Tel. 938-2244

AUSTRIA – AUTRICHE
Gerold and Co., Graben 31, WIEN 1. Tel. 52.22.35

BELGIUM – BELGIQUE
LCLS
44 rue Otlet, B 1070 BRUXELLES. Tel. 02-521 28 13

BRAZIL – BRÉSIL
Mestre Jou S.A., Rua Guaipà 518,
Caixa Postal 24090, 05089 SAO PAULO 10. Tel. 261-1920
Rua Senador Dantas 19 s/205-6, RIO DE JANEIRO GB.
Tel. 232-07. 32

CANADA
Renouf Publishing Company Limited,
2182 St. Catherine Street West,
MONTREAL, Quebec H3H 1M7 Tel. (514) 937-3519

DENMARK – DANEMARK
Munksgaards Boghandel,
Nørregade 6, 1165 KØBENHAVN K. Tel. (01) 12 85 70

FINLAND – FINLANDE
Akateeminen Kirjakauppa
Keskuskatu 1, 00100 HELSINKI 10. Tel. 625.901

FRANCE
Bureau des Publications de l'OCDE,
2 rue André-Pascal, 75775 PARIS CEDEX 16. Tel. (1) 524.81.67
Principal correspondant :
13602 AIX-EN-PROVENCE : Librairie de l'Université.
Tel. 26.18.08

GERMANY – ALLEMAGNE
Alexander Horn,
D - 6200 WIESBADEN, Spiegelgasse 9
Tel. (6121) 37-42-12

GREECE – GRÈCE
Librairie Kauffmann, 28 rue du Stade,
ATHÈNES 132. Tel. 322.21.60

HONG-KONG
Government Information Services,
Sales and Publications Office, Beaconsfield House, 1st floor,
Queen's Road, Central. Tel. H-233191

ICELAND – ISLANDE
Snaebjörn Jönsson and Co., h.f.,
Hafnarstraeti 4 and 9, P.O.B. 1131, REYKJAVIK.
Tel. 13133/14281/11936

INDIA – INDE
Oxford Book and Stationery Co.:
NEW DELHI, Scindia House. Tel. 45896
CALCUTTA, 17 Park Street. Tel.240832

ITALY – ITALIE
Libreria Commissionaria Sansoni:
Via Lamarmora 45, 50121 FIRENZE. Tel. 579751
Via Bartolini 29, 20155 MILANO. Tel. 365083
Sub-depositari:
Editrice e Libreria Herder,
Piazza Montecitorio 120, 00 186 ROMA. Tel. 674628
Libreria Hoepli, Via Hoepli 5, 20121 MILANO. Tel. 865446
Libreria Lattes, Via Garibaldi 3, 10122 TORINO. Tel. 519274
La diffusione delle edizioni OCSE è inoltre assicurata dalle migliori
librerie nelle città più importanti.

JAPAN – JAPON
OECD Publications and Information Center
Akasaka Park Building, 2-3-4 Akasaka, Minato-ku,
TOKYO 107. Tel. 586-2016

KOREA - CORÉE
Pan Korea Book Corporation,
P.O.Box n° 101 Kwangwhamun, SÉOUL. Tel. 72-7369

LEBANON – LIBAN
Documenta Scientifica/Redico,
Edison Building, Bliss Street, P.O.Box 5641, BEIRUT.
Tel. 354429–344425

MEXICO & CENTRAL AMERICA
Centro de Publicaciones de Organismos Internacionales S.A.,
Av. Chapultepec 345, Apartado Postal 6-981
MEXICO 6, D.F. Tel. 533-45-09

THE NETHERLANDS – PAYS-BAS
Staatsuitgeverij
Chr. Plantijnstraat
'S-GRAVENHAGE. Tel. 070-814511
Voor bestellingen: Tel. 070-624551

NEW ZEALAND – NOUVELLE-ZÉLANDE
The Publications Manager,
Government Printing Office,
WELLINGTON: Mulgrave Street (Private Bag),
World Trade Centre, Cubacade, Cuba Street,
Rutherford House, Lambton Quay, Tel. 737-320
AUCKLAND: Rutland Street (P.O.Box 5344), Tel. 32.919
CHRISTCHURCH: 130 Oxford Tce (Private Bag), Tel. 50.331
HAMILTON: Barton Street (P.O.Box 857), Tel. 80.103
DUNEDIN: T & G Building, Princes Street (P.O.Box 1104),
Tel. 78.294

NORWAY – NORVÈGE
Johan Grundt Tanums Bokhandel,
Karl Johansgate 41/43, OSLO 1. Tel. 02-332980

PAKISTAN
Mirza Book Agency, 65 Shahrah Quaid-E-Azam, LAHORE 3.
Tel. 66839

PORTUGAL
Livraria Portugal, Rua do Carmo 70-74,
1117 LISBOA CODEX.
Tel. 360582/3

SPAIN – ESPAGNE
Mundi-Prensa Libros, S.A.
Castelló 37, Apartado 1223, MADRID-1. Tel. 275.46.55
Libreria Bastinos, Pelayo, 52, BARCELONA 1. Tel. 222.06.00

SWEDEN – SUÈDE
AB CE Fritzes Kungl Hovbokhandel,
Box 16 356, S 103 27 STH, Regeringsgatan 12,
DS STOCKHOLM. Tel. 08/23 89 00

SWITZERLAND – SUISSE
Librairie Payot, 6 rue Grenus, 1211 GENÈVE 11. Tel. 022-31.89.50

TAIWAN – FORMOSE
National Book Company,
84-5 Sing Sung Rd., Sec. 3, TAIPEI 107. Tel. 321.0698

UNITED KINGDOM – ROYAUME-UNI
H.M. Stationery Office, P.O.B. 569,
LONDON SEI 9 NH. Tel. 01-928-6977, Ext. 410 or
49 High Holborn, LONDON WC1V 6 HB (personal callers)
Branches at: EDINBURGH, BIRMINGHAM, BRISTOL,
MANCHESTER, CARDIFF, BELFAST.

UNITED STATES OF AMERICA
OECD Publications and Information Center, Suite 1207,
1750 Pennsylvania Ave., N.W. WASHINGTON, D.C.20006.
Tel. (202)724-1857

VENEZUELA
Libreria del Este, Avda. F. Miranda 52, Edificio Galipàn,
CARACAS 106. Tel. 32 23 01/33 26 04/33 24 73

YUGOSLAVIA – YOUGOSLAVIE
Jugoslovenska Knjiga, Terazije 27, P.O.B. 36, BEOGRAD.
Tel. 621-992

Les commandes provenant de pays où l'OCDE n'a pas encore désigné de dépositaire peuvent être adressées à :
OCDE, Bureau des Publications, 2 rue André-Pascal, 75775 PARIS CEDEX 16.
Orders and inquiries from countries where sales agents have not yet been appointed may be sent to:
OECD, Publications Office, 2 rue André-Pascal, 75775 PARIS CEDEX 16.

OECD PUBLICATIONS, 2 rue André-Pascal, 75775 Paris Cedex 16 - No. 40.191 1979
PRINTED IN FRANCE
(96 79 01 1) ISBN 92-64-11889-3